Copyright Notice

CCNA v3 Routing and Switching 200-125

600+ Questions and Answers

Disclaimer

This book was written as a study guide to Cisco CCNA 200-125 certification. While every effort has been made to make this book as accurate as possible no warranty is implied. The author shall not be liable or responsible for any loss or damage arising from the information contained in this book.

About The Author

Shaun Hummel is a Senior Network Engineer with 15 years enterprise network planning, design and implementation experience. He has worked for various public and private companies in Canada and the United States improving infrastructure, security and network management. Author of Cisco Design Fundamentals and Cloud Design Fundamentals.

Contents

Introduction

Cisco CCNA 200-125 Routing and Switching is a study guide for prospective CCNA candidates. The book covers new and updated subject matter for the 200-125 exam. The study guide is comprised of 678 questions and answers. There are seven learning modules based on the official new Cisco published guidelines for CCNA v3. Each question includes a detailed explanation that covers all of the CCNA exam requirements. There are significant changes to the CCNA routing and switching curriculum. CCNA 200-125 exam includes ICND 100-105 and ICND 200-105 exams. The question and answer format used in this book is an effective technique to learn and prepare for CCNA v3 certification. *CCNA v3 Lab Guide* is available online at cisconetsolutions.com

Official CCNA 200-125 Exam Topics

The following is a list of the official Cisco CCNA 200-125 exam topics published at cisco.com for prospective CCNA candidates.

Network Fundamentals

Compare and contrast OSI and TCP/IP models

Compare and contrast TCP and UDP protocols

Describe the impact of infrastructure components in the enterprise
- Firewalls
- Access points
- Wireless LAN controllers

Describe the effects of cloud resources on network architecture

- Traffic path to internal and external cloud services
- Virtual services
- Basic virtual network infrastructure

Compare and contrast collapsed core and three-tier architectures

Compare and contrast network topologies
- Star
- Mesh
- Hybrid

Select the appropriate cabling type based on requirements

Apply troubleshooting methodologies to resolve problems
- Perform and document fault isolation
- Resolve or escalate
- Verify and monitor resolution

Configure, verify and troubleshoot IPv4 addressing and subnetting

Compare and contrast IPv4 address types

- Unicast
- Broadcast
- Multicast

Describe the need for private IPv4 addressing

Select appropriate IPv6 addressing based on requirements

Configure, verify and troubleshoot IPv6 addressing

Configure and verify IPv6 Stateless Address Auto Configuration

Compare and contrast IPv6 address types

- Global unicast
- Unique local
- Link-local
- Multicast
- Modified EUI 64
- Autoconfiguration
- Anycast

LAN Switching Technologies

Describe and verify switching concepts

- MAC learning and aging
- Frame switching
- Frame flooding
- MAC address table

Interpret Ethernet frame format

Troubleshoot interface and cabling (collisions, runts, duplex, speed)

Configure, verify and troubleshoot normal/extended range VLANs

- Access ports (data and voice)
- Default VLAN

Configure, verify and troubleshoot inter-switch connectivity

- Trunk ports
- Add and remove VLANs on a trunk
- DTP, VTPv1, VTPv2 and 802.1q
- Native VLAN

Configure, verify and troubleshoot STP protocols

- STP mode (PVST+ and RPVST+)
- STP root bridge selection

Configure, verify and troubleshoot Spanning Tree Protocol (STP)

- PortFast
- BPDU guard

Configure and verify Layer 2 protocols

- Cisco Discovery Protocol
- LLDP

Configure, verify and troubleshoot EtherChannel

- Static
- PAgP
- LACP

Describe the benefits of switch stacking and chassis aggregation

Routing Technologies

Describe the routing concepts

- Packet handling along the path through a network
- Forwarding decision based on route lookup
- Frame rewrite

Interpret the components of a routing table

- Prefix
- Network mask
- Next hop
- Routing protocol code
- Administrative distance
- Metric
- Gateway of last resort

Describe routing table selection based on multiple routing sources

Configure, verify and troubleshoot Inter-VLAN routing

- Router on a stick
- Switch Virtual Interface (SVI)

Compare and contrast static routing and dynamic routing

Compare distance vector and link-state routing protocols

Compare and contrast interior and exterior routing protocols

Configure, verify and troubleshoot IPv4 and IPv6 static routing

- Default route
- Network route
- Host route
- Floating static

Configure, verify and troubleshoot single and multi-area OSPFv2

Configure, verify and troubleshoot single and multi-area OSPFv3

Configure, verify and troubleshoot EIGRP for IPv4

Configure, verify and troubleshoot EIGRP for IPv6

Configure, verify and troubleshoot RIPv2 for IPv4

Troubleshoot basic Layer 3 end-to-end connectivity issues

WAN Technologies

Configure and verify PPP and MLPPP WAN connectivity

Configure, verify and troubleshoot PPPoE client-side interfaces

Configure, verify and troubleshoot GRE tunnel connectivity

Describe WAN topology options

- Point-to-point
- Hub and spoke
- Full mesh
- Single vs Dual-Homing

Describe WAN access connectivity options

- MPLS
- Metro Ethernet
- Broadband PPPoE
- DMVPN
- IPsec VPN
- Client VPN

Configure and verify single-homed branch connectivity with eBGP

Describe basic QoS concepts

- Marking
- Device trust
- Prioritization (voice, video, data)
- Shaping
- Policing
- Congestion management

Infrastructure Services

Describe DNS lookup operation

Troubleshoot client connectivity issues involving DNS

Configure and verify DHCP on a router

- Server
- Relay
- Client
- TFTP, DNS and default gateway options

Troubleshoot client and router-based DHCP connectivity issues

Configure, verify and troubleshoot basic HSRP

- Priority
- Preemption
- Version

Configure, verify and troubleshoot inside source NAT

- Static
- Pool
- Port Address Translation (PAT)

Configure and verify NTP operating in a client/server mode

Infrastructure Security

Configure, verify and troubleshoot port security

- Static
- Dynamic
- Sticky
- Max MAC addresses
- Violation actions
- Errdisable recovery

Describe common access layer threat mitigation techniques

- 802.1X Port-Based Authentication
- DHCP snooping
- Nondefault Native VLAN

Configure, verify and troubleshoot IPv4 and IPv6 access lists

- Standard
- Extended
- Named

Verify ACLs using the APIC-EM Path Trace ACL Analysis tool

Configure, verify and troubleshoot basic device hardening

- Local authentication
- Secure password
- Access to device (Source address, Telnet/SSH)
- Login banner

Describe device security using AAA with TACACS+ and RADIUS

Infrastructure Management

Configure and verify device-monitoring protocols

- SNMPv2
- SNMPv3
- Syslog

Troubleshoot network connectivity with ICMP echo-based IP SLA

Configure and verify device management

- Backup and restore device configuration
- Using Cisco Discovery Protocol or LLDP for device discovery
- Licensing
- Logging
- Time zone
- Loopback

Configure and verify initial device configuration

Perform device maintenance

- IOS upgrades, recovery and verify (SCP, FTP, TFTP, MD5)
- Password recovery and configuration register
- File system management

Use Cisco IOS tools to troubleshoot and resolve problems

- Ping and traceroute with extended option
- Terminal monitor
- Log events
- Local SPAN

Describe network programmability in enterprise network architecture

- Function of an SDN controller
- Separation of control plane and data plane
- Northbound and southbound APIs

All People Seem TU Need Data Protection

Application:

Presentation

Session:

Transport:

Network : L3

Data Link : L2

Physical : bits 1,0

    TCP/IP model = 4 layers

Layer 4 = Session, Presentation, Application

Layer 3 : Transport, TRANSPOT layer

Layer 2 : Internet, Network layer

Layer 1 = Network, Physical + Data Link

Module 1: Network Fundamentals

1. What layer of the OSI reference model provides compression and encryption?

    A. session layer

    B. network layer

    C. presentation layer

    D. application layer

Correct Answer (C)
Subject Matter: OSI Model

The presentation layer services include compression, encryption, formatting and encoding at layer 6 of the OSI model. The presentation layer translates data sent from the application layer of a host so it is readable by the application layer of the remote host.

2. What layer of the OSI reference model is associated with TCP and UDP?

    A. physical layer

    B. network layer

    C. data link layer

    D. transport layer

Correct Answer (D)
Subject Matter: OSI Model

TCP and UDP are transport protocols (layer 4). The transport layer encapsulates upper OSI layers in a segment.

3. Select the correct Protocol Data Unit (PDU) associated with each OSI model reference layer?

    A. Layer 1 = bits, Layer 2 = data, Layer 3 = bytes, Layer 4 = packets

    B. Layer 1 = frames, Layer 2 = packets, Layer 3 = segments, Layer 4 = data

    C. Layer 1 = bits, Layer 2 = frames, Layer 3 = packets, Layer 4 = segments

    D. Layer 1 = bytes, Layer 2 = data, Layer 3 = packets, Layer 4 = segments

Correct Answer (C)
Subject Matter: OSI Model

Layer 1 are bits, Layer 2 are frames, Layer 3 are packets and Layer 4 are segments. The Protocol Data Unit (PDU) is based on the headers added as data is encapsulated from the application layer data to the physical layer. The encapsulation process adds a header at each layer. For instance a frame PDU is comprised of all headers added including frame header. The application, presentation and session layers add or modify data. The transport, network and data link layers add headers. The physical layer converts it all to binary (ones and zero bits).

4. What layer of the OSI reference model is MAC hardware addressing?

    A. layer 2

    B. layer 3

    C. layer 1

    D. frame layer

Correct Answer (A)
Subject Matter: OSI Model

The data link (layer 2) creates a frame with a source MAC address and destination MAC address. The most popular layer 2 protocol is Ethernet.

5. What are the four layers of the new TCP/IP reference model from lowest to highest?

   A. network, transport, internet, application

   B. internet, network, transport, application

   C. application, transport, internet, network

   D. network, internet, transport, application

Correct Answer (D)
Subject Matter: TCP/IP Reference Model

The newer TCP/IP model is based on the popularity of TCP with internet connectivity and network applications. The network layer maps to the OSI model physical and data link layers. In addition there is the internet layer transport layer and application layer. The internet layer is the same as OSI network layer. The transport layer maps to the OSI transport layer. The application layer collapses the session, presentation and application layer of the OSI model to a single application layer.

- Network Layer = OSI Physical Layer, Data Link Layer
- Internet Layer = OSI Network Layer
- Transport Layer = OSI Transport Layer
- Application Layer = OSI Session, Presentation and Application Layer

6. Select the answer that correctly describes the network services provided at each layer of the OSI reference model?

   A. **application:** network services to applications
      presentation: data formatting, translation, encoding, encryption
      session: session setup and tear down between applications
      transport: host-to-host, flow control, reliability, error recovery
      network: logical addressing, routing and path selection
      data link: media access and physical (mac) addressing
      physical: binary signaling, encoding, putting bits on physical media

B. **application:** network services to applications
   presentation: data formatting, translation, encoding, encryption
   session: host-to-host, flow control, reliability, error recovery
   transport: session setup and tear down between applications
   network: logical addressing, routing and path selection
   data link: media access and physical (mac) addressing
   physical: binary signaling, encoding, putting bits on the physical media

C. **application:** data formatting, translation, encoding, encryption
   presentation: network services to applications
   session: session setup and tear down between applications
   transport: host-to-host, flow control, reliability, error recovery
   network: media access and physical (mac) addressing
   data link: logical addressing, routing and path selection
   physical: binary signaling, encoding, putting bits on the physical media

D. **application:** network services to applications
   presentation: data formatting, translation, encoding, encryption
   session: session setup and tear down between applications
   transport: logical addressing, routing and path selection
   network: host-to-host, flow control, reliability, error recovery
   data link: binary signaling, encoding, putting bits on the physical media
   physical: media access and physical (mac) addressing

Correct Answer (A)
Subject Matter: OSI Model

The following describe the network services at each layer of the OSI model. Each lower OSI layer provided services to the next higher layer. Effective troubleshooting should start from the physical layer and verify connectivity to the application layer.

application layer 7: network services to applications
presentation layer 6: data formatting, translation, encoding, encryption
session layer 5: session setup and tear down between applications
transport layer 4: host-to-host, flow control, reliability, error recovery
network layer 3: logical addressing, routing and path selection
data link layer 2: media access and physical (mac) addressing
physical layer 1: binary signaling, encoding, putting bits on physical media

7. What statement is true concerning OSI model data encapsulation?

   A. each higher OSI layer adds a header to the PDU from a lower layer

   B. each lower OSI layer adds a header to the PDU from an upper layer

   C. frame adds a header to a TCP segment

   D. packet adds a header to a frame

Correct Answer (B)
Subject Matter: OSI Model

- Segment encapsulates data from upper OSI layers (5-7)
- Packet encapsulates upper layer segment (layer 4)
- Frame encapsulates upper layer packet (layer 3)
- Physical layer converts all to binary bits for transmission across the wire

8. Where does routing occur within the TCP/IP reference model?

   A. transport layer

   B. data link layer

   C. internet layer

   D. network layer

Correct Answer (C)
Subject Matter: TCP/IP Reference Model

Routing occur at the Internet layer of the TCP/IP reference model. The new TCP/IP reference model is comprised of four layers:

   Layer 4: Application = OSI Session, Presentation and Application Layers

   Layer 3: Transport = OSI Transport Layer

   Layer 2: Internet = OSI Network Layer

   Layer 1: Network = OSI Physical Layer and Data Link Layer

9. What two statements describe the OSI data encapsulation process?

   A. presentation layer translates frame into bits before sending across the physical link

   B. network layer add IP addressing and control information header to a segment

   C. data link layer adds source and destination MAC addressing with FCS to the segment

   D. network layer encapsulates a frame with source and destination IP addressing

   E. transport layer divides a data stream into segments. Reliability and flow control information is added when the transport protocol is TCP

Correct Answers (B,E)
Subject Matter: OSI Model

Lower layers encapsulate higher layers for the OSI and TCP/IP reference model. The transport layer 4 divides a data stream into segments. The network layer packet encapsulates the upper transport layer segment.

10. The network administrator is testing connectivity of a new application by establishing an HTTP connection to a web server. What is the highest layer of the OSI protocol stack required for testing purposes?

   A. transport

   B. session

   C. presentation

   D. application

   E. internet

Correct Answer (D)
Subject Matter: OSI Model

HTTP is an example of an application layer protocol. Verifying network connectivity requires testing to the application layer. That will confirm all layers of the OSI reference model are working. Some additional application layer protocols include FTP, Telnet, SSH, TFTP and NTP.

11. Match the OSI reference model layer on the left with the associated network services on the right?

application layer	windowing, error control, segmentation, host-to-host
presentation layer	network services to applications
session layer	logical communication between host processes
transport layer	IP addressing
network layer	data formatting, translation, encryption
data link layer	binary bits, electrical signaling, 802.3ae
physical layer	framing, media access control (MAC)

Correct Answers.
Subject Matter: OSI Model

The following describe the network services provided at each OSI model layer.

application layer	**network services to applications**
presentation layer	**data formatting, translation, encryption**
session layer	**logical communication between host processes**
transport layer	**windowing, error control, segmenting, host-to-host**
network layer	**IP addressing**
data link layer	**framing, media access control (MAC)**
physical layer	**binary bits, electrical signaling, 802.3ae**

12. What layers of the OSI reference model do WAN protocols use?

A. transport, session

B. network, data link

C. application, transport

D. session, network

E. physical, data link

Correct Answer (E)
Subject Matter: OSI Model

WAN protocols are often associated with the lower layers of the OSI model to include physical layer 1 and data link layer 2. The router provides WAN interface options for connecting to a variety of WAN services. The routing protocols provide packet forwarding based on IP addressing and best path selection. As a result WAN protocols strip off Ethernet framing and add new framing based on the WAN protocol.

13. What layer of the OSI reference model provides logical addressing, path selection and packet forwarding?

    A. physical layer

    B. session layer

    C. transport layer

    D. network layer

Correct Answer (D)
Subject Matter: OSI Model

The OSI network layer 3 is associated with routing packets. The routing protocols are responsible for assigning IP addresses, providing best path selection and next hop forwarding. The routing table is used as the source for selecting the preferred next hop to a destination subnet.

14. What layer of the OSI model provides reliability and error recovery between network devices using flow control?

    A. physical layer

    B. data link layer

    C. transport layer

    D. network layer

    E. session layer

Correct Answer (C)
Subject Matter: OSI Model

The OSI transport layer provides host-to-host reliability and error recovery with flow control. The flow control techniques include TCP sliding window, packet sequencing and acknowledgements. Flow control enables the receiving host to control the amount of data from the sender. The primary transport layer protocols include UDP and TCP. Note that only TCP provides error recovery and retransmission. UDP is a best effort transmission that only detects errors with CRC/FCS checksum from the frame. Any UDP datagrams with errors are discarded instead of being retransmitted.

15. What transport layer protocol provides best-effort delivery service with no acknowledgment receipt?

    A. UDP

    B. TCP

    C. FTP

    D. HTTP

Correct Answer (A)
Subject Matter: OSI Model

The transport layer provides host-to-host peering connectivity with TCP or UDP protocols. TCP provides reliable, connection-oriented connectivity with error recovery techniques and retransmission. UDP is connectionless with best effort transmission and error detection only. The CRC/FCS checksum from the frame is checked and any UDP datagrams with errors are discarded.

16. Match the network protocols on the left with the correct OSI reference model layer on the right?

PAP, CHAP	transport layer
FTP, HTTP, Telnet, SSH, DNS	application layer
TCP, UDP	physical layer
SSL, TLS	network layer
802.3ae, T1, T3	presentation layer
Ethernet, PPP, DSL, CDP, STP	data link layer
IP, ARP, ICMP, Ping	session layer

Correct Answers.
Subject Matter: OSI Model

The following correctly match network protocols with the associated OSI reference model layer.

PAP, CHAP	**session layer**
FTP, HTTP, Telnet, SSH, DNS	**application layer**
TCP, UDP	**transport layer**
SSL, TLS	**presentation layer**
802.3ae, T1, T3	**physical layer**
Ethernet, PPP, DSL, CDP, STP	**data link layer**
IP, ARP, ICMP, Ping	**network layer**

17. Match the network message type with correct description on the right?

Unicast	packets sent from a single source to a destination group
Multicast	packets sent from a single source to the nearest destination
Broadcast	packets sent from a single source to a single destination
Anycast	packets sent from a single source to all hosts on a VLAN

Correct Answers.
Subject Matter: IPv4 Address Types

The following describe standard network messages types:

Unicast	**packets sent from a single source to a single destination**
Multicast	**packets sent from a single source to a destination group**
Broadcast	**packets sent from a single source to all hosts on a VLAN**
Anycast	**packets sent from a single source to nearest destination**

18. Select the Gigabit Ethernet physical layer standard that supports full-duplex SMF (Single-mode Fiber) across single strand?

A. 1000Base-TX

B. 1000Base-LX

C. 1000Base-SX

D. 1000Base-BX

E. 1000Base-ZX

Correct Answer (D)
Subject Matter: Cabling Type

The following are all Ethernet physical layer signaling standards for Gigabit network connectivity. Each standard is based on a media type supported (copper or fiber), network distance limitations, maximum speed and transceiver support. Most fiber media is designed for full-duplex with multi-strands. 1000Base-BX provides full-duplex with a single strand.

1000Base-TX = Gigabit Copper (Cat6/Cat7), 100 meters, 1000 Mbps

1000Base-LX = Gigabit Fiber, MMF (550 meters), SMF (5 km), 1000 Mbps

1000Base-SX = Gigabit Fiber, MMF, 100 meters, 1000 Mbps

1000Base-BX = Gigabit Fiber (Single Strand), SMF, 10 km, 1000 Mbps

1000Base-ZX = Gigabit Fiber, SMF, 70 km, 1000 Mbps

19. Select the network protocol assigned to UDP port 123?

A. SSH

B. Telnet

C. NTP

D. FTP

Correct Answer (C)
Subject Matter: UDP Protocol

UDP-based protocols such as NTP are connectionless with no guaranteed service delivery. NTP is poll-oriented sending a request for time at regular intervals. SSH, Telnet and FTP run over TCP and are connection-oriented with the TCP handshake and flow control.

20. Match the network protocol on the left with the correct TCP/UDP port number on the right?

Telnet	TCP 22
SMTP	TCP 21
FTP	TCP 23
HTTP	TCP/UDP 53
SNMP	TCP 80
DNS	TCP 25
HTTPS	UDP 161
SSH	TCP 443
TFTP	UDP 69

Correct Answers.
Subject Matter: TCP/UDP Protocols

The following correctly match network protocol with TCP/UDP port assignment. DNS can use TCP or UDP transport protocol.

Telnet	**TCP 23**
SMTP	**TCP 25**
FTP	**TCP 21**
HTTP	**TCP 80**
SNMP	**UDP 161**
DNS	**TCP/UDP 53**
HTTPS	**TCP 443**
SSH	**TCP 22**
TFTP	**UDP 69**

21. Select the network protocol that is connection-oriented?

    A. TFTP

    B. NTP

    C. SNMP

    D. FTP

    E. ICMP

    F. EIGRP

Correct Answer (D)
Subject Matter: TCP/UDP Protocols

FTP is the only network protocol from the list of options that is run over TCP transport. As a result it is connection-oriented with packet acknowledgement and error recovery. The other listed network protocols are UDP-based.

22. What cable type is required when connecting to the console port of a Cisco network device?

    A. DB25

    B. rollover

    C. crossover

    D. 1000Base-SX

    E. 802.3ae

Correct Answer (B)
Subject Matter: Cabling Type

The rollover cable is a proprietary cable available from Cisco for connecting locally to the console port. It is often used for initial configuration and where remote management isn't an option.

straight-through = connect dissimilar network devices (router to firewall)

rollover = console port

crossover = connect same class devices (switch to switch)

serial = WAN interface (DTE/DCE)

23. What two of the following transport layer techniques are used to detect lost packets?

    A. queuing

    B. sliding window

    C. acknowledgements

    D. FCS

    E. CRC

    F. sequencing

Correct Answers (C,F)
Subject Matter: TCP Protocol

Packet loss occurs when there is network congestion. Acknowledgements and sequencing are TCP flow control techniques that track when packets arrive at the destination host. The destination host sends an alert to the source when a packet does not arrive. Any dropped packets are detected and retransmitted.

Queuing/Buffering - prevents packet loss instead of detecting it by storing packets to memory instead of discarding them.

CRC/FCS - some protocols will verify the checksum of a frame. The frame is discarded where there is a mismatch between the original checksum value and the value when arriving at the destination. The packet is discarded if there is a mismatch. Data integrity is verified however there is no detection of packet loss.

TCP Sliding Window - flow control technique that prevents packet loss instead of detecting it. The send and receive window size are negotiated to manage data forwarding rate. That prevents packet overrun and retransmissions.

24. What feature allows an FTP server to support multiple downloads?

    A. sequence number

    B. IP address

    C. port number

    D. session ID

    E. MAC address

Correct Answer (D)
Subject Matter: OSI Model

The session ID provides logical communication for each application process. It is an OSI session layer service that would manage multiple FTP downloads for instance. Each download session is then assigned a unique session ID. The port number or socket number identifies different applications running on the same server. For instance a web browser (HTTP) would be assigned a unique session ID as well. The server distinguishes where to forward arriving packets to each application based on port number.

25. What application layer feature enables a network server with multiple applications to route inbound requests to the correct application?

   A. IP address

   B. sequence number

   C. routing protocol

   D. port number

   E. session ID

Correct Answer (D)
Subject Matter: OSI Model

The port number or socket number identifies different applications running on the same server. The server would distinguish where to forward arriving packets to each application based on port number.

26. The network administrator has configured two new switches each with a unique assigned VLAN and a single host connected. What network topology and cable type is required to enable packet forwarding between switches?

   A. connect switches with a straight-through cable

   B. connect switches to a single router using a straight-through cable

   C. connect switches to separate routers with a crossover cable

   D. connect switches with a crossover cable

   E. connect the switches to a single router using a rollover cable

Correct Answer (B)
Subject Matter: Cabling Type

The router is required for Inter-VLAN routing between different VLANs. The connectivity between network devices that are dissimilar such as switch to router requires a straight through cable. Connecting the same device type such as switch to switch for instance requires a crossover cable.

27. What network protocol supports TCP and UDP?

   A. DNS

   B. SSH

   C. FTP

   D. TFTP

   E. Telnet

Correct Answer (A)
Subject Matter: TCP/UDP Protocols

DNS is unique with support for either transport protocol. TCP is preferred where there are larger DNS records resulting from IPv6 addresses.

28. What are three primary differences between TCP and UDP?

   A. TCP provides flow control and error correction

   B. TCP is connection-oriented

   C. TCP provides sequencing numbering of packets

   D. TCP provides best effort delivery model

   E. TCP is faster than UDP

   F. TCP is preferred for video streaming

Correct Answers (A,B,C)
Subject Matter: TCP/UDP Protocols

TCP is connection-oriented with handshake setup, flow control and sequencing. The purpose is to detect, prevent and correct packet drops. It is less efficient than UDP with increased overhead and packet processing.

UDP is faster than TCP however it is connectionless with no guarantee of packet delivery (best effort). Some applications such as video streaming prefer UDP where there is less latency resulting from retransmissions.

29. There are two switches connected with a straight-through cable in the lab. What is required to enable connectivity where the network administrator can ping the neighbor interface from each switch? (select two)

    A. replace the straight-through cable with a crossover cable

    B. replace the straight-through cable with a rollover cable

    C. assign switch interfaces to the same subnet

    D. configure classless subnet masks only

    E. configure public IP addressing only

Correct Answers (A,C)
Subject Matter: Cabling Type

Connecting the same network device type such as switch to switch requires a crossover cable to flip the Tx and Rx pins. In addition, assigning the same subnet enables communication between the network devices without any routing required. Assignment to the same subnet requires the same subnet mask and subnet within that range.

30. Select three advantages of a hierarchical network addressing scheme?

    A. reduces routing table entries

    B. ease of management and troubleshooting

    C. auto-negotiation of media interface speed

    D. effective utilization of MAC addresses

    E. network scalability

Correct Answers (A,B,E)
Subject Matter: IPv4 Addressing

Hierarchical network addressing enables optimized route summarization at each network layer (access, distribution, core). The number of routes are decreased creating a smaller routing table with improved scalability.

Summarization requires contiguous addressing assignment for best results. Network management and troubleshooting is much easier with contiguous, summarized addressing. Layer 3 routing problems can then be easily identified.

31. Refer to the network topology drawing. What is the best explanation for why Host-1 cannot ping Server-1?

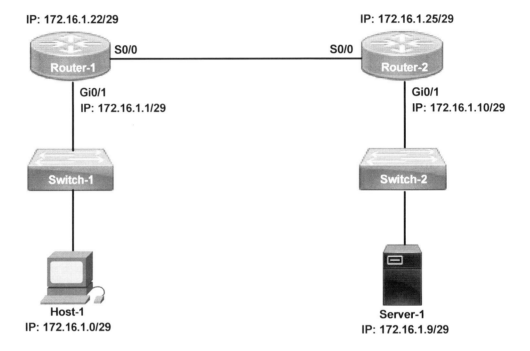

IP: 172.16.1.22/29

S0/0

Router-1

Gi0/1
IP: 172.16.1.1/29

Switch-1

Host-1
IP: 172.16.1.0/29

IP: 172.16.1.25/29

S0/0

Router-2

Gi0/1
IP: 172.16.1.10/29

Switch-2

Server-1
IP: 172.16.1.9/29

A. Host-1 and Server-1 are not on the same subnet

B. routing is not enabled on any switch

C. router serial interfaces are assigned to different subnets

D. IP address of Server-1 is incorrect

Correct Answer (C)
Subject Matter: IPv4 Addressing

The physical network interfaces for directly connected links must be assigned to the same subnet. That applies to LAN or WAN interfaces. The subnet mask and subnet within that range determines the subnet assigned to the network interface. The number of subnets available is based on subnet mask length.

Router-1 = 172.16.1.22/29
Router-2 = 172.16.1.25/29

The /29 subnet mask assigns 29 bits to the network portion and 3 bits (2 power 3 = 8) to the host portion. The number of host addresses assignable = 6 (8 - 2). The network address (zero) and broadcast address (all ones) can't be assigned.

network portion (/29) | hosts (1-6)
11111111.11111111.11111111.11111 000

- Router-1 = 172.16.1.22/29
- Network address = 172.16.1.16/29
- Broadcast address = 172.16.1.23/29

- Router-2 = 172.16.1.25/29
- Network address = 172.16.1.24/29
- Broadcast address = 172.16.1.31/29

- IP subnet range 1 = 172.16.1.16-172.16.1.23
- IP subnet range 2 = 172.16.1.24-172.16.1.31

The result is that Router-1 is within IP subnet range 1 while Router-2 is within IP subnet range 2. The serial interfaces are assigned to different subnets and cannot communicate. The ping is discarded at Router-1 as a result.

32. What is the binary conversion of 192.168.64.10?

Correct Answer.
Subject Matter: IPv4 Addressing

It is important to understand how to convert from IPv4 decimal notation to binary for subnetting and summarization.

- The binary system is based on ones (1) and zeros (0).
- There are 8 bits per octet, 4 octets per IPv4 address.
- The bit value is based on position.
- The bit set to 1 sets the value. The bit set to zero = 0
- There are 8 bits with 2 (nth power) so 2 power of 8 = 255
- Per octet: set all bits to 1 = 255, set all bits to 0 = 0

0	0	0	0	0	0	0	0 = 0
1	1	1	1	1	1	1	1 = 255
128	64	32	16	8	4	2	1

Example:
decimal 10 = from right to left, set 2nd bit (2) and 4th bit (8) to a (1) and everything else to a zero (0).

00001010 = 10

10.0.0.0 = 00001010 | 00000000 | 00000000 | 00000000

Converting IPv4 address 10.100.40.128 to an equivalent binary number requires setting specific bits for each octet to (1) value. The sum of each octet must add up to the decimal value for each octet.

192 . 168 . 64 . 10

11000000 . **1**0**1**0**1**000 . 0**1**000000 . 0000**1**0**1**0

(128+64) | (128+32+8) | 64 position | (8+2)

33. Convert the following binary number to IPv4 decimal equivalent?

00001010.01100100.00101000.10000000

Correct Answer.
Subject Matter: IPv4 Addressing

It is important to understand decimal to binary conversion for subnetting and route summarization.

- The binary system is based on ones (1) and zeros (0).
- There are 8 bits per octet, 4 octets per IPv4 address.
- The bit value is based on position.
- The bit set to 1 sets the value. The bit set to zero = 0
- There are 8 bits with 2 (nth power) so 2 power of 8 = 255
- Per octet: set all bits to 1 = 255, set all bits to 0 = 0

0	0	0	0	0	0	0	0	= 0
1	1	1	1	1	1	1	1	= 255
128	64	32	16	8	4	2	1	

Example:
decimal 100 = from right to left, set 3rd bit (4), 6th bit (32) and 7th bit (64) to a (1) and everything else to a zero (0).

01100100 = 100

Converting the following IPv4 binary number to decimal equivalent requires adding bits for each octet that are set to (1) value:

10 . 100 . 40 . 128

00001010 . 01100100 . 01000000 . 10000000

(8+2) | (64+32+4) | (32+8) | 128 position

10.100.40.128

34. What is the binary conversion of hexidecimal FDA4?

Correct Answer.
Subject Matter: IPv6 Addressing

IPv6 use hexidecimal format instead of the IPv4 octets. The IPv4 address is comprised of 4 octets that are 8 bits each (32 bit length). The IPv6 address is comprised of 32 hexidecimal values of 4 bits each. The length of an IPv6 address is then 128 bits (4 bits x 32 hexidecimal values).

Each hexidecimal number has 16 possible values that range from 0 to F derived from the lower 4 bits of an octet. The same values from 0 -9 are used for IPv4 and IPv6 binary to decimal conversion. The values 10 to 15 however are A to F.

Example binary 5 = 0 **1** 0 **1**
               0 **4** 0 **1** = 4 + 1 = 5

Example binary 13 = 1 1 0 1
                8 4 0 **1** = 8 + 4 + 1 = 13 (hexidecimal **D)**

A = 10 (1010)
B = 11 (1011)
C = 12 (1100)
D = 13 (1101)
E = 14 (1110)
F = 15 (1111)

Converting FDA4 to binary:

FDA4 = 1111 1101 1010 0100
           F   D   A   4

35. Select the correct order of bit values for binary numbering?

    A. 1 2 4 8 16 32 64 128

    B. 128 64 32 16 8 4 2 1

    C. 128 64 32 16 8 4 2 0

    D. 0 2 4 8 16 32 64 128

Correct Answer (B)
Subject Matter: IPv4 Addressing

The binary numbering system is based on an octet (8 bits) with zero and one possible values. When set to one, the value is based on the position. When set to zero it is zero (0). For instance all ones (1) for the octet is a value of 256 (128+64+32+16+8+4+2+1). All zeros (0) is of course zero.

    0   0   0   0   0   0   0   0

    1   1   1   1   1   1   1   1

    128 64 32 16 8 4 2 1

36. Select the default Class A, Class B and Class C subnet masks?

    A. Class A = 255.255.255.0
        Class B = 255.255.0.0
        Class C = 255.255.255.0

    B. Class A = 255.255.255.255
        Class B = 255.255.255.0
        Class C = 255.255.0.0

    C. Class A = 255.0.0.0
        Class B = 255.255.0.0
        Class C = 255.255.255.0

    D. Class A = 0.0.0.0
        Class B = 255.255.0.0
        Class C = 255.255.255.0

Correct Answer (C)
Subject Matter: IPv4 Addressing

The default subnet mask is deployed when no subnetting is required for that specific address class. The CIDR notation denotes the number of bits in the subnet mask. In addition where there is subnetting the CIDR notation is based on all ones that define the subnet mask. For instance a Class C address with subnet mask 255.255.255.240 = /28

- Class A = 255.0.0.0 (/8)
- Class B = 255.255.0.0 (/16)
- Class C = 255.255.255.0 (/24)

37. What is the maximum number of IP addresses available for host assignment with network address 192.168.34.0 and subnet mask 255.255.255.0?

   A. 255

   B. 254

   C. 253

   D. 252

Correct Answer (B)
Subject Matter: IPv4 Addressing

It is a Class C default subnet mask so the 4th octet (most right 8 bits) are not subnetted and assigned for host addressing. Any octet has 8 bits and provides binary 2 power 8 = 256 IP addresses. The result is 256 - 2 = 254 usable IP addresses are available. The network address and broadcast address are never assignable to network hosts (desktop, server, switch, router, mobile etc).

- network address = 192.168.34.0
- host addresses = 192.168.34.1 - 192.168.34.254
- broadcast address = 192.168.34.255

38. What additional subnets are enabled with **ip subnet-zero** feature?

A. The first subnet of any network address

B. The last subnet for any subnetted range of IP addresses

C. The first subnet for any subnetted range of IP addresses

D. The first and last subnet for any subnetted range of IP addresses

E. **ip subnet-zero** command is no longer supported

Correct Answer (D)
Subject Matter: IPv4 Addressing

The **ip subnet-zero** command is now the default with current IOS. That provides two additional subnets based on the zero subnet and broadcast subnet. It applies to subnettted IP addresses and not default subnet masks.

Consider IP address 192.168.1.1 255.255.255.224 for instance. The 3 leftmost bits of the 4th octet are subnetted based on a Class C address. The 3 bits provide 8 subnets with ip subnet-zero enabled instead of 6 subnets. There are the standard 254 hosts per subnet. The network address and broadcast address for each individual subnet are not assignable to hosts.

The rightmost bit of the subnet mask (/27) determines the subnet multiple. That is bit 6 of the 4th octet with a binary value of 32. As a result the subnets are multiples of 32 (0, 32, 64, 96, 128, 160, 192, 224).

192.168.1.0 - 192.168.1.31 (zero subnet)

192.168.1.32 - 192.168.1.63

192.168.1.64 - 192.168.1.95

192.168.1.96 - 192.168.1.127

192.168.1.128 - 192.168.1.159

192.168.1.160 - 192.168.1.191

192.168.1.192 - 192.168.1.223

192.168.1.224 - 192.168.1.255 (broadcast subnet)

39. Select the IP subnet that summarizes the network address range from 172.33.0.0/24 to 172.33.40.0/24?

A. 172.33.0.0/18

B. 172.33.0.0/24

C. 172.33.40.0/14

D. 172.33.0.0/14

Correct Answer (A)
Subject Matter: IPv4 Addressing

The example is based on a default subnet mask for a Class B address. The purpose of summarization is to aggregate multiple IP addresses to a single address that includes all of them. The single IP address advertises all of them. Modify the subnet mask so it includes both IP addresses will summarize the range to a single IP address. The third octet is being summarized and relevant bits are noted.

172.33.0.0/24 = **10101010.00100001.00** 000000.00000000

172.33.40.0/24 = **10101010.00100001.00** 101000.00000000

172.33.0.0/18 = 10101010.00100001.00 000000.00000000

Move from left to right and identify where all bits match for the IP addresses. The point where they don't match defines the subnet mask. For instance the bits no longer match at bit 19 (/19). They do match at bit 18 (/18) and that defines the summary address (**172.33.0.0/18)**

40. What is the usable range of host IP addresses within 172.16.3.0/23 subnet?

A. 172.16.3.1 to 172.16.4.254

B. 172.16.2.0 to 172.16.3.255

C. 172.16.0.0 to 172.16.4.254

D. 172.16.1.0 to 172.16.3.254

Correct Answer (B)
Subject Matter: IPv4 Addressing

The subnet mask defines the network portion and the host portion for the IP address. The example is a Class B using a non-default subnet mask. The 3rd octet is subnetted with 255.255.254.0 (/23).

The rightmost bit of the /23 subnet mask (network bits) determines the subnet multiple and where it starts. That is bit 2 of the third octet with a binary value of 2. The subnets are multiples of 2 (0, 2, 4, 6 etc.) so the subnet starts at 172.16.2.0 as the network address for the subnet. In addition 172.16.3.0 is a host address of the .2 subnet. The broadcast address is 172.16.3.255 derived from setting all ones(1) for the 9 bit host portion.

```
                       network             |   host
172.16.3.0    = 10101100.00010000.0000001 1.00000000
255.255.254.0 = 11111111.11111111.1111111 0.00000000
```

- network address = 172.16.2.0

- host addresses = 172.16.2.1 - 172.16.3.254

- broadcast address = 172.16.3.255

41. Select the subnet masks that are classless?

   A. 255.0.0.0

   B. 255.255.224.0

   C. 255.255.255.248

   D. 255.255.0.0

   E. 255.255.255.0

Correct Answers (B,C)
Subject Matter: IPv4 Addressing

Classless subnet masks are of variable length. Classful subnet masks are based on default subnet masks for each address Class (A,B,C).

- 255.0.0.0 = classful (default Class A subnet mask)
- **255.255.224.0 = classless**
- **255.255.255.248 = classless**
- 255.255.0.0 = classful (default Class B subnet mask)
- 255.255.255.0 = classful (default Class C subnet mask)

42. What network address would allow the maximum number of subnets for 172.16.1.0/23 with 30 hosts?

A. 172.16.1.0/27

B. 172.16.1.0/29

C. 172.16.1.0/26

D. 172.16.1.0/25

E. 172.16.1.0/28

Correct Answer (A)
Subject Matter: IPv4 Addressing

The subnet mask defines the network portion (bold) and host portion of an IP address. The subnet mask /23 (255.255.254.0) assigns 23 bits to the network portion and 9 bits to the host portion. The number of assignable hosts is 2 power 9 = 512 - 2.

```
                          network        |  host
172.16.1.0      = 10101100.00010000.0000000 1.00000000
255.255.254.0   = 11111111.11111111.1111111 0.00000000

                          network          |  host
255.255.255.224 = 11111111.11111111.11111111.111 00000
```

The question asked for a maximum of 30 hosts. The subnet mask is used to modify the network portion and consequently the host portion as well. Moving the subnet mask to the right will increase the network portion and decrease the host portion assignable. Assigning the rightmost 5 bits provides a maximum of 30 hosts (32 - 2). The network address and broadcast address cannot be assigned to hosts.

binary 32 = 5 bits = 00000000

The host portion must be decreased from 9 bits to 5 bits. That will require increasing the subnet mask from /23 to /27.

Subnet with 30 hosts = **172.16.1.0/27**

43. What is the second IP address available for host assignment from 172.33.1.64/30?

    A. 172.33.1.64

    B. 172.33.1.65

    C. 172.33.1.66

    D. 172.33.1.1

Correct Answer (C)
Subject Matter: IPv4 Addressing

The IP address is a nondefault Class A address. The subnet mask defines the number of bits assigned to the network portion and host portion. The /30 subnet mask creates a network portion of 30 bits and a host portion of 2 bits. The number of host assignments available with 2 bits = 2 power 2 = 4. The network address and broadcast address are not assignable to hosts. As a result the number of host assignments = 4 - 2 = 2 IP addresses.

- network address = 172.33.1.64
- first usable host IP address = 172.33.1.65
- second usable host IP address = 172.33.1.66
- broadcast address = 172.33.1.67

```
                            network              | host
172.33.1.64     = 10101100.00100001.00000001.010000 00
255.255.255.252 = 11111111.11111111.11111111.111111 00
```

The rightmost bit of the subnet mask (network bits) determines the multiple and where it starts. For this example it is bit 3 of the 4th octet that has a binary value of 4. The maximum number of bits assigned to the host portion (4 bits) is the subnet multiple (0, 4, 8, 12 etc). The next available subnet is 172.33.1.68 address (64 + 4).

44. Select the IP address that is part of RFC 1918 assigned address space?

    A. 192.169.0.0/23

    B. 10.0.0.0/7

    C. 172.16.0.0/12

    D. 172.33.0.0/24

Correct Answer (C)
Subject Matter: IPv4 Addressing

RFC 1918 defines private IP address space from each address class. The private IP addressing is not public routable across the internet. The standard practice is for companies to assign private addressing to all inside hosts. NAT is deployed at the internet edge where private addresses are translated to public routable addresses.

The following are the RFC 1918 private IP address ranges:

10.0.0.0 - 10.255.255.255 /8

172.16.0.0 - 172.31.255.255 /12

192.168.0.0 - 192.168.255.255 /16

45. What is the wildcard mask for subnet mask 255.255.224.0?

A. 0.0.0.255

B. 0.0.0.0

C. 0.0.255.255

D. 0.0.31.255

Correct Answer (D)
Subject Matter: IPv4 Addressing

The wildcard mask is a technique for matching specific IP address or range of IP addresses. It is used by routing protocols and access control lists (ACL) to manage routing and packet filtering.

The wildcard mask is an inverted mask where the matching IP address or range is based on 0 bits. The additional bits are set to 1 as no match required. The wildcard 0.0.0.0 is used to match a single IP address.

The wildcard mask for 255.255.224.0 is 0.0.31.255 (invert the bits so zero=1 and one=0)

11111111.11111111.111 00000.00000000 = subnet mask
00000000.00000000.000 **11111.11111111** = wildcard mask

Example: Classful Wildcard

The following wildcard will only match on the 192.168.3.0 subnet and not match on everything else. This could be used with an ACL for instance to permit or deny a subnet. It could define a single subnet to advertise from OSPF as well.

192.168.3.0 0.0.0.255

    192.   168.   3.   0
11000000.10101000.00000011.00000000
00000000.00000000.00000000.**11111111** = 0.0.0.255

Example: Classless Wildcard

The classless wildcard can filter based on any network boundary. The following wildcard mask matches on the subnet 192.168.4.0 serial link only. It is the equivalent of 255.255.255.252 subnet mask.

    192.   168.   4.   0
11000000.10101000.00000100.00000000
00000000.00000000.00000000.000000**11** = 0.0.0.3

192.168.4.0 0.0.0.3 = match on 192.168.4.1 and 192.168.4.2

46. What is the minimum subnet mask required on a Cisco switch that would enable 440 host IP address assignments on the same subnet?

   A. 255.255.255.0

   B. 255.255.255.192

   C. 255.255.255.224

   D. 255.255.254.0

Correct Answer (D)
Subject Matter: IPv4 Addressing

Defining the number of IP addresses required for any particular subnet is fundamental to any new deployment. The subnet mask defines the network portion and host portion. The longer subnet mask decreases the IP addresses available for host assignment. Some typical network hosts include desktops, servers, switches, routers, wireless and mobile devices.

The Cisco switch requirement is 440 available host assignments. The Class C address (with default subnet mask) provides a maximum of 254 host addresses. That is derived from all 8 bits of the 4th octet. Subnetting will always decrease the number of host IP addresses available.

To enable 440 host addresses will require a Class B address with a smaller subnet mask length than the default Class C (255.255.255.0)

11111111.11111111.11111110.00000000 = 255.255.254.0 = /23
     255.   255.   254.   0

Subnetting 9 bits instead of 8 bits provides 510 host assignments. The binary value for 9 bits is 2 power 9 = 512 however the network address and broadcast address are not assignable to hosts.

       0.   0   0   0   0   0   0   0   0
      256   128   64   32   16   8   4   2   1 = 510

47. The ISP has assigned public routable IP address 71.83.34.0/25 for your internet connectivity. What subnet mask would create two additional subnets for the DMZ where a maximum 60 host assignments are required?

   A. 255.255.255.128

   B. 255.255.255.224

   C. 255.255.255.0

   D. 255.255.255.192

Correct Answer (D)
Subject Matter: IPv4 Addressing

The Class A address of 71.83.34.0/25 is subnetting to the 4th octet. There are 126 host assignments per subnet. There are already two subnets including 71.83.34.0 and 71.83.34.128 subnets.

- network address = 71.83.34.0
- host addresses = 71.83.34.1-126
- broadcast address = 71.83.34.127

- network address = 71.83.34.128
- host addresses = 71.83.34.129-254
- broadcast address = 71.83.34.255

```
            network              |  host
11111111.11111111.11111111.1 0000000
   255.       255.      255.     128 = /25 (7 bits = 126 hosts)
```

Adding two new subnets require increasing the subnet mask length to **255.255.255.192 (/26)** mask. That borrows a single bit from the host portion. The result is two bits are now assigned to the subnet portion of the 4th octet. That increases the number of available subnets from two to four subnets. Adding 30 new subnets would have required /29 subnet.

```
            network              |  host
11111111.11111111.11111111.11 000000
   255.       255.      255.     192 = /26 (6 bits = 64 hosts)
```

48. What two IP addresses are assignable to hosts from subnet 172.16.8.0/21?

   A. 172.16.10.0

   B. 172.16.12.254

   C. 172.16.7.0

   D. 172.16.15.255

   E. 172.16.16.1

Correct Answers (A,B)
Subject Matter: IPv4 Addressing

The /21 subnet mask assigns 5 bits (bold) from the 3rd octet for 32 available subnets. There are 11 bits from the 3rd and 4th octet for 2,046 assignable host addresses.

```
                            network        |    host
172.16.8.0         = 10101100.00010000.00001 000.00000000
255.255.248.0 (/21) = 11111111.11111111.11111 000.00000000
```

The rightmost bit of the subnet mask (network bits) determines the multiple and where it starts. In this case it is bit 4 of the 3rd octet that has a binary value of 8. The subnets will then start at 0 (ip subnet-zero) with multiples of 8 (0, 8, 16, 24 etc). The network address 172.16.8.0/21 is the .8 subnet that extends to .15 based on the 8 multiple. The next subnet starts at .16 and extends to .23 for that subnet. The network address and broadcast address are not assignable to hosts for each subnet. Note as well the Class B address can subnet the range from bit 17 to bit 31 based on the subnet mask length.

46

- network address = 172.16.8.0
- host address range = 172.16.8.1 - 172.16.15.254
- broadcast address = 172.16.15.255

The two host IP addresses within range for IP address 172.16.8.0/21 include 172.16.10.0/21 and 172.16.12.254/21

49. What is the network address of a host assigned 192.168.1.42/29?

A. 192.168.1.8/29

B. 192.168.1.32/27

C. 192.168.1.40/29

D. 192.168.1.16/28

E. 192.168.1.48/29

Correct Answer (C)
Subject Matter: IPv4 Addressing

The network address is the first address assigned to a subnet range. The IP address 192.168.1.42 is a Class C address. The nondefault subnet mask 255.255.248.0 (/29) provides the subnetting.

```
                        network               | host
192.168.1.42    = 11000000.10101000.00000001.00101 010
255.255.255.248 = 11111111.11111111.11111111.11111 000
```

The host portion is the rightmost 3 bits of the 4th octet. The subnetted portion is the 5 bits of the 4th octet (bold). It is a Class C address so subnetting is only done on the 4th octet. The IP address class is key with subnetting questions.

The rightmost bit of the subnet mask (network bits) determines the multiple and where it starts. In this case it is bit 4 that has a binary value of 8. The 5 subnetted bits (bold) enable 32 subnets with the first network address starting at subnet bit (.0) and multiples of 8. (0, 8, 16, 24, 32, **40**, 48, 56 etc). The nearest subnet is 192.168.1.40 as the network address for 192.168.1.42

- network address = 192.168.1.40
- host addresses = 192.168.1.41 - 192.168.1.46
- broadcast address = 192.168.1.47

The next subnet of 192.168.1.48 is out of range.

50. The network administrator must assign a static IP address to the web server for the DMZ. The router is assigned the first host IP address from 192.168.34.16/28 while the web server is assigned the next available host IP address. Select the correct IP address configuration for the web server?

   A. IP address = 192.168.34.17/28
       default gateway = 192.168.34.16

   B. IP address = 192.168.34.18/28
       default gateway = 192.168.34.17

   C. IP address = 192.168.34.19/28
       default gateway =192.168.34.18

   D. IP address: 192.168.34.23/24
       default gateway = 192.168.34.16

   E. IP address = 192.168.34.254/24
       default gateway = 192.168.34.1

Correct Answer (B)
Subject Matter: IPv4 Addressing

The network address of 192.168.34.16/28 is a Class C address with subnetting of the 4th octet. The /28 subnet mask (255.255.255.240) assigns the leftmost 4 bits of the 4th octet to the network (subnet) address. The rightmost 4 bits are assigned to the host portion.

```
                         network (subnet)           | hosts (1-14)
192.168.34.16   = 11000000.10101000.00100010.0001 0000
255.255.255.240 = 11111111.11111111.11111111.1111 0000
```

The 4 bits of the subnetted (bold) portion provide 16 subnet addresses. The rightmost bit of the subnet mask (network bits) determines the subnet multiple. In this case the rightmost bit is position 5 with a binary value of 16. The subnet numbering will then start at zero with multiples of 16 (0, 16, 32, 48 etc). The .16 subnet, for instance, extends from .16 to .31 with the next subnet starting at .32 subnet.

The 4 bits of the host portion provides 16 assignable host addresses per subnet. The question requested assignment from the .16 subnet only.

   • network address = 192.168.34.16
   • host address range = 192.168.34.17 - 192.168.34.30
   • broadcast address = 192.168.34.31

The first available IP address of 192.168.34.17/28 is assigned to the router. The next IP address of 192.168.34.18/28 is assigned to the web server.

- web server IP address = 192.168.34.18/28
- router (default gateway) = 192.168.34.17

51. Select the valid IPv6 address from the following list?

   A. 2001:0000:12D4::043D::1

   B. 2001:1234:4567:AD:12DE:1

   C. FEC0:ABCD:9WCD:0067::2A4

   D. 2001:AD:654C:1234::9

Correct Answer (D)
Subject Matter: IPv6 Addressing

Options A, B and C have features that are not valid with IPv6 addressing. The following explains the issues with each address.

Option A - has double colons :: occurring twice. The double colon is only permitted once per IPv6 address. 2001:0000:12D4**::**043D**::**1

Option B - has only 6 groups. IPv6 requires 8 groups (8 x 16 bits = 128 bits). Any IPv6 address with less than 8 groups must have double colon to summarize zero groups. 2001:1234:4567:AD:12DE:1

Option C - has an illegal value (W). IPv6 is based on hexidecimal notation with values from 0 to F hexidecimal. FEC0:ABCD:9**W**CD:0067::2A4

52. Select four primary strategies that enable IPv4 to IPv6 address migration?

   A. ISATAP Tunneling

   B. NAT Proxy and Translation (NAT-PT)

   C. IPv4 to IPv6 static mapping

   D. IPv6 Autoconfiguration

   E. Teredo Tunneling

   F. 6to4 Tunneling

Correct Answers (A,B,E,F)
Subject Matter: IPv6 Addressing

The solutions available for IPv4 to IPv6 transition include tunneling and translation. Tunneling enables forwarding of IPv6 packets across an IPv4 network. IP address migration and re-addressing is often done over a period of time. The strategies allow network engineers to make a gradual transition to IPv6. In addition they can sharpen their skills with IPv6 deployment and troubleshooting. The following techniques provide IPv4 to IPv6 migration.

- ISATAP Tunneling
- NAT Proxy and Translation (NAT-PT)
- Teredo Tunneling
- 6to4 Tunneling

53. What IOS command enables IPv6 packet forwarding on a Cisco router?

A. ipv6 host

B. ipv6 local

C. ipv6 neighbor

D. ipv6 unicast-routing

Correct Answer (D)
Subject Matter: IPv6 Addressing

The global command used to enable IPv6 routing is **ipv6 unicast-routing.** It is the standard first command to enable before assigning IPv6 addresses.

54. Select the correct statement concerning IPv6 addressing?

A. IPv6 address is 32 bits long and represented as decimal digits

B. IPv6 address is 128 bits long and represented as decimal digits

C. IPv6 address is 128 bits long and represented as hexadecimal character

D. IPv6 address is 64 bits long and represented as hexadecimal character

Correct Answer (C)
Subject Matter: IPv6 Addressing

Any IPv6 address is comprised of 8 groups each with 4 hexidecimal values of 4 bits each. The hexidecimal group **AF23** for example is 16 bits x 8 groups that equals 128 bits.

55. What three statements accurately describe IPv6 addressing?

    A. IPv6 address is divided into eight 16-bit groups

    B. double colon (::) can only be used once in a single IPv6 address

    C. IPv6 addresses are 196 bits in length

    D. leading zeros cannot be omitted in an IPv6 address

    E. groups with zero (0) value can be summarized with a single zero

Correct Answers (A,B,E)
Subject Matter: IPv6 Addressing

The IPv6 is comprised of eight hexidecimal groups with 4 values per group of 4 bits each. The hexidecimal numbering is from 0 to F (4 bits). The 16 bit group x 8 groups = 128 bits. The double colon :: can summarize multiple consecutive zeros for multiple groups, however only once per address. In addition multiple zeros in a single group can be summarized with a single zero.

56. What are three characteristics of an IPv6 Anycast address?

    A. one-to-many communication model

    B. one-to-nearest communication model

    C. any-to-many communication model

    D. unique IPv6 address for each device in the group

    E. same address for multiple devices in the group

    F. delivery of packets to the group interface closest to the sending device

Correct Answers (B,E,F)
Subject Matter: IPv6 Address Types

Anycast is a network messaging technique supported with IPv6. It is deployed as a cloud solution for load balancing as well. Anycast is based on the nearest reply from multiple receivers configured with the same address. The packets are then forwarded to the nearest responding device for optimized performance.

57. What three network messaging techniques are supported with IPv6?

    A. multicast

    B. broadcast

    C. anycast

    D. limited broadcast

    E. unicast

    F. dynamic broadcast

Correct Answers (A,C,E)
Subject Matter: IPv6 Address Types

The network messaging techniques supported by IPv6 include multicast, anycast and unicast. The features that used broadcast messaging is now provided with multicast.

58. Select the IPv6 link-local address from the following?

    A. FE80::1234:AE43:4567:1D34

    B. FFFE::1234:AE43:4567:0000

    C. FF08::1234:AE43:0000:0000

    D. FFF0::/64

Correct Answer (A)
Subject Matter: IPv6 Addressing

The IPv6 link-local address always start with the FE80::/64 prefix. It is an address that is only routable within the local network segment where it is assigned. In addition every IPv6 enabled interface must have a link-local address even where there are routable IPv6 addresses assigned.

- **unique local address** is a company private routable address that routers forward with prefix FC00::/7

- **global unicast address** is an internet public routable address with prefix 2000::/3

59. Select two characteristics of IPv6 unicast addressing that are correct?

   A. global address prefix is 2000::/3

   B. link-local address prefix is FE00:/12

   C. unique local address prefix is FF00::/10

   D. universal loopback address is ::1

   E. IPv6 only supports a single IP address per interface

Correct Answers (A,D)
Subject Matter: IPv6 Addressing

IPv6 addressing is based on a hexidecimal address 128 bits in length. There is a prefix (64 bits) and interface identifier (64 bits). The prefix includes a variable length subnet mask. The interface identifier is unique for the network device where it is assigned. The global address prefix is **2000::/3** and the loopback address is **::1**

- link-local address prefix is **FE80::/64**
- unique local address prefix is **FC00::/7**
- multiple IPv6 addresses are assignable per interface

60. What two features are unique to IPv6 addressing?

   A. IPsec

   B. address autoconfiguration

   C. broadcasts

   D. DMVPN

   E. no checksum

   F. NAT

Correct Answers (B,E)
Subject Matter: IPv6 Addressing

The correct answers are auto-configuration (B) and no checksum (E). IPv6 supports address Auto-configuration (SLAAC) with link-local addressing. In addition checksum error detection is done by upper layer protocols for each IPv6 packet.

Broadcast messaging technique is not supported or required with IPv6. The multicast messages provide that service for network protocols. IPsec and DMVPN are WAN protocols supported with IPv4 and IPv6. NAT isn't required with IPv6 at all. It is used with IPv4 address space to increase public routable connections to the internet.

61. What two of these features are supported with IPv6 addressing?

    A. unique local addresses are public (internet) routable

    B. multiple IPv6 addresses are supported per interface

    C. at least one loopback address is assigned to any interface

    D. leftmost 64 bits represent the interface identifier

Correct Answers (B,C)
Subject Matter: IPv6 Addressing

IPv6 does support multiple IPv6 address types per interface. In addition there is at least one loopback address (**::1**) assigned to each interface as well. Unique local addresses are only routable across the company private network. The leftmost 64 bits of an IPv6 address represent the prefix with subnet mask.

62. What is the alternate equivalent notation for the IPv6 address
2001:25D3:0000:0000:009F:CD2A:0000:332E?

    A. 2001:25D3:009F::CD2A:0000:332E

    B. 2001:25D3:009F:CD2A:332E

    C. 2001:25D3::009F:CD2A:0:332E

    D. 2001:25D3:0:009F:CD2A:332E

Correct Answer (C)
Subject Matter: IPv6 Addressing

The correct IPv6 address **2001:25D3::009F:CD2A:0:332E** does the following:

1. Minimizes multiple zero groups of the IPv6 address to a double colon **::** (group 3 and 4)

2. Minimize a single group with zeros to **:0:** (group 7)

Incorrect Answers (A,B,D)

2001:25D3:009F**::**CD2A:**0000**:332E
(double colon in wrong location and group 7 not summarized)

2001:25D3:009F:CD2A:332E
(zero groups removed instead of being summarized)

2001:25D3:**0**:009F:CD2A:**332E**
(group 3 and group 4 should summarizes to double colon :: instead of a single zero. In addition group 7 was removed instead of using single zero notation)

63. What are three primary reasons for migrating to IPv6?

    A. scalability

    B. NAT support

    C. no broadcasts

    D. no multicasts

    E. CDP

    F. address autoconfiguration

Correct Answers (A,C,F)
Subject Matter: IPv6 Addressing

The primary reason for migrating to or enabling support for IPv6 is scalability. The IPv4 public routable address space is near depleted. In addition there is increasing demand for public addresses resulting from new cloud services and mobile devices. Enabling IPv6 support now will ease migration over so that public routable addresses will be available for internet connectivity.

IPv6 decreases network traffic by eliminating broadcast messages with multicasting. The ease of management with address Autoconfiguration is an advantage as well.

64. Select the correct network address and subnet mask that allows at least 10 web servers (hosts) to be assigned to the same subnet?

   A. 192.168.100.0 255.255.255.252

   B. 192.168.100.16 255.255.255.248

   C. 192.168.100.16 255.255.255.240

   D. 192.168.252.16 255.255.255.252

   E. 192.168.100.8 255.255.255.252

Correct Answer (C)
Subject Matter: IPv4 Addressing

The subnet mask defines the network portion and host portion of a subnetted address. Increasing the subnet mask length will increase the number of subnets available. Creating ten host assignments for web servers requires at least 4 host bits. That allows for 14 host assignments where the network address and broadcast address are not assignable.

Example:

2 power 3 = 3 host bits = 8 - 2 = 6 host assignments

2 power 4 = 4 host bits = 16 - 2 = 14 host assignments

network portion = 32 bits - 4 bits = 28 bits (/28)
                       = **255.255.255.240**

            network (28 bits) | host (4 bits)
       11111111.11111111.11111111.**1111** 0000
          255.   255.   255.   240

The 255.255.255.240 (/28) subnet mask starts at the bit 5 of the 4th octet and has a binary value of 16. The subnets are multiples of 16 (0, 16, 32, 48 etc).

Correct Answer: **192.168.100.16/28**

65. You are asked to develop an IP address schema for 100 new branch offices using the IP network address 10.10.32.0/23. There are a maximum of 28 hosts required per branch office. In addition the subnet mask must enable the maximum number of subnets?

A. 10.10.32.0/26

B. 10.10.32.0/29

C. 10.10.32.0/27

D. 10.10.32.0/25

E. 10.10.32.0/28

Correct Answer (C)
Subject Matter: IPv4 Addressing

The subnet mask divides the network portion from the host portion. The 10.10.32.0/23 address has 255.255.254.0 subnet mask with 23 bits assigned to the network portion and 9 bits for the host portion. 9 bits = 2 power 9 = 512 - 2 = 510 host assignments. The requirement for 30 hosts will require less host bits.

            network (23 bits) | host (9 bits)
       11111111.1111111.1111111 0.00000000

Assigning 4 host bits from the host portion to the network portion increases the subnet mask from /23 -> /27.

The nearest is 5 bits = 2 power 5 = 32 - 2 = 30 host assignments. The network address and broadcast address can't be assigned to hosts.

            network (27 bits) | host (5 bits)
       11111111.1111111.11111111.111 00000
            255.   255.   255.   224 (/27)

Correct Answer: **10.10.32.0/27**

66. The network administrator is asked to configure multiple point-to-point WAN links. Select the optimized subnet mask that enabled the minimum number of host IP address assignments?

    A. 192.168.1.0/25

    B. 192.168.1.0/30

    C. 192.168.1.0/24

    D. 192.168.1.0/27

    E. 192.168.1.0/23

Correct Answer (B)
Subject Matter: IPv4 Addressing

The question asks for the most effective addressing of point-to-point (PTP) WAN links. Most current WAN links today are PTP where only two host assignments (IP address) are required on a WAN link. There is an IP address on each router WAN physical interface. In addition each WAN link is assigned to a separate subnet.

The number of host bits required for 2 host IP addresses = 2
The number of network bits (subnet mask) = 30

           network bits (/30) | host (1-2)
   11111111.11111111.11111111.111111 00

The rightmost bit of the subnet mask (network bits) determines the subnet multiple. That is bit 3 of the 4th octet with a binary value of 4. As a result the subnets are multiples of 2 (0, 4, 8, 12 etc). The zero subnet is included as a result of the default ip subnet zero feature. The following are the first assignable host IP addresses for the zero subnet.

- network address = 192.168.1.0
- router interface addresses = 192.168.1.1/30, 192.168.1.2/30
- broadcast address = 192.168.1.3

Correct Answer: **192.168.1.0/30**

67. Refer to the network topology drawing. A new switch with 75 hosts has been added to the network. What is the optimized subnet mask that will provide enough IP addresses?

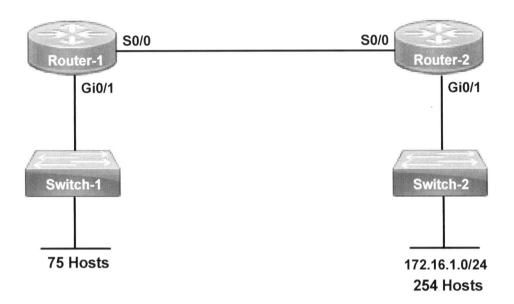

A. 192.168.1.128/25

B. 192.168.1.64/27

C. 192.168.1.65/27

D. 192.168.1.192/26

Correct Answer (A)
Subject Matter: IPv4 Addressing

The Class C address assigns all hosts from the 4th octet only. The subnet mask must support 75 new hosts that will connect to a new switch. That requires at least 7 bits for hosts (2 power 7 = 128) from the 4th octet. The rightmost 6 bits of 4th octet provide a maximum of only (2 power 6 = 64) host IP addresses.

The network portion (subnet mask length) is 25 bits or (/25 for CIDR notation) based on the fact that 7 bits are assigned to the host portion. It is a Class C address so the 4th octet is being subnetted only. There is a single bit (leftmost bit of 4th octet) that provides subnets 192.168.1.0 and 192.168.1.128 so the correct answer is 192.168.1.128/25

      network portion (/25) | host (7 bits)
11111111.11111111.11111111.1 0000000

68. Refer to the network topology drawing and select the IP address that will summarize the routes shown?

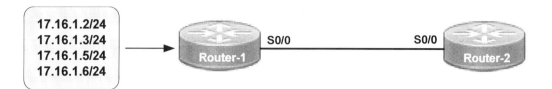

17.16.1.2/24
17.16.1.3/24
17.16.1.5/24
17.16.1.6/24

A. 172.16.1.0/21

B. 172.16.1.0/29

C. 172.16.1.0/23

D. 172.16.1.0/24

Correct Answer (B)
Subject Matter: IPv4 Addressing

Summarization aggregates (includes) all bits that are common to all IP addresses. The example has four different IP addresses with /24 subnet mask. Start from the left and move right until the bits are mismatched (non-common). The common bits all occur up to and including bit 29. That translates to a /29 subnet mask (255.255.255.248) assigning 29 bits to the network portion. The /29 subnet mask can summarize IP address range 172.16.1.0 - 172.16.1.7

common bits (/29)
172.16.1.2/24 = **10101100.00010000.00000001.00000** 010
172.16.1.3/24 = **10101100.00010000.00000001.00000** 011
172.16.1.5/24 = **10101100.00010000.00000001.00000** 101
172.16.1.6/24 = **10101100.00010000.00000001.00000** 110

The summary address is obtained from the common bits that include all IP addresses ignoring the 3 non-common bits. The single summarized address is an aggregate that can advertise all included IP addresses.

Summary Address = **172.16.1.0/29**

69. Select two subnet masks that provide a minimum of 300 Class B subnets with a maximum of 50 host IP addresses per subnet?

A. 255.255.248.0

B. 255.255.255.224

C. 255.255.255.192

D. 255.255.255.128

E. 255.255.252.0

F. 255.255.255.0

Correct Answers (C,D)
Subject Matter: IPv4 Addressing

The default Class B subnet mask is 255.255.0.0 (/16)

>   network (16 bits) | host (16 bits)
>   **11111111.11111111**.00000000.00000000

The number of subnets (network portion) and number of hosts per subnet (host portion) is based on the subnet mask. The fact that it is a Class B address indicates the 3rd octet and/or 4th octet is being subnetted. The subnetting will decrease the number of host bits and assign them to the network portion. Binary values make it easy to determine the minimum number of bits. The examples include the next lower to show why the number of bits were not enough.

9 bits = 2 power 9 = 512 subnets > 300 subnets = **Yes**
8 bits = 2 power 8 = 256 < 300 subnets No

6 bits = 2 power 6 = 62-2 = 60 > 50 hosts **Yes**
5 bits = 2 power 5 = 32 < 50 hosts No

Add the minimum 9 bits to the default /16 bits of a Class B address = /25 subnet mask (bold). In addition the question asks for two subnet masks so add an additional bit (/26) as well. That doesn't affect the host portion where 6 bits are still available for the 50 hosts.

11111111.1111111.11111111.10000000 = 255.255.255.128 = (/25)

11111111.1111111.11111111.11000000 = 255.255.255.192 = (/26)

Correct Answers: **255.255.255.128** and **255.255.255.192**

70. Refer to the network topology drawing. Summarize all routes advertised from Router-1 and Router-2 to minimize the routing table of Router-3?

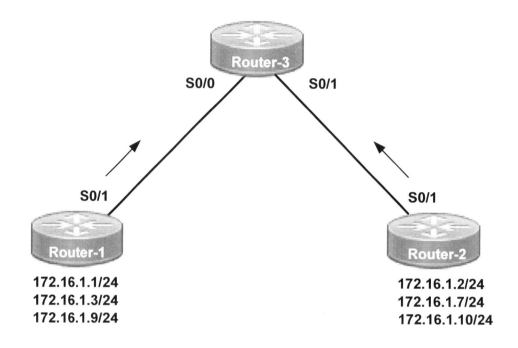

A. 172.16.0.0/27

B. 172.16.1.0/28

C. 172.16.1.0/29

D. 172.16.1.0/30

Correct Answer (B)
Subject Matter: IPv4 Addressing

Summarization aggregates (includes) all bits that are common to all IP addresses. The example has six different IP addresses with /24 subnet mask from two routers. Start from the left and move right until the bits are mismatched (non-common). The common bits all occur up to and including bit 28. That translates to a /28 subnet mask assigning 28 bits to the network portion. The /28 subnet mask summarize IP address range 172.16.1.0 - 172.16.1.15

Router-1   common bits (/28)
    172.16.1.1/24 = **10101100.00010000.00000001.0000** 0001
    172.16.1.3/24 = **10101100.00010000.00000001.0000** 0011
    172.16.1.9/24 = **10101100.00010000.00000001.0000** 1001

Router-2

    172.16.1.2/24 = **10101100.00010000.00000001.0000** 0010
    172.16.1.7/24 = **10101100.00010000.00000001.0000** 0111
    172.16.1.10/24 = **10101100.00010000.00000001.0000** 1010

The summary address is obtained from the common bits that include all IP addresses ignoring the 4 non-common bits. The single summarized address is an aggregate that can advertise all included IP addresses.

Summary Address = **172.16.1.0/28**

71. Refer to the network topology drawing. What is the most efficient summarization that Router-1 can use to advertise all subnets/routes to Router-2?

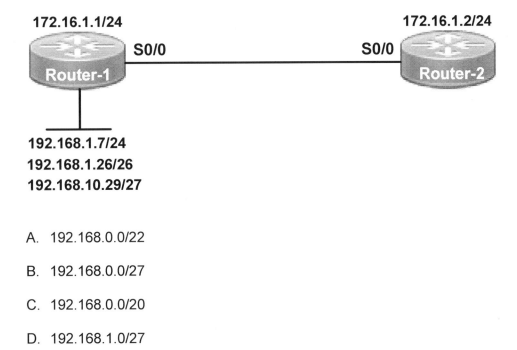

172.16.1.1/24   **172.16.1.2/24**

S0/0   **S0/0**

Router-1   **Router-2**

192.168.1.7/24
192.168.1.26/26
192.168.10.29/27

   A. 192.168.0.0/22

   B. 192.168.0.0/27

   C. 192.168.0.0/20

   D. 192.168.1.0/27

Correct Answer (C)
Subject Matter: IPv4 Addressing

Summarization aggregates (includes) all bits that are common to all IP addresses. The example has three different IP addresses with variable subnet masks (/24, /25 and /27). **Start from the left and move right** until the bits are mismatched (non-common). The common bits all occur up to and including bit 20. That translates to a /20 subnet mask (255.255.240.0)

common bits (/20)

192.168.1.7/24   = **11000000.10101000.0000** 0001.00000111
192.168.1.26/25 = **11000000.10101000.0000** 0001.00011010
192.168.10.29/27 = **11000000.10101000.0000** 1010.00011101

The summary address is obtained from the common bits for all IP addresses. Ignore the 12 non-common bits when writing the summary address. The single summarized address is an aggregate that can advertise all included IP addresses.

Summary Address = **192.168.0.0/20**

72. Select the two network devices that can provide routing services from the following list?

   A. layer 2 switch

   B. wireless access point

   C. router

   D. firewall

   E. wireless LAN controller (WLC)

Correct Answers (C,D)
Subject Matter: Infrastructure Components

The only devices that provide routing services are routers and firewalls. Firewall routed mode is required to enable routing. The switch, access point and wireless LAN controller (WLC) are layer 2 devices. The layer 2 switch does allow configuring a single SVI with an IP address.

73. Match the network device on the left with the OSI model layer on the right?

firewall (transparent mode)	layer 2
wireless access point	layer 3
wireless LAN controller	layer 2
firewall (routed mode)	layer 3
switch	layer 2
router	layer 2

Correct Answers.
Subject Matter: Infrastructure Components

Network devices that forward packets based on MAC address are layer 2. They include bridges, switches, access points and wireless LAN controller. In addition the firewall can support both layer 2 (bridging) mode and routed mode. The router is a layer 3 device.

firewall (transparent mode)	**layer 2**
wireless access point	**layer 2**
wireless LAN controller	**layer 2**
firewall (routed mode)	**layer 3**
switch	**layer 2**
router	**layer 3**

74. What four network devices with a default configuration create a single broadcast domain?

A. firewall (transparent mode)

B. wireless LAN controller (WLC)

C. switch

D. wireless access point

E. router

F. firewall (routed mode)

Correct Answers (A,B,C,D)
Subject Matter: Infrastructure Components

Layer 2 network devices create a single broadcast domain with their default configuration. Assigning VLANs creates multiple broadcast domains per VLAN. The transparent firewall, wireless LAN controller, switch and wireless access point all create a single broadcast domain. Routers and firewalls configured with routed mode create a single broadcast domain per interface.

75. What two devices and/or topology enable multiple collision domains?

A. router with two switches connected

B. wireless access point connected to a switch

C. switch uplink to a router

D. switch VLAN

E. 4-port EtherChannel between switches

F. wireless access point with 100 wireless hosts connected

Correct Answer (A,E)
Subject Matter: Infrastructure Components

Collision domains are created based on separate Ethernet links. Multiple collision domains require at least two Ethernet links. Wireless access points are half-duplex media that share a single collision domain among multiple clients. There is a single collision domain however on the switch side. The 48 port switch creates 48 separate collision domains however the uplink to the router is only a single collision domain. VLANs create a single broadcast domain.

- **Router with two switches connected = 2 collision domains**
- Wireless access point connected to a switch = single collision domain
- Switch uplink connected to router = single collision domain
- Layer 2 switch VLAN = single broadcast domain
- **4-port EtherChannel = 4 collision domains (1 per port)**
- Wireless access point with 100 clients = single collision domain

76. What is the effect of deploying a firewall configured in transparent mode to the network? (select three)

A. firewall is a layer 2 device

B. single broadcast domain

C. routing protocol traffic is forwarded

D. broadcast traffic is dropped

E. provides default gateway services

F. default mode for Cisco firewall

Correct Answers (A,B,C)
Subject Matter: Infrastructure Components

The Cisco firewall supports transparent mode and routed mode. Deploying a firewall in transparent mode is similar to a bridge. It functions as a layer 2 device with a single broadcast domain. The inside and outside interfaces are assigned to the same subnet. Routing protocol traffic is forwarded enabling neighbor adjacencies across the firewall.

Network broadcast traffic is forwarded as with a switch. There is no support for providing layer 3 default gateway service. The default mode for Cisco firewalls is routed mode and not transparent mode.

77. What is the effect of firewall routed mode on the network? (select two)

   A. multiple broadcast domains

   B. routing protocol traffic is forwarded

   C. broadcast traffic is forwarded

   D. default gateway enabled

   E. ARP, HSRP, IPsec, BPDU traffic forwarded

Correct Answers (A,D)
Subject Matter: Infrastructure Components

Firewall routed mode has the same effect as deploying a router. The routed mode firewall creates multiple broadcast domains based on subnets. The inside and outside interface are assigned to different subnets. There is support for default gateway services. Connected network devices such as switches can be configured to use the firewall as their default gateway.

The routed mode firewall (as with routers) won't forward broadcast traffic. As a result routing protocol traffic isn't forwarded across the firewall. The routing protocols can be enabled on interfaces however and establish adjacencies with neighbor devices. Network protocols including ARP, HSRP, IPsec and BPDU traffic are not forwarded.

78. Select three characteristics of a Cisco wireless access point?

    A. half-duplex mode

    B. bridge traffic

    C. CSMA/CD

    D. PortFast support

    E. layer 2 switching

Correct Answers (A,B,D)
Subject Matter: Infrastructure Components

The wireless access point is essentially a bridge where packets arrive and are forwarded based on MAC address. The access point however is a single broadcast domain with a shared collision domain. The wireless RF cell is not equivalent to a dedicated Ethernet port on a network switch. It is half-duplex media with CSMA/CA required for collision detection. CSMA/CD is a method for detecting Ethernet collisions on older hubs and bridges. It is no longer required with full-duplex switch ports. There is a wired side of an access point with an Ethernet port uplink to a switch. The access point is similar to a desktop or IP phone where PortFast is typically enabled.

79. Select the four characteristics of a wireless LAN controller (WLC)?

    A. layer 2

    B. DHCP relay agent

    C. MAC forwarding

    D. CSMA/CA

    E. Spanning Tree Protocol (STP) node

    F. No Proxy ARP

Correct Answer (A,B,C,E)
Subject Matter: Infrastructure Components

The wireless LAN controller (WLC) is a layer 2 network device. The purpose of WLC is to manage wireless access points. It does not route packets however it does rewrite layer 2 frame headers. The layer 2 frame between wireless 802.11n and Ethernet format. The MAC source and destination address are updated as well.

- For inbound frames the source MAC address is the switch and destination MAC address is the WLC.

- For outbound frames the source MAC address is the WLC and the destination MAC address is the switch.

- For inbound packets, the source IP address is the wireless client and the destination IP address is the WLC.

- For outbound packets, the source IP address is the WLC and the destination IP address is the wireless client.

- The wireless access point is a bridge and as with a layer 2 switch doesn't rewrite frame header MAC address or IP header packet address.

- DHCP relay service is supported with wireless LAN controller (WLC) to forward client DHCP requests to the nearest DHCP server.

- The CSMA/CA wireless collision detection method does not apply to WLC. The purpose of CSMA/CA is to detect collisions across the RF cell. The WLC is a wired device that connects typically with a trunk link to a switch.

- The WLC supports multiple links with VLANs assigned for redundancy. As a result Spanning Tree Protocol (STP) is supported to prevent layer 2 loops. The WLC does provide Proxy ARP service for clients.

80. What device rewrites MAC address for both Ethernet and 802.11n header?

A. wireless access point

B. wireless LAN controller (WLC)

C. router

D. switch

E. laptop

F. firewall

Correct Answer (B)
Subject Matter: Infrastructure Components

The wireless LAN controller (WLC) strips off and rewrites headers between the wireless and wired network. The source and destination MAC addresses are rewritten and forwarded to the switch.

For outbound (egress) packets to the switch, the 802.11n wireless header is stripped off and replaced with an Ethernet frame header. The source MAC address is the WLC and destination MAC address is the switch.

For inbound (ingress) packets from the switch, the Ethernet frame header is stripped off and replaced with 802.11n header. The source MAC address is the switch and destination MAC address is the WLC.

Wireless Access Point (outer IP header)

- Outbound packet sent from access point to WLC have IP source address of access point and destination IP address of WLC.

- Inbound packet sent from WLC to access point have IP source address of WLC and destination IP address of access point.

Wireless Host (inner IP header)

- For outbound packets sent from a wireless host to a server, the source IP address is the wireless host and destination IP address is the server.

- For inbound packets sent from a server to a wireless host, the source IP address is the server and destination IP address is the wireless host.

- The inner IP header is unaltered between source and destination as per the standard routing rules. The exception is encapsulation/tunneling where an outer IP header is added or NAT.

81. Refer to the network topology drawing. The wireless host has established a session with the server. What is the source and destination MAC address when the packet is outbound from the wireless host?

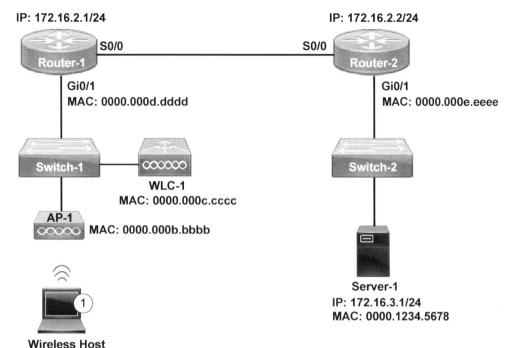

IP: 172.16.2.1/24

IP: 172.16.2.2/24

S0/0

S0/0

Router-1

Router-2

Gi0/1
MAC: 0000.000d.dddd

Gi0/1
MAC: 0000.000e.eeee

Switch-1

Switch-2

WLC-1
MAC: 0000.000c.cccc

AP-1
MAC: 0000.000b.bbbb

Server-1
IP: 172.16.3.1/24
MAC: 0000.1234.5678

Wireless Host
IP: 172.16.1.1/24
MAC: 0000.000a.aaaa

A. source MAC address = 0000.000a.aaaa
destination MAC address = ffff.ffff.ffff

B. source MAC address = 0000.000a.aaaa
destination MAC address = 0000.000b.bbbb

C. source MAC address = 0000.000b.bbbb
destination MAC address = 0000.1234.5678

D. source MAC address = 0000.000a.aaaa
destination MAC address = 0000.000c.cccc

Correct Answer (D)
Subject Matter: Infrastructure Components

The source and destination MAC address change per layer 3 hop between host and server. The source MAC address of the outbound packet is the wireless host. The destination MAC address is the wireless LAN controller (WLC). The source MAC address is assigned to the wireless network interface of the host. The destination MAC address is the device MAC address of the WLC.

- source MAC address = wireless host adapter
- destination MAC address = wireless LAN controller (WLC)

- source IP address = wireless host
- destination IP address = server

The wireless access point (AP-1) does not change the source and destination MAC address. Traffic from the wireless host (802.11n client) is bridged to the wireless LAN controller (WLC). The purpose of the WLC is to manage LWAPP enabled access points. AP-1 establishes a layer 3 CAPWAP tunnel for communicating with the WLC. The 802.11n wireless frame arriving from the host is stripped off. The WLC adds an Ethernet header and rewrites the source and destination MAC address. The packet is forwarded to the connected switch (wired network). WLC does not forward broadcasts or multicasts between wireless clients.

82. What are three primary traffic flows for connecting the enterprise network to the cloud?

A. backhaul branch office traffic through the data center to cloud service

B. broadband point-to-point connectivity between branch office and cloud service provider

C. multipoint connectivity between data center routers and cloud service

D. leased line WAN connectivity between branch offices and cloud service

E. metro ethernet connectivity from remote users to cloud service

Correct Answers (A,B,C)
Subject Matter: Cloud Services

The cloud is essentially an internet based service enabling connectivity from any device and from any location. That includes remote users, mobile devices, data center, branch offices and customers. There are a variety of options and solutions for connecting the enterprise to the cloud that affect traffic flows. In addition the traffic flows have implications for network security, performance and redundancy. The three primary traffic flows include the following:

1. Backhauling traffic from branch offices and even customers is available. The traffic is routed through the data center DMZ and forwarded over direct links to the cloud. This topology often increases network latency and utilization on the internet routers.

2. Broadband point-to-point connectivity between branch offices and cloud service. This is becoming the de facto standard for branch office connectivity. The DSL provides internet access for direct connectivity to cloud services.

3. Multipoint connectivity between data center routers and cloud services. The internet routers at the data center are hubs for multiple WAN links to the same or different cloud services. It is effective in that each links is a direct point-to-point connection. Redundancy is available as well to failover traffic to a secondary cloud service. Any backhaul traffic from branch offices would increase CPU utilization and affect latency to hub routers. In addition there is a significant single point of failure with a single internet router only.

Leased line WAN connectivity between branch offices and cloud service is being replaced with broadband connections (DSL, Cable etc). Metro Ethernet is typically deployed for branch offices and increasingly for point-to-point cloud connectivity. It provides bandwidth on demand with easy internet access. Remote users connect to the internet with broadband and wireless connections.

83. Select two optimized traffic flows when deploying client/server applications to the cloud?

   A. web, application and database servers at cloud data center.

   B. web, application and database servers on same switch.

   C. web servers in cloud
      application and database servers at enterprise data center

   D. web servers and application servers in cloud
      database servers at enterprise data center

   E. database servers in cloud
      web servers and application servers at enterprise data center

Correct Answers (A,B)
Subject Matter: Cloud Services

Most cloud applications today are based on a client/server application traffic model. The client web browser makes a small request to a web server. The web server forwards the request to an application server. The application server then processes and requests data from a database server. The database server returns the data to the application server where it is forwarded to the web server. The data is then sent to the client from the web server. It is often a web page URL updated with some requested data. The primary advantage of the client/server traffic model is lower WAN bandwidth utilization.

Servers are located significantly affects network performance. Most data center traffic, sometimes called east-west, flows between application servers and database servers.

Optimized traffic flow for cloud applications would have all servers colocated at the same cloud data center **(Public Cloud)**. In addition deploying the server to the same switch would optimize performance as well. Web servers comprise most of the server count for any client/server application. As a result they require cloud scalability and elasticity to spin up new web servers on demand. Anytime the server are separated across a WAN link will affect performance particularly with application servers and database servers. There is the expense of higher speed WAN links for throughput. In addition point-to-point links for decreasing network latency.

Hybrid Cloud is based on locating some servers in the cloud and some at the enterprise data center. An example is where there are security compliance requirements for an application. Companies will often decide to deploy database servers at the enterprise data center. That provides maximum security where data is company managed and protected The web servers and application servers are located at a cloud provider such as Amazon AWS for instance.

84. What two network message types are supported with cloud services?

    A. layer 2 unicast support

    B. layer 2 broadcast

    C. layer 3 unicast support

    D. layer 3 broadcast

    E. Layer 3 multicast

Correct Answers (A,C)
Subject Matter: Cloud Services

Layer 3 broadcasts and multicasts require layer 2 broadcasts not supported within the cloud infrastructure. The enterprise network require broadcasts and multicasts. The cloud only permits unicast messages. The cloud provider drops all broadcasts, multicasts and ARP packets from the enterprise.

85. What four network protocols are not supported with public cloud services?

A. HSRP

B. OSPF

C. EtherChannel

D. IPv6

E. BGP

F. VPN

Correct Answers (A,B,C,D)
Subject Matter: Cloud Services

Some network protocols require broadcast and multicast messages to work correctly. Cloud providers do not permit broadcasts or multicasts. As a result HSRP, OSPF, EtherChannel and IPv6 aren't supported in a cloud environment. BGP routing protocol does not require broadcasts or multicasts. VPN is an internet-based service external to the cloud infrastructure.

86. Select three common methods for segmenting cloud traffic between tenants, enterprise servers and applications for security purposes?

A. routing table

B. VLAN

C. virtual security gateway (VSG)

D. firewall

E. static routes

F. web application firewall (WAF)

Correct Answers (A,C,D)
Subject Matter: Cloud Services

Segmenting tenant traffic in the cloud is a primary security requirement. The techniques include routing tables (VRF) and firewall appliances. There are north-south firewalls (ASA 5500-X) and east-west firewalls (VSG). Where virtual appliances are not supported, access control lists (ACL) are configured.

87. What are two disadvantages of public cloud services?

    A. shared infrastructure

    B. network security

    C. scalability

    D. ease of deployment

    E. support costs

Correct Answers (A,B)
Subject Matter: Cloud Services

The shared infrastructure can affect performance and limits the management options available to tenants. In addition the tenant isn't managing all aspects of network security. The public cloud provides configuration of ACLs only. In addition VPN appliances are shared among multiple tenants. There is added security with Amazon AWS virtual private cloud service. The tenant can deploy virtual appliances for optimized security.

88. What are two preferred options for connecting the branch offices to the cloud where latency and bandwidth utilization is minimized?

    A. internet broadband

    B. data center backhaul

    C. point-to-point topology

    D. serial leased line (private)

Correct Answers (A,C)
Subject Matter: Cloud Services

The optimized topology for connecting branch offices to the cloud is internet point-to-point connectivity. Broadband provides internet access at significantly higher speed and lower cost than private leased lines. The broadband services enables easier connectivity to the cloud. The internet point-to-point access minimizes latency as well. Any backhaul through the data center increases network latency and throughput across internet routers and WAN links.

89. Select three components that are common to a virtualized environment?

A. hypervisor

B. WAN

C. virtual machines (VM)

D. virtual appliances

E. VPN

F. server

Correct Answers (A,C,F)
Subject Matter: Cloud Services

The primary components of a virtualized solution include hypervisor, virtual machine (VM) and server hardware.

Hypervisor - manages requests from multiple virtual machines for server hardware. The hypervisor abstracts (separates) the hardware layer from operating system. That enables applications and operating system software to run on any hardware platform.

Virtual Machine (VM) - virtual server with bundled applications and operating systems. Sends requests to hypervisor for hardware services. The virtual appliances (switch, firewall etc) are network services bundled as a VM.

Server - hardware including CPU, memory, hard drive and NIC.

90. What three items will limit the number of virtual machines (VM) that can be supported on a single network server?

A. server memory and CPU capacity

B. server uplink capacity

C. hypervisor support

D. encryption support

E. server hard disk space

Correct Answers (A,B,E)
Subject Matter: Cloud Services

The migration from physical servers with applications to virtual machines has shifted network capacity considerations to the network server. There are now more applications running on fewer network servers. In addition physical network devices are running as virtual machines as well. They both provide the same services however now they are bundled as virtual machines. The hardware requirements for virtual machines include memory, CPU cycles, hard disk space and a network interface. The limiting factor to network performance is now based on server hardware capacity. The network interface card (NIC) is often limited to a single Gigabit port providing the uplink to a switch port.

91. What are four advantages of virtualization?

    A. cost effective

    B. faster deployment

    C. optimize hardware utilization

    D. network performance

    E. network management

    F. encryption

Correct Answers (A,B,C,E)
Subject Matter: Cloud Services

The primary advantages of virtualization include cost effectiveness, faster deployment, optimal hardware utilization and network management.

Cost Effective - fewer physical servers are required for the same number of applications. Less data center cabling, power and cooling is required.

Faster Deployment - virtual machines make deployment faster with bundled application that can be copied, distributed and activated when required. Virtualization enables easier disaster recovery as well with virtual machines.

Optimized Hardware Usage - server hardware is utilized at much higher rates with multiple virtual machines. That is preferable to physical servers staying idle when a single application is deployed.

Network Management - virtual servers (VMs) are abstracted from hardware making them agile, easier to manage and assign to servers.

The network performance provided by virtualization is a disadvantage. The virtualized environment is a shared infrastructure model. There is often some increased network latency and less throughput than with a physical server. Encryption is available with physical and virtual servers as a network service.

92. What three Cisco software platforms supports virtual appliances?

    A. NX-OS

    B. IOS

    C. IOS-XE

    D. IOS-XR

    E. VMware

    F. ASA

Correct Answer (A,C,F)
Subject Matter: Cloud Services

Cisco virtual appliances are now available for switching, routing, firewall, WAAS, firewall and load balancer. The switch is based on Nexus (NX-OS) platform. The router is from the ASR 1000 platform with IOS-XE. The firewall is ASA software and WAAS is based on the software for that platform. The purpose of virtual appliances is for cloud deployment however they are supported at the enterprise data center. Cisco modified the IOS software for each platform to support network services in the virtualized environment and bundle as a virtual machine.

93. What are three primary characteristics of cloud services?

    A. resource pooling

    B. elastic capacity

    C. broadcast support

    D. multi-tenancy

    E. router redundancy

Correct Answers (A,B,D)
Subject Matter: Cloud Services

The five primary characteristics of cloud computing include resource pooling (shared infrastructure), elastic capacity, metered billing services, multi-tenancy and anywhere access. There is no support for broadcasts or router redundancy that requires broadcast messages.

94. What three Cisco network services are available as a virtualized service?

A. firewall

B. WAN optimization

C. wireless access point

D. web application firewall

E. IPsec

F. wireless LAN controller (WLC)

Correct Answers (A,B,F)
Subject Matter: Cloud Services

The virtual appliances now available from Cisco include switch, router, firewall, wireless LAN controller, WAAS, Inter-Cloud and virtual security gateway.

ASA 1000V Firewall - ASA 5500-X platform

vWAAS - WAN optimization platform

Wireless LAN Controller (WLC) - WLC 7.3+ software

Nexus 1000V Switch for VMware - Nexus layer 2 switch

CSR 1000V Router - ASR 1000 router platform

Nexus 1000V Inter-Cloud – Nexus layer 2 switch

Virtual Security Gateway (VSG) - application filtering (east-west)

95. How are Cisco virtual appliances managed?

    A. hypervisor

    B. Prime Network Services Controller

    C. VMware vCenter

    D. Prime Infrastructure

    E. vMotion

    F. vSphere

Correct Answer (B)
Subject Matter: Cloud Services

Cisco virtual appliances are the virtual machine counterpart to the physical network devices. The virtual appliance are managed by Prime Network Services Controller (PNSC). In fact PNSC is a virtual machine as well that works in tandem with VMware vCenter. The purpose of vCenter is primarily to manage virtual machines (VM) that have applications and operating systems. There are virtual appliances for switching, routing, firewall and load balancing services.

Hypervisor - manages requests for hardware among multiple VMs.

Prime Infrastructure - management platform for Cisco physical devices.

vMotion - dynamic assignment of VMs across the virtualized infrastructure.

vSphere - commercial brand name for VMware hypervisor.

96. Match the Ethernet cabling standard on the left with the associated media type, speed and distance limitations for network connectivity on the right?

1000Base-LX/LH	Multi-mode Fiber (MMF), 1000 Mbps, 220-550 meters
1000Base-SX	Copper, 100 Mbps, 100 meters
Cat 5	Copper, 1000 Mbps, 100 meters
Cat 5e	Multi-mode Fiber (MMF), 1000 Mbps, 550 meters
Cat 6	Single-mode Fiber (SMF), 1000 Mbps, 70 km
1000Base-LX	Single-mode Fiber (SMF), 1000 Mbps, 10 km
1000Base-ZX	Copper, 10 Gbps, 55 meters

Correct Answers.
Subject Matter: Cabling Type

The following are the most common Ethernet cabling standards with supported media type, speed and distance specifications.

1000Base-LX/LH	**Single-mode Fiber (SMF), 1000 Mbps, 10 km**
1000Base-SX	**Multi-mode Fiber (MMF), 1000 Mbps, 220 m - 550 m**
Cat 5	**Copper, 100 Mbps, 100 m**
Cat 5e	**Copper, 1000 Mbps, 100 m**
Cat 6	**Copper, 10 Gbps, 55 m**
1000Base-LX	**Multi-mode Fiber (MMF), 1000 Mbps, 550 m**
1000Base-ZX	**Single-mode Fiber (SMF), 1000 Mbps, 70 km**

97. What are the three layers of the traditional Cisco three tier architecture?

    A. access layer, distribution layer, core layer

    B. access layer, aggregation layer, internet layer

    C. access layer, core layer, internet layer

    D. access layer, distribution layer, internet layer

Correct Answer (A)
Subject Matter: Network Architecture Models

The traditional Cisco network design model is comprised of three distinct layers (tiers). They include access layer, distribution layer and core layer. Each layer provides network services for performance, redundancy, security and scalability.

98. What three statements accurately describe the difference between Cisco collapsed core architecture and the traditional three tier model?

    A. collapsed core architecture redefines core layer

    B. collapsed core architecture removes core layer

    C. collapsed core architecture removes distribution layer

    D. collapsed core architecture is comprised of a single layer

    E. collapsed core architecture is comprised of two layers

Correct Answers (A,C,E)
Subject Matter: Network Architecture Models

The traditional Cisco network design model is comprised of access, distribution and core layer. The newest architecture promotes a collapsed core architecture. The collapsed core is comprised of an access layer and a core layer. The distribution layer is collapsed into the core layer along with associated services.

99. What are three advantages of the Cisco collapsed core architecture model?

  A. scalable

  B. easier to manage

  C. layer 2 optimization

  D. redundancy

  E. cost effective

  F. designed for larger data centers

Correct Answer (B,C,E)
Subject Matter: Network Architecture Models

Three advantages of the collapsed core architecture include easier management, layer 2 optimization and cost effectiveness. Collapsing (combining) the distribution layer and core layer into a single core layer requires fewer network devices and uplinks. Layer 2 topology is simplified and STP issues have less effect on the switching infrastructure. It isn't as scalable as the 3-tier model making it preferable for smaller data centers.

100. Select three network services provided by the access layer as defined with the Cisco three tier hierarchical model?

  A. layer 2 switching

  B. quality of service (QoS)

  C. port security

  D. routing

  E. access control lists (ACL)

  F. traffic aggregation

Correct Answers (A,B,C)
Subject Matter: Network Architecture Models

The access layer provides connectivity primarily for desktops and servers. Cisco IP phones and often wireless access points are connected to access switches as well. The network services include the following:

- Layer 2 switching
- Quality of Service (QoS)
- Port security
- High availability
- Dynamic ARP inspection
- Spanning Tree
- VLAN ACLs (VACLs)
- Power over Ethernet (PoE)

101. Select three network services provided by the distribution layer as defined with the Cisco three tier hierarchical model?

A. traffic aggregation

B. ARP

C. access control lists (ACL)

D. Inter-VLAN routing

E. quality of service (QoS)

F. power over ethernet (PoE)

Correct Answers (A,C,D)
Subject Matter: Network Architecture Models

The distribution layer is sometimes called the aggregation layer where north-south traffic is forwarded between the access layer and core layer. In addition the distribution layer forwards east-west traffic between access switches. The distribution layer provide switching and routing services. Inter-VLAN routing is a Layer 2 / Layer 3 boundary where packets are routed between access switches. The network services provided by the distribution layer include the following:

- Traffic aggregation
- Policy-based security (ACLs)
- Inter-VLAN routing
- Redundancy and load balancing
- Routing to core layer
- Route summarization (aggregation) to core
- Broadcast domain segmentation

102. Select three network services provided by the core layer as defined with the Cisco three tier hierarchical model?

A. high speed switching

B. quality of service (QoS)

C. reliability

D. access control lists (ACL)

E. minimized network services

Correct Answers (A,C,E)
Subject Matter: Network Architecture Models

The core layer provides connectivity between the distribution layer and the DMZ or internet edge devices. The core layer switches provide fast switching with minimized network services. The network services (QoS, ACLs, encryption, packet inspection etc) increase processor utilization. The following describe typical characteristics of the core layer.

- High speed switching
- Reliability
- Minimized network services
- Scalability
- Neighbor route peering

103. What network topology provides no redundancy and most cost effective?

A. star

B. partial mesh

C. full mesh

D. hybrid

Correct Answer (A)
Subject Matter: Network Topologies

The star topology or sometimes called hub and spoke is a point-to-point connection between multiple endpoints and a hub. It is most often deployed for connecting smaller branch offices to a core office or data center. There is no link redundancy making it the most cost effective.

104. What network topology provides maximum link redundancy between multiple data centers?

A. full mesh

B. partial mesh

C. hybrid

D. star

E. DMVPN

Correct Answer (A)
Subject Matter: Network Topologies

The full mesh topology is referred to as any-to-any connectivity where there is a link between a single endpoint and all neighbor endpoints. It provides maximum redundancy and most expensive. Deployed for WAN core connectivity including multiple data centers.

105. What network topology is comprised of star and partial mesh topology for increased link redundancy?

A. hybrid

B. star

C. mesh

D. hub and spoke

E. DMVPN

Correct Answer (A)
Subject Matter: Network Topologies

The hybrid topology is a customized solution comprised of at least two different topology types. For instance combining a partial mesh topology with a star topology. The partial mesh has at least two paths to a single or multiple upstream neighbor endpoint/s. It is used where additional link redundancy is required. There is however increased cost compared with the star topology.

106. Order the seven steps for the Cisco troubleshooting methodology?

1. Identify problem

2. Propose hypothesis

3. Gather information

4. Solve problem

5. Analyze data

6. Verify with test plan

7. Eliminate causes not relevant

Correct Answer.
Subject Matter: Troubleshooting Methodology

The following describes the standard Cisco recommended troubleshooting methodology.

Step 1: Identify problem

Step 2: Gather information

Step 3: Analyze data

Step 4: Eliminate causes not relevant

Step 5: Propose hypothesis

Step 6: Verify with test plan

Step 7: Solve problem

107. What three statements are correct concerning IPv6 Stateless Address Autoconfiguration (SLAAC)?

A. supports EUI-64 modified address format

B. link-local address is automatically created

C. no support for assigning DNS servers to hosts

D. no support for assigning multiple IPv6 addresses to the same interface

E. requires DHCP

Correct Answers (A,B,C)
Subject Matter: IPv6 Addressing (SLAAC)

IPv6 makes IP addressing easier when stateless Autoconfiguration is enabled. There is a unique link-local address assigned automatically to the interface. The IPv6 Autoconfiguration default is EUI-64 modified address format (/64 prefix). In addition enabling SLAAC does not support assignment of DNS servers to clients. The feature only provides an IP address and default gateway to clients.

108. What two statements correctly describe IPv6 addressing?

    A. ARP broadcasts are required

    B. stateful DHCPv6 is most similar to DHCPv4

    C. stateless DHCPv6 does not support SLAAC

    D. IPv6 Autoconfiguration (SLAAC) is not supported with WAN interfaces

    E. IPv6 support is automatically enabled on an interface as soon as an IPv6 address is assigned

    F. stateless DHCPv6 enables configuration of DNS server only

Correct Answers (B,E)
Subject Matter: IPv6 Addressing

The methods available for assigning IPv6 addresses include manually, stateful DHCPv6, stateless DHCPv6 and stateless (SLAAC).

Stateful DHCPv6 is most similar to DHCPv4 for IPv4 addressing. The IPv6 client sends a broadcast request to the nearest DHCPv6 server for IP address configuration. The DHCPv6 server assigns the IPv6 address and any additional required addressing configuration such as default gateway, DNS server etc.

Stateless DHCPv6 feature uses stateless address Autoconfiguration (SLAAC) for assigning IPv6 address and default gateway to clients. The feature does however require a DHCPv6 server for sending a variety of additional IP configuration settings including DNS server to clients.

Stateless Autoconfiguration (SLAAC) generates a unique link-local address based on EUI-64 format. The IPv6 address is based on the network prefix sent in Router Advertisement (RA) from the local router. In addition SLAAC obtains the default gateway from Router Advertisements as well to configure clients. IPv6 supports Autoconfiguration on any campus and WAN interfaces.

IPv6 processing is automatically enabled on an interface as soon as an IPv6 address is assigned to the interface. In addition the auto configured address (SLAAC) will enable the interface automatically as well. The **ipv6 enable** command is not required when an IPv6 address is already assigned to interface.

109. What are the two parts of an IPv6 address?

    A. subnet + interface identifier

    B. prefix + interface identifier

    C. prefix + MAC address + interface identifier

    D. interface identifier + EUI-64

Correct Answer (B)
Subject Matter: IPv6 Addressing

The IPv6 address is comprised of a 64 bit network prefix and a 64 bit interface identifier. The 64 bit network prefix is comprised of a 48 bit routing prefix and 16 bit local subnet ID. The network prefix is similar to the IPv4 network address portion. The interface identifier is similar to the IPv4 host address portion. The subnet ID allows for deploying local subnets that identify departments, buildings and city for instance.

110. Select the best description for how an EUI-64 modified IPv6 address is created?

    A. host divides its MAC address into two 24-bits components. The 16-bit hexidecimal value 0xFFEE is inserted between the MAC address halves. The most significant bit 7 is then changed to zero.

    B. host divides its MAC address into two 24-bits components. The 16-bit hexidecimal value 0xFFFE is inserted between the MAC address halves.

    C. host divides its MAC address into two 24-bits components. The 16-bit hexidecimal value 0xFFFE is inserted between the MAC address halves. The most significant bit 7 is then inverted.

    D. host divides its MAC address into two 24-bits components. The 16-bit hexidecimal value 0xFFFF is inserted between the MAC address halves. The most significant bit 7 is then changed to one.

Correct Answer (C)
Subject Matter: IPv6 Addressing

The interface identifier is the host portion of an IPv6 address comprised of the rightmost 64 bits. The EUI-64 modified address is the current standard for host portion address format. It is uniquely derived from the MAC address of the host.

The host divides its MAC address into two 24-bits components. The 16-bit hexidecimal value 0xFFFE is inserted between the MAC address halves. The most significant bit 7 is then inverted.

111. What three protocols and/or advertisement types are required for proper IPv6 Stateless Address Autoconfiguration (SLAAC)?

    A. router advertisement messages

    B. router solicitation messages

    C. neighbor discovery protocol

    D. link-local broadcast enabled

    E. MAC flooding

    F. ARP requests

Correct Answer (A,B,C)
Subject Matter: IPv6 Addressing (SLAAC)

Neighbor Discovery Protocol is a layer 2 protocol that provides a variety of network messaging services. It is based on five ICMPv6 packet types that enable stateless address Autoconfiguration (SLAAC), node discovery, duplicate address detection and DNS server. The following are specific message types required for address Autoconfiguration (SLAAC).

- Router advertisement
- Router solicitation

112. What interface states are supported with IPv6 address Autoconfiguration?

    A. tentative, preferred, deprecated, valid, invalid

    B. tentative, valid, deprecated, invalid, unknown, duplicate

    C. learning, valid, preferred, unknown, invalid

    D. valid, listening, duplicate, preferred, deprecated, invalid

Correct Answer (A)
Subject Matter: IPv6 Addressing (SLAAC)

The IPv6 interface state refers to the current status of interface based on the Autoconfiguration (SLAAC) address request.

Tentative: address is being verified with duplicate address detection.

Valid: address can send and receive unicast traffic.

Preferred: address can send and receive unicast traffic.

Deprecated: address can send/receive unicasts though not recommended.

Invalid: address cannot be used to send or receive unicast traffic.

113. What IOS commands enable IPv6 address Autoconfiguration on Gi1/1?

   A. router(config)# interface gigabitethernet1/1
      router(config-if)# enable ipv6
      router(config-if)# ipv6 autoconfig

   B. router(config)# interface gigabitethernet1/1
      router(config)# ipv6 auto-config

   C. router(config)# interface gigabitethernet1/1
      router(config-if)# enable ipv6 auto

   D. router(config)# interface gigabitethernet1/1
      router(config-if)# ipv6 address autoconfig

Correct Answer (D)
Subject Matter: IPv6 Addressing (SLAAC)

IPv6 address Autoconfiguration requires the **autoconfig** command to enable it on any interface. The **ipv6 enable** command is not required.

   router(config)# interface gigabitethernet1/1
   router(config-if)# ipv6 address autoconfig

114. What IOS command will verify the status of an IPv6 interface?

   A. router# show ipv6 interface

   B. router# show interface ipv6

   C. router# show interface

   D. router# show ipv6

Correct Answer (A)
Subject Matter: IPv6 Addressing

The following IOS command will show the status of an IPv6 enabled interface. That includes interface and line protocol state, IPv6 link-local addressing and global unicast addressing.

    router# show ipv6 interface

115. Match the IPv6 address type on the left with the description on the right?

global unicast address	send to any member of a group that is nearest and available, typically the default route ::/0
multicast address	internet routable with global routing prefix
unique local address	prefix FF00::/8 (send to group members)
link-local address	auto configured for local subnet, not internet routable, prefix FE80::/64
modified eui-64 address	IPv6 host interface identifier, EUI-64 + msb 7th bit inverted
anycast address	private globally unique and not internet routable, starts with FD

Correct Answers.
Subject Matter: IPv6 Addressing

The following are IPv6 address types with associated descriptions.

global unicast address	**internet routable with global routing prefix**
multicast address	**prefix FF00::/8 (send to group members)**
unique local address	**private globally unique, not internet routable, starts with FD**
link-local address	**auto configured for local subnet, not internet routable prefix FE80::/64**
modified eui-64 address	**IPv6 host interface identifier, EUI-64 + msb 7th bit inverted**
anycast address	**send to any member of a group that is nearest and available, typically default route ::/0**

116. Match the IPv6 route type with the correct example on the right?

network prefix	ipv6 route 2001:345:213:FDAE::0/64 serial1/0 FE80::CA0A:01FF:33A9:2
default route	ipv6 route ::/0 A:F:A:D::3 200
WAN point-to-point address	/126
floating static route	/64
static route	/128
host route	ipv6 route ::/0 C:D:C:D::2
directly connected static route	ipv6 route 2001:DE3::/32 serial 1/0

Correct Answers.
Subject Matter: IPv6 Addressing

The following correctly match IPv6 route types with examples. The egress interface must be specified when the next hop is a link-local IPv6 address.

network prefix	**/64**
default route	**ipv6 route ::/0 C:D:C:D::2**
WAN point-to-point address	**/126**
floating static route	**ipv6 route ::/0 A:F:A:D::3 200**
static route	**ipv6 route 2001:345:213:FDAE::0/64 serial1/0 FE80::CA0A:01FF:33A9:2**
host route	**/128**
directly connected static route	**ipv6 route 2001:DE3::/32 serial 1/0**

117. Select two network protocols that use UDP?

    A. SNMP

    B. SMTP

    C. DNS

    D. DHCP

Correct Answers (A,C)
Subject Matter: UDP Protocol

User Datagram Protocol (UDP) is a connectionless transport protocol that doesn't provide reliable packet delivery. The following are some popular UDP-based protocols.

- SNMP
- DNS
- TFTP
- NTP

118. Select the two sublayers of the OSI data link layer?

    A. media access control

    B. media link control

    C. logical link control

    D. data link control

Correct Answers (A,C)
Subject Matter: OSI Model

The OSI data link layer is comprised of two sublayers. The lower sublayer is Media Access Control (MAC) while the upper sublayer is Logical Link Control (LLC). The following describe the network services provided by each sublayer.

Media Access Control (MAC) - manages access to the network media for upper layers.

Logical Link Control (LLC) - manage network media access for devices on the local segment, error detection, framing and MAC addressing. The data link PDU is created by the LLC as well.

119. Match the following OSI reference model layers on the left with the network services performed on the right?

data link	convert data to 0s and 1s, bit signaling and synchronization
physical	logical device identification, path selection
network	logical topology, hardware addresses, media access, framing
transport	flow control, reliable delivery, windowing, segmentation, sequencing

Correct Answers.
Subject Matter: OSI Model

The following correctly describe the network services provided by each OSI reference model layer.

data link	**logical topology, hardware addresses, media access, framing**
physical	**convert data to 0s and 1s, bit signaling and synchronization**
network	**logical device identification, path selection**
transport	**flow control, reliable delivery, windowing, segmentation, sequencing**

120. Match the cabling type on the left required for connecting the network devices on the right?

straight-through	console port
rollover	switch to router
crossover	router to CSU/DSU
serial (DTE/DCE)	switch to switch

Correct Answers.
Subject Matter: Cabling Type

The following describes the correct usage for each cable type.

Straight-Through

- switch to router
- switch to server
- switch to desktop
- switch to firewall
- switch to wireless access point
- switch to wireless LAN controller

Cisco Rollover

- desktop to console port

Crossover

- switch to switch
- router to router
- firewall to firewall
- host to host

Serial (DTE/DCE)

- router to CSU/DSU

121. Select the valid IPv6 address from the following examples?

A. 2001:CDCD:1357::D234:59:AD12

B. 2001:1C43:0000:123X:0000:0000:5678:12

C. 2301:443G:1:2345::CD34:5

D. 2201::1234::6789:EF42:3456

Correct Answer (A)
Subject Matter: IPv6 Addressing

Option A is the only valid IPv6 address that could be assigned to an interface.

The following describes why the IPv6 addresses are not valid.

Option B - has **X** in the address. 2001:1C43:0000:123**X**:0000:0000:5678:12

Option C - has **G** in the address. 2301:443**G**:1:2345::CD34:5

Option D - has double colons occurring twice. 2201**::**1234**::**6789:EF42:3456

122. Identify the IPv6 address that is not valid?

    A. 2000::

    B. ::

    C. 2001:AE25:1234:2943::

    D. ::172:33:0:1

    E. 2001:CD43:1234::4567

Correct Answer (A)
Subject Matter: IPv6 Addressing

The option **2000::** is a prefix only for a global unicast address with no interface identifier. The **::** is an unspecified address used as source address for a device requesting an IPv6 address (valid).

123. What three statements accurately describe how IPv6 duplicate address detection works?

    A. IPv6 state is tentative while duplicate address detection is active

    B. IPv6 duplicate address detection is performed on global addresses first

    C. device address solicitation messages are required

    D. neighbor solicitation messages are required

    E. IPv6 duplicate address detection is verified on link-local addresses first

Correct Answers (A,D,E)
Subject Matter: IPv6 Addressing

IPv6 duplicate address detection is required on all unicast IPv6 addresses assigned to an interface. The detection starts with Stateless Autoconfiguration (SLAAC) assigning an IPv6 link-local address to a node. The network interface state is tentative during the detection process. The network administrator can enable duplicate address detection again by assigning a new IPv6 address.

The network device or host (node) sends a neighbor solicitation message with an unspecified source address and proposed link-local IP address. Any network device or host that is already assigned the link-local address sends a neighbor advertisement to notify the source device. In addition any IPv6 node that is simultaneously verifying the address will send a neighbor solicitation to alert the source device. Any additional IPv6 addresses including global routable require duplicate address detection after the link-local address is verified.

124. What is the state of an IPv6 address when the interface is admin down?

   A. tentative

   B. pending

   C. unassigned

   D. suspended

Correct Answer (B)
Subject Matter: IPv6 Addressing

There are a variety of IPv6 address states based on the operational status of the interface and duplicate address detection. The IPv6 address state is pending while the associated network interface is administratively down.

125. Name three advantages of private IPv4 addressing?

   A. IP address space conservation

   B. support for multiple IP addresses per interface

   C. enable private routing domains and address space management

   D. network security

   E. minimize routing table size

Correct Answers (A,C,D)
Subject Matter: Private IPv4 Addressing

There are a variety of advantages to private IP addressing that has enabled deployment across the enterprise network. The number of public IP addresses available has decreased over the past 10 years where they are now only assignable for internet access.

RFC 1918 private address space cannot be routed across the internet. There are thousands of private IP addresses that are mapped to a single public IP address with Network Address Translation (NAT). As a result public address space conservation is a primary advantage. The reuse of IP address space maximizes the private IP addressing available to all enterprise companies. In addition there is granular management of private routing domains. There is network security for private IP addresses that are hidden from the public internet. Any duplicate addressing errors are minimized with management of public addressing by the ISP.

- IP address space conservation
- Management of private routing domains
- Network security
- Minimize duplicate IP address errors

126. What happens when an IPv6 duplicate address is detected? (select three)

    A. duplicate global address is not used on the network interface where it is assigned

    B. duplicate global address can only forward packets on local segment

    C. IPv6 packet forwarding is disabled on any interface that has a duplicate link-local address

    D. packets are forwarded on the local segment for any available IPv6 address until resolved

    E. all IPv6 addresses are disabled on the IPv6 interface that has a duplicate link-local address until resolved

Correct Answers (A,C,E)
Subject Matter: IPv6 Addressing

The following statements correctly describe what happens when a router detects an IPv6 duplicate address.

- Duplicate global address is not used on a network interface where it is assigned.

- IPv6 packet forwarding is disabled on any interface that has a duplicate link-local address.

- All IPv6 addresses are disabled on the IPv6 interface that has a duplicate link-local address until it is resolved.

127. Select the correct IOS command to manually assign an IPv6 address to a router interface?

A. ipv6 auto ::1/64

B. ipv6 address 2001:AF42:1212:4F32::32/64

C. ipv6 autoconfig 2001:AF42:1212:4F32::32/64

D. ipv6 autoconfig

Correct Answer (B)
Subject Matter: IPv6 Addressing

The following interface level IOS command assigns a static IPv6 address to a router interface.

router(config-if)# ipv6 address 2001:AF42:1212:4F32::32/64

The IPv6 address is manually assigned to an interface. There is dynamic IP address Stateless Autoconfiguration (SLAAC) and DHCPv6 server as well.

128. Refer to the network topology drawing. What default gateway address should be assigned to Host-1?

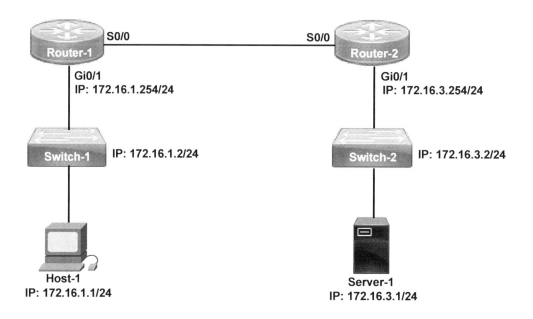

A. 172.16.3.254

B. 172.16.1.2

C. 172.16.1.254

D. 172.16.3.2

Correct Answer (C)
Subject Matter: IPv4 Addressing

The default gateway is the upstream layer 3 device (router) that provides routing services. The default gateway for Host-1 is 172.16.1.254. The IP address of the directly connected interface (Gi0/0) to the layer 2 switch is assigned as default gateway for the host. The host, switch and default gateway must be in the same subnet.

129. Refer to the routing table for router-3. What network address and subnet mask is a summary of the routes learned by EIGRP?

router-3# show ip route

Gateway of last resort is not set

172.33.1.0/28 is subnetted, 4 subnets
D   172.33.1.12 [90/2681856] via 192.168.1.1, 00:00:10, Serial0/0
D   172.33.1.16 [90/1823638] via 192.168.1.1, 00:00:30, Serial0/0
D   172.33.1.32 [90/3837233] via 192.168.1.1, 00:05:13, Serial0/0
D   172.33.1.60 [90/8127213] via 192.168.1.1, 00:06:31, Serial0/0
C   192.168.32.1/30 is directly connected, Serial0/1
C   192.168.2.0/24 is directly connected, GigabitEthernet0/0

A. 172.33.1.0 255.255.255.252

B. 172.33.1.0 255.255.255.192

C. 172.33.1.0 255.255.255.240

D. 172.33.1.64 255.255.255.192

E. 172.33.1.16 255.255.255.224

F. 172.33.1.28 255.255.255.224

Correct Answer (B)
Subject Matter: IPv4 Addressing

There are 4 successive subnets associated with 172.33.1.0/28 address. The 4 subnets = (2 power 2) so move the subnet mask left by 2 bits (28 − 2 = 26) and the summarized address is **172.33.1.0 255.255.255.192 (/26)**

common bits (/26)
172.33.1.60 = **10101100.00100001.00000001.00** 111100
172.33.1.12 = **10101100.00100001.00000001.00** 001100
172.33.1.16 = **10101100.00100001.00000001.00** 010000
172.33.1.32 = **10101100.00100001.00000001.00** 100000

130. Refer to the results of the following IOS command. Summarize the RIPv2 routes learned from 172.16.1.1?

router# show ip route

172.16.200.0/27 is subnetted, 4 subnets

R   172.16.200.12 [120/1] via 172.16.1.1, 00:00:05, Serial0/2
R   172.16.200.16 [120/1] via 172.16.1.1, 00:00:03, Serial0/2
R   172.16.200.32 [120/3] via 172.16.1.1, 00:05:32, Serial0/2
R   172.16.200.24 [120/2] via 172.16.1.1, 00:06:51, Serial0/2

A. 172.16.0.0/27

B. 172.16.0.0/26

C. 172.16.200.0/26

D. 172.16.200.64/26

E. 172.16.200.128/25

Correct Answer (C)
Subject Matter: IPv4 Addressing

The result of **show ip route** provides the following information:

172.16.200.0/27 is subnetted, 4 subnets

RIPv2 has 4 routes:

172.16.200.12 = **10101100.00010000.11001000.00** 001100

172.16.200.16 = **10101100.00010000.11001000.00** 010000

172.16.200.32 = **10101100.00010000.11001000.00** 100000

172.16.200.24 = **10101100.00010000.11001000.00** 011000

255.255.255.192 = /26 mask
The bits are common up to and including bit 26

Summarized Address = **172.16.200.0/26**

131. The ISP has assigned your company 2001:AD7:4312:0000::/48 for migrating to IPv6 addressing. There are ten regions spanning four continents with a maximum of 16 data centers per region. In addition there is a requirement for 200 subnets per data center. Select the IPv6 addressing that would provide the correct subnet allocation?

   A. regions = 2001:AD7:4312:0000::/52
      data centers = 2001:AD7:4312:0000::/56
      subnets = 2001:AD7:4312:0000::/64

   B. regions = 2001:AD7:4312:0000::/48
      data centers = 2001:AD7:4312:0000::/64
      subnets = 2001:AD7:4312:0000::/126

   C. regions = 2001:AD7:4312:0000::/56
      data centers = 2001:AD7:4312:0000::/60
      subnets = 2001:AD7:4312:0000::/64

   D. regions = 2001:AD7:4312:0000::/48
      data centers = 2001:AD7:4312:0000::/64
      subnets = 2001:AD7:4312:0000::/56

Correct Answer (A)
Subject Matter: IPv6 Addressing

The /48 network address block is a typical assignment to an enterprise network. It provides 16 bits for subnetting as part of the /64 network prefix. In addition there is a /64 (64 bits) available for host address portion.

- IPv6 address = 2001:AD7:4312:1D34.0000:0000:0000:0001/128
- single subnet = 2001:AD7:4312:1D34::/64
- 65,535 subnets (16 bits) = 2001:AD7:4312::/48

- network prefix = 2001:AD7:4312::/48
- network prefix + subnets = 2001:AD7:4312:**0**000::/64
- host identifier = 0000:0000:0000:0000/64 - FFFF:FFFF:FFFF:FFFF/64

regions	data centers	subnets
0000	0000	0000 0000

Each number or letter of an IPv6 address is a hexidecimal value comprised of 4 bits with 16 possible values from 0 to F. The subnet portion has 16 bits that can be assigned with variable subnet masks. For instance the first 4 bits (49 - 52) can be assigned to identify regions (bold).

The second group of 4 bits (53 - 56) can be assigned to identify data centers. The remaining group of 8 bits (57 - 64) are assigned to subnets for each data center.

- **regions** = /52
- data centers = /56
- data center subnets = /64

The number of regions, data centers and number of subnets per data center determine the subnets masks selected. For example where there are only 3 regions, the /50 subnet mask with 2 bits (49-50) would provide the required 4 region identifiers. The following IPv6 address ranges are assigned to regions, data centers and subnets per data center.

- 16 regions: 2001:AD7:4312:1000::/52 - 2001:AD7:4312:F000::/52

- 16 data centers: 2001:AD7:4312:0000::/56 - 2001:AD7:4312:0F00::/56

- data center subnets: 2001:AD7:4312:0000::/64 - 2001:AD7:4312:00FF::/64

Module 2: LAN Switching Technologies

1. Select three statements that accurately describe network switches?

    A. switches forward data link layer traffic

    B. switches create and maintain the MAC address table

    C. switches create extended collision domains from VLANs

    D. switches support segmenting collision domains

    E. switches forward packets based on IP address and MAC address

Correct Answers (A,B,D)
Subject Matter: Switching Concepts

The primary purpose of a switch is to make forwarding decisions based on destination MAC address. The MAC address table is created with a list of destination MAC address for each connected device. In addition the switch port assigned and VLAN membership. The Gigabit Ethernet ports are full-duplex that define a single collision domain per switch port.

2. What IOS command disables CDP on a specific network interface only?

    A. cdp off

    B. no cdp

    C. no cdp enable

    D. no cdp run

Correct Answer (C)
Subject Matter: Layer 2 Protocols

CDP is enabled on Cisco devices globally by default including the network interfaces. Disable CDP on a specific interface only with the following IOS interface level command.

    switch(config-if)# no cdp enable

The following IOS command disables CDP globally on the network device including all interfaces.

    switch(config)# no cdp run

3. What command lists the IOS version running on a neighbor switch?

    A. show version

    B. show neighbor ios

    C. show cdp neighbor

    D. show cdp neighbor detail

Correct Answer (D)
Subject Matter: Layer 2 Protocols

There is additional neighbor configuration information available with the **detail** keyword used with **show cdp neighbor** IOS command. The detail keyword includes IOS version of connected neighbors.

    switch# show cdp neighbor detail

4. What statement is correct concerning Cisco Discovery Protocol (CDP)?

    A. CDP is disabled by default on all network interfaces

    B. CDP is enabled by default on all Ethernet interfaces

    C. CDP requires an IP address to be assigned to network devices

    D. CDP is enabled on network devices globally only

Correct Answer (B)
Subject Matter: Layer 2 Protocols

CDP is enabled by default both globally and on all network interfaces.

5. What is the Cisco default CDP timer update interval (seconds)?

    A. 30 seconds

    B. 60 seconds

    C. 180 seconds

    D. 120 seconds

Correct Answer (B)
Subject Matter: Layer 2 Protocols

The default CDP update timer = 60 seconds.

6. What is the purpose of the CRC in an Ethernet frame?

    A. reorder frames at the destination

    B. correct data errors

    C. request retransmission of lost packets

    D. detect data errors

    E. detect lost packets

Correct Answer (D)
Subject Matter: Ethernet Frame Format

The Cyclic Redundancy Check (CRC) is a number (FCS) calculated on each frame received to verify data integrity. The layer 2 frame is discarded if the received FCS number doesn't match the original. It is an error detection technique and not error recovery. Any layer 3 device such as a router will write an IP header to create a packet with source and destination IP address. Any error detection and/or error recovery is managed by transport layer 4 protocols.

7. Select the two statements that best describe standard switch operation?

    A. switches are based on logical addressing to forward packets to VLANs

    B. switches repeat frames to all ports

    C. switches use the MAC address in a frame to make forwarding decisions

    D. switches forward frames and do not rewrite source or destination MAC address

Correct Answers (C,D)
Subject Matter: Switching Concepts

The host connected to a switch is assigned a MAC address used for network connectivity. The MAC address of the host sending a packet becomes the source MAC address. The destination MAC address is typically the default gateway (router). The switch builds a MAC address table comprised of host MAC address, assigned switch port and VLAN membership.

The layer 2 network switch does not rewrite the frame header MAC addressing. It examines the source MAC address and destination MAC address. The source MAC address and associated port is added to the MAC address table if it isn't listed. The switch then does a lookup of the destination MAC address.in the MAC address table to makes a forwarding decision. The frame is forwarded out the switch port associated with the destination MAC address.

MAC address learning occurs when the destination MAC address isn't listed in the MAC address table. The switch floods (broadcasts) the packet out all ports except the port where the MAC address was learned. That is of course the port assigned to the host that sent the frame (source MAC address).

The host sends packets with an IP header encapsulated in a frame. The source and destination IP address are required for end-to-end connectivity. Layer 2 switches do not examine or understand IP addressing. The router or any layer 3 enabled network device rewrite frame MAC addressing. The forwarding decisions for routers are based on destination IP address and not destination MAC address. The source and destination IP address do not change between source and destination hosts.

8. What are two advantages of network switches?

    A. switches examine IP address and make a forwarding decision

    B. host connected to a full-duplex switch port creates a collision domain

    C. VLANs create separate broadcast domains on a switch

    D. all network devices connected to the switch create a single collision domain

    E. switches forward broadcast and multicast traffic between VLANs

Correct Answer (B,C)
Subject Matter: Switching Concepts

The Gigabit Ethernet switch port supports full-duplex traffic between the host and network switch. That eliminates collisions and creates a collision domain per port. The fact that there are no collisions increases throughput and decreases network latency for host connections.

The VLAN creates a broadcast domain that is defined by assigning switch port/s to the same VLAN. All hosts connected to assigned switch ports are part of the same broadcast domain. Creating multiple VLANs will then define multiple broadcast domains. Switches do not forward broadcast or multicast traffic between VLANs minimizing bandwidth utilization.

9. Refer to the network topology drawing. What is the source MAC address of the Ethernet frame sent from Host-1 that arrives at Server-1?

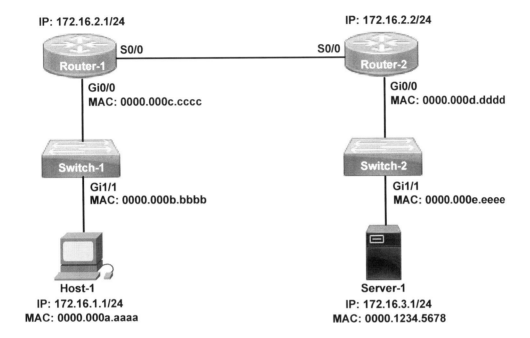

A. 0000.000d.dddd

B. 0000.000a.aaaa

C. 0000.1234.5678

D. 0000.000e.eeee

E. 0000.000c.cccc

Correct Answer (A)
Subject Matter: Switching Concepts

Router-2 rewrites the frame with the MAC address of Gi0/0 as source MAC address before forwarding it to Server-1. That is the egress network interface. The destination MAC address for the frame is the network interface card of Server-1. That was obtained from the ARP request sent to start the session with Server-1. WAN serial interfaces do not have a MAC address assigned.

10. Refer to the network topology drawing. Host-1 has established a session with Server-1 and sending a new file. What is the destination MAC address as the packet leaves Host-1 toward Router-1?

IP: 172.16.2.1/24

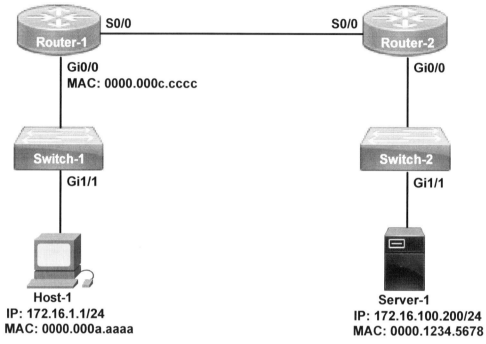

Host-1
IP: 172.16.1.1/24
MAC: 0000.000a.aaaa

Server-1
IP: 172.16.100.200/24
MAC: 0000.1234.5678

A. 0000.1234.5678

B. 0000.0000.0000

C. 0000.000c.cccc

D. 0000.000a.aaaa

E. ffff.ffff.ffff

Correct Answer (C)
Subject Matter: Switching Concepts

Host-1 sends all frame with the MAC address assigned to its network interface card as the source MAC address. The destination MAC address for the frame is the Gi0/0 Ethernet interface of Router-1. That was obtained from the ARP request sent before the session started with Server-1. Switches forward frames and are never a destination. In addition the directly connected upstream router interface (Gi0/0) is the default gateway as well.

11. Refer to the network topology drawing. Select three network devices that use the destination MAC address to make a forwarding decision?

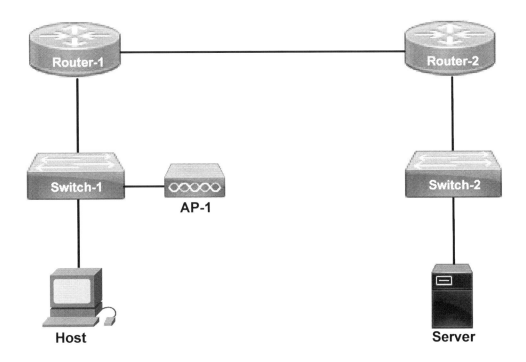

A. Switch-1

B. AP-1

C. Router-1

D. Switch-2

E. Router-2

Correct Answers (A,B,D)
Subject Matter: Switching Concepts

Switches and wireless access points are network devices that make forwarding decisions based on the destination MAC address in the frame. They do not change MAC addressing in the frame. Wireless access points are essentially bridges. Routers update/rewrite the source and destination MAC address in the frame. In addition routers make forwarding decisions based on source and destination IP address.

12. Select three correct statements concerning CDP?

    A. CDP is data link layer

    B. CDP is open standard protocol

    C. CDP is Cisco proprietary

    D. CDP is network layer

    E. CDP discovers directly connected neighbor Cisco devices only

    F. CDP supports discovery of Cisco devices that are not directly connected

Correct Answer (A,C,E)
Subject Matter: Layer 2 Protocols

CDP is a data link layer Cisco proprietary neighbor discovery protocol. The purpose is to discover connectivity and configuration information for directly connected Cisco devices. The open standard counterpart to CDP that supports multi-vendor discovery is LLDP.

13. Refer to the network topology drawing. What destination MAC address will Host-1 use when sending packets for the first time to Server-1?

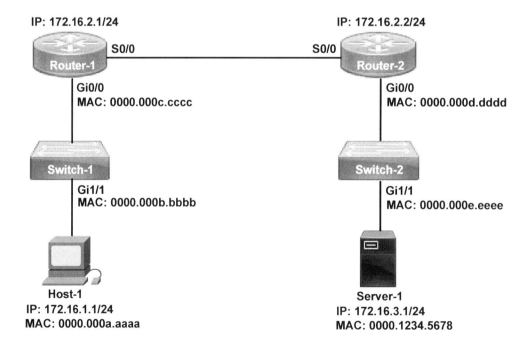

A. 0000.000a.aaaa

B. 0000.000b.bbbb

C. 0000.000c.cccc

D. 0000.000d.dddd

E. ffff.ffff.ffff

F. 0000.1234.5678

Correct Answer (E)
Subject Matter: Switching Concepts

Host-1 sends a layer 2 ARP broadcast frame on the local VLAN (network segment) to request the MAC address of the default gateway. That is required before sending an ARP request to the default gateway for the MAC address of Server-1. The host will first verify the MAC address of the default gateway is not already in the local ARP cache. The following describes the network addressing of the broadcast packet sent from Host-1.

- source MAC address = host-1 network interface card
- destination MAC address = ffff.ffff.ffff
- source IP address = host-1 assigned IP address
- destination IP address = server-1 assigned IP address

14. What network protocol detects whether a connected IP phone is from Cisco or a third party vendor?

A. RTP

B. CDP

C. 802.1q

D. 802.3ae

Correct Answer (B)
Subject Matter: Layer 2 Protocols

The purpose of CDP is to detect and relay device network configuration information to neighbor devices. In addition Cisco CDP can only detect Cisco devices including IP phones. The Cisco IP phone appears to CDP as a unique neighbor device with an IP address. During bootup, the IP phone receives voice VLAN configuration from the switch.

15. Refer to the network topology. Host-1 has sent a packet to Server-1 on Switch-1. What will Switch-1 do with the frame when it arrives?

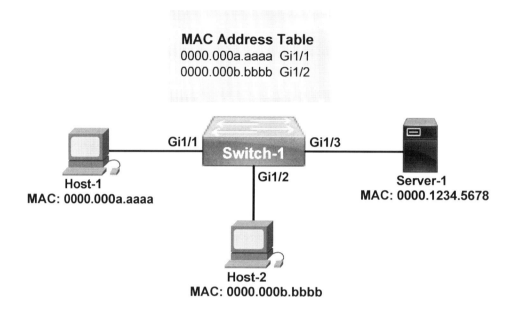

A. drop the frame

B. flood the frame out all ports except port Gi1/3

C. send an ARP request to Host-1

D. flood the frame out all ports except port Gi1/1

E. send an ICMP host unreachable message to Host-1

F. send the frame to the nearest router

Correct Answer (D)
Subject Matter: Switching Concepts

The destination MAC address is unknown. The switch will unicast flood (MAC learning) the frame out all ports except the port where the frame was learned from (Gi1/1). Server-1 with the matching destination MAC address receives the frame. The switch updates the MAC address table with the MAC address and associated port (Gi1/3) of Server-1. That occurs when packets are sent from Server-1 to Host-1.

16. The network administrator has configured a switch with a single VLAN. The switch receives a frame with no MAC address table entry for the destination MAC address. What will the switch do with the frame?

    A. drop the frame

    B. flood it out all active ports

    C. send an ARP request

    D. forward it out of all active ports except the port where it was learned

    E. send a broadcast ARP

Correct Answer (D)
Subject Matter: Switching Concepts

The switch will flood the frame out of all active ports except the switch port where it was learned.

17. What address is used by a layer 2 network switch to make forwarding decisions?

    A. source IP address

    B. destination IP address

    C. destination MAC address

    D. source and destination IP address

    E. source and destination MAC address

Correct Answer (C)
Subject Matter: Switching Concepts

The switch examines the frame header for the destination MAC address and forwards it out the associated port.

18. Refer to the network topology drawing. Host-2 is sending a packet to Server-1. What will Switch-1 do with the arriving frame? (select two)

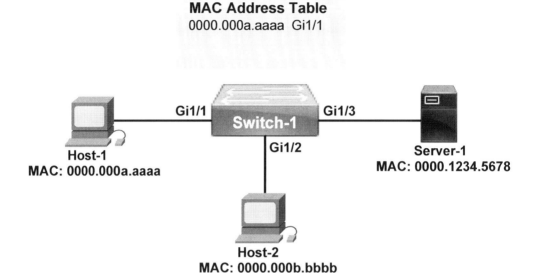

MAC Address Table
0000.000a.aaaa Gi1/1

Gi1/1   Switch-1   Gi1/3

Gi1/2

Host-1
MAC: 0000.000a.aaaa

Server-1
MAC: 0000.1234.5678

Host-2
MAC: 0000.000b.bbbb

A. switch will forward the frame out Gi0/0 and Gi0/1 ports only

B. 0000.000b.bbbb will be added to the MAC address table

C. switch will drop a frame with this destination MAC address

D. frame will be forwarded out all active switch ports except port Gi1/2

E. 0000.000a.aaaa will be added to the MAC address table

F. frame will be flooded out all switch ports

Correct Answers (B,D)
Subject Matter: Switching Concepts

The switch will examine the source and destination MAC address of the frame arriving on port Gi1/2 from Host-2. The MAC address table has no entry for either MAC address. The switch will then add the source MAC address (Host-2) to the MAC table. In addition the switch will unicast flood (MAC learning) the frame out all ports except the port where the frame was learned from (Gi1/2). Server-1 with the matching destination MAC address receives the frame. The switch updates the MAC address table with the MAC address and associated port (Gi1/3) of Server-1. That occurs when Server-1 sends a packet to Host-2.

19. What does a host on an Ethernet network do when it is sending a frame to a server where the destination MAC (physical) address is unknown?

A. drops the frame

B. ARP broadcast

C. sends layer 3 broadcast message

D. send an ICMP message to router requesting the MAC address

E. sends DNS request to server

Correct Answer (B)
Subject Matter: Switching Concepts

The host will send an ARP broadcast for the MAC address of the default gateway first. It is the default gateway (router) that eventually does the ARP request for the server MAC address.

20. How many collision domains and broadcast domains exist on a 24-port Gigabit switch with 4 VLANs?

A. 4 collision domains, 48 broadcast domains

B. 24 collision domains, 4 broadcast domains

C. 24 collision domains, 1 broadcast domain

D. 1 collision domain, 24 broadcast domains

E. 1 collision domain, 4 broadcast domains

Correct Answer (B)
Subject Matter: Switching Concepts

Each switch port is a separate collision domain and each VLAN is a separate broadcast domain. The 24-port switch configured with 4 VLANs has 24 collision domains and 4 broadcast domains.

21. Refer to the network drawing. Host-2 is sending a packet to Server-1. What will Switch-1 do with the frame when it arrives? (select two)

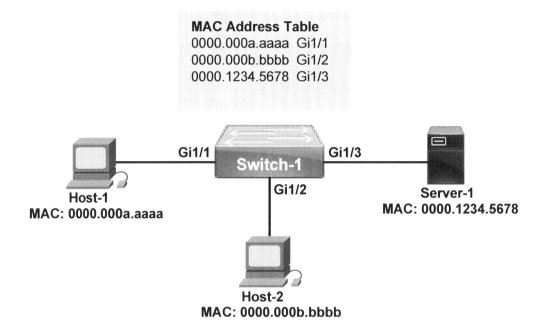

MAC Address Table
0000.000a.aaaa Gi1/1
0000.000b.bbbb Gi1/2
0000.1234.5678 Gi1/3

Host-1
MAC: 0000.000a.aaaa

Gi1/1   Switch-1   Gi1/3

Gi1/2

Server-1
MAC: 0000.1234.5678

Host-2
MAC: 0000.000b.bbbb

A. frame is forwarded out port Gi1/1 only

B. frame is forwarded out port Gi1/3

C. frame will be forwarded out all active ports

D. switch will send an ARP request

E. switch will examine the frame and do a MAC table lookup

Correct Answers (B,E)
Subject Matter: Switching Concepts

Switch-1 will examine the incoming frame from Host-2 arriving on port Gi1/2. The switch will do a MAC table lookup based on the destination MAC address. The switch determines the destination MAC address is assigned to Server-1. The frame is forwarded to port Gi1/3 associated with Server-1.

22. What two network protocols support the dynamic establishment of an EtherChannel link between switches?

A. PAgP

B. STP

C. LACP

D. DTP

E. 802.1q

Correct Answers (A,C)
Subject Matter: EtherChannel

EtherChannel bundles multiple physical switch links that exist between two switches into a single logical link. It is sometimes referred to as switch port aggregation. The advantages include fault tolerance (redundancy) and high speed links between switches. Traffic from a previously single Gigabit Ethernet port can now forward traffic across a logical link at higher speed. For instance bundling four separate Gigabit Ethernet links into a single EtherChannel creates a 4 Gbps link. In addition alll traffic is forwarded across all existing links when any single link isn't available.

The options for configuring EtherChannel include static or dynamic protocols.

1. Static trunks do not require any negotiation protocol. The channel-group is configured with **on** keyword for all switches ports on both switches assigned to the EtherChannel.

2. PAgP is a Cisco proprietary protocol for dynamic negotiation of an EtherChannel link. It supports Cisco network devices only and configured with the **channel-group** command. The four PAgP modes include **on, off, auto and desirable.**

3. LACP is an open standard that supports EtherChannel between different switch vendors. It supports negotiating of dynamic EtherChannel links as well. The four modes supported include **on**, **off, active and passive.**

23. What spanning tree port type is the facing port to the elected root bridge with the least cost path?

A. designated port

B. disabled

C. root port

D. blocking port

Correct Answer (C)
Subject Matter: Spanning Tree Protocol (STP)

The Spanning Tree election assigns root bridge along with designated ports, root ports and alternate ports to neighbor switches. The root port is a switch port on a neighbor switch that has the least cost path to the root bridge. It is a primary forwarding link to the root bridge.

24. What network switch table builds a list of learned MAC addresses and associated switch ports for connected devices?

A. routing table

B. MAC address table

C. VLAN table

D. ARP table

Correct Answer (B)
Subject Matter: Switching Concepts

The switch builds a MAC address table that is comprised of the MAC address for each connected host along with the assigned switch port and VLAN membership. The purpose is to make layer 2 forwarding decisions.

25. Refer to the network topology drawing. What switch ports from the topology drawing are Spanning Tree Protocol (STP) designated ports?

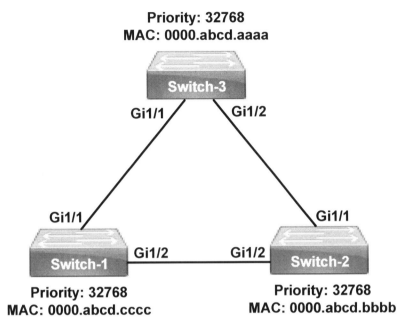

Priority: 32768
MAC: 0000.abcd.aaaa

Switch-3

Gi1/1   Gi1/2

Gi1/1   Gi1/1

Switch-1   Gi1/2   Gi1/2   Switch-2

Priority: 32768   Priority: 32768
MAC: 0000.abcd.cccc   MAC: 0000.abcd.bbbb

A. Switch-3 Gi1/1, Switch-3 Gi1/2, Switch-2 Gi1/2

B. Switch-2 Gi1/1, Switch-2 Gi1/2, Switch-3 Gi1/1

C. Switch-1 Gi1/2, Switch-2 Gi1/2, Switch-3 Gi1/2

D. Switch-1 Gi1/1, Switch-2 Gi1/2, Switch-3 Gi1/1

Correct Answer (A)
Subject Matter: Spanning Tree Protocol (STP)

The root bridge switch ports are all assigned as designated ports by STP. The switch with the lowest bridge ID is assigned as root bridge. The switch priorities are all equal (32768) so the switch with the lowest MAC address is elected root bridge. The designated ports of a root bridge connect to the root port of non-root bridge (switch) neighbors. The root port of a non-root bridge is the switch port with the lowest cost to the root bridge. That is a directly connected switch port with the highest bandwidth. That creates the primary links for switch traffic.

The lowest MAC address is calculated from left to right per hexidecimal number. All numbers match until number 9 where Switch-3 has the lower (a) compared with Switch-2 (b) and Switch-1 (c). As a result, Switch-3 is elected as root bridge. In addition all switch ports on a root bridge are all designated ports.

Switch-1 = 0000.abcd.cccc
Switch-2 = 0000.abcd.bbbb
Switch-3 = 0000.abcd.**aaaa** = **root bridge**

The non-root switches are assigned a designated port as well to forward BPDUs on the network segment. The designated port connects to a neighbor non-root bridge. The non-root switches compare link cost (bandwidth) for that switch link (network segment). The switch port with the lower cost (highest bandwidth) is the designated port for that link. When the switch ports are equal-cost, the port of the non-root switch with the lower bridge ID is assigned as a designated port.

The two non-root switches are Switch-1 and Switch-2. There is a single Gigabit Ethernet link connecting the non-root switches. As a result the switch port cost to the network segment is equal. The port of the non-root switch with the lower bridge ID is assigned as a designated port when path costs are equal. Switch-2 has a lower bridge-ID than Switch-1. As a result Switch-2 port Gi1/2 is a designated port as well. Switch-1 port Gi1/2 is blocking/alternate port type to prevent layer 2 loops.

Switch-1
- Gi1/1 = Root Port
- Gi1/2 = Blocking/Alternate Port

Switch-2
- Gi1/1 = Root Port
- Gi1/2 = Designated Port

Switch-3
- Gi1/1 = Designated Port
- Gi1/2 = Designated Port

26. Refer to the network topology drawing. Based on the results of **show vlan brief**, why can't the hosts in VLAN 11 and VLAN 12 of Switch-1 communicate with hosts in the same VLANs on Switch-2?

switch-1# **show vlan brief**

VLAN	Name	Status	Ports
1	default	active	Gi1/1, Gi1/2, Gi1/3
			Gi1/4, Gi1/5, Gi1/6
			Gi1/7, Gi1/8, Gi1/9
10	data	active	Gi1/1, Gi1/2, Gi1/3
11	server	active	Gi1/4, Gi1/5, Gi1/6
12	wireless	active	Gi1/7, Gi1/8, Gi1/9

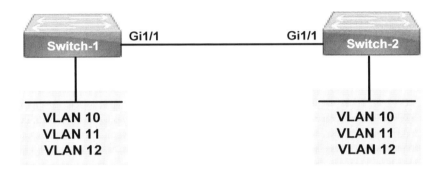

A.   routing is required to connect VLANs between switches

B.   at least two links are required where there are multiple VLANs

C.   EtherChannel is not enabled between the switches

D.   GigabitEthernet1/1 (Gi1/1) interface is not configured as a trunk

Correct Answer (D)
Subject Matter: Inter-Switch Connectivity

The purpose of a switch trunk is to forward multiple VLANs between two switches. The network engineer must configure a trunk link to enable forwarding of multiple VLANs. That allows hosts assigned to the same VLAN across different switches to communicate. VLAN 10 is assigned to access port Gi1/1 of Switch-1 allowing connectivity for that VLAN to Switch-2 hosts. Forwarding traffic across the switch link between VLAN 11 and VLAN 12 would require a trunk. That would allow all VLANs across the switch link unless pruned. The interface level IOS command **switchport mode trunk** is required on port Gi1/1 of Switch-1 and Switch-2.

27. What IOS show command will display the port channel interface status?

    A. show etherchannel summary

    B. show interface port-channel

    C. show etherchannel port-channel

    D. show interfaces pagp

Correct Answer (B)
Subject Matter: EtherChannel

The following IOS show command lists the port channel and line protocol interface status (up/up). In addition the port channel members are listed along with interface errors.

    switch# show interface port-channel

The port channel is an aggregation of up to 8 physical interfaces to create a single logical interface. There are layer 2 and layer 3 port channels. The layer 2 port channels are comprised of access ports or trunk ports. The layer 3 port channel bundles multiple routed interfaces. The port settings must match for both sides of a switch link that is part of a port channel.

EtherChannel refers to the bundling (aggregation) of layer 2 interfaces. The layer 2 port channel is the same as an EtherChannel. The layer 3 port channel is a virtual interface that assigns an IP address to an EtherChannel group.

28. What switch feature enables multiple VLANs to span switches?

    A. PortFast

    B. EtherChannel

    C. Trunk

    D. Spanning Tree

Correct Answer (C)
Subject Matter: Inter-Switch Connectivity

The trunk enables a switch to forward multiple VLANs across a switch link. That allows communication between hosts assigned to the same VLAN that spans switches.

29. What possible problems can occur when deploying redundant links between campus switches? (select three)

A. additional frames sent

B. broadcast storms

C. MAC address table instability

D. VLAN mismatch errors

E. trunk port flapping

Correct Answers (A,B,C)
Subject Matter: Inter-Switch Connectivity

The redundant topology is characterized by multiple paths that could cause layer 2 loops. STP is deployed to forward and block specific ports to eliminate forwarding loops between switches. Specific problems caused by redundant topology include sending multiple frames, broadcast storms and MAC address table instability.

30. What is the purpose of 802.1q?

A. trunk negotiation

B. enable switch port security

C. spanning tree root bridge selection

D. forwarding multiple VLANs across a switch trunk

E. VLAN pruning

Correct Answer (D)
Subject Matter: Inter-Switch Connectivity

Trunking enables forwarding of multiple VLANs across a switch link. The 802.1q protocol is an encapsulation type that enables tagging of VLANs across the switch link. Ethernet frames have an 802.1q field that is used for identifying VLAN membership. That allows the switch to identify VLAN membership for each frame.

31. What two IOS show commands are used to verify trunk status on a switch interface?

A. show interface switchport

B. show interface [interface]

C. show interfaces trunk

D. show ip interface brief

E. show interface vlan

Correct Answers (A,C)
Subject Matter: Inter-Switch Connectivity

The following IOS show commands display configuration information for all trunk interfaces. That includes switch port operational status, encapsulation type, trunking mode, dynamic protocol negotiation (PAgP, LACP) and native VLAN.

switch# show interfaces trunk
switch# show interface switchport

32. What IOS command enables PortFast on a switch access port?

A. spanning-tree portfast

B. spanning-tree portfast default

C. spanning-tree portfast bpduguard default

D. spanning-tree bpduguard enable

Correct Answer (A)
Subject Matter: Spanning Tree Protocol (STP)

PortFast is a Spanning Tree Protocol (STP) enhancement designed for access layer network devices. Any host or even network device connected to an access layer switch does not receive STP BPDUs. The uplinks that connect each switch are part of STP election and any messaging. That is where layer 2 loops if any would occur. PortFast is enabled on switch ports where hosts are connected. That allows the ports to transition from disabled or blocking state to forwarding immediately on startup. The following is the interface level IOS command to enable PortFast.

switch(config-if)# spanning-tree portfast

33. What statement best describes the PVST+ network protocol?

   A. provides fast convergence

   B. defines a separate 802.1d spanning tree instance for each VLAN

   C. defines a single 802.1d spanning tree instance for all VLANs

   D. faster convergence with a single spanning tree instance per switch

Correct Answer (B)
Subject Matter: Spanning Tree Protocol (STP)

Per VLAN Spanning Tree Plus (PVST+) enables an 802.1d spanning tree instance per VLAN. It was developed to support 802.1q encapsulation for Cisco devices only. The original 802.1d standard was designed for a single broadcast domain. STP prevents broadcast storms caused by layer 2 loops.

34. Select four standard VLAN design considerations when deploying a switching infrastructure?

   A. maximum number of VLANs is 1004

   B. VLAN 10 is the Cisco default Ethernet VLAN

   C. native VLAN configured on a trunk link must match between connected switches

   D. change the native VLAN from the default VLAN 1 for security purposes

   E. DTP provides dynamic trunk negotiation and is enabled by default

   F. configure an SVI on the switch for management purposes

Correct Answers (C,D,E,F)
Subject Matter: Inter-Switch Connectivity

There are requirements and best practices when deploying trunks between switches.

   • The native VLAN configured on a trunk link must match between each switch. That is required to forward untagged packets across the trunk.

   • Change the native VLAN from the default VLAN 1 for security purposes. Layer 2 loops caused by extending the default VLAN 1 across trunks is minimized as well.

- DTP provides dynamic trunk negotiation and is enabled by default.

- Configure an SVI on the switch for management purposes (Telnet, SSH, SNMP, Syslog etc.) instead of the default VLAN 1.

- The purpose of VLAN 1 is to forward control traffic (CDP, VTP, PAgP etc.) between switches. All switch ports are assigned to default VLAN 1.

35. What statement describes the operation of Dynamic Trunking Protocol (DTP) in auto mode?

A. trunking is disabled

B. enables trunking on the interface

C. trunk setup is based on the DTP request from the neighbor switch

D. DTP frame requests are dropped before sending to neighbor switch

E. sends a DTP message request to create a trunk with neighbor switch

Correct Answer (C)
Subject Matter: Inter-Switch Connectivity

DTP is a network protocol that enables dynamic negotiation of a trunk between two switches. The DTP modes are **nonegotiate**, **desirable** and **auto**. DTP is enabled by default and can be disabled with the interface level IOS command **switchport nonegotiate**.

The DTP request frames are sent to the neighbor switch to negotiate the trunk setup. Cisco switches use the default **auto** mode. The switch port configured with **desirable** or **auto** mode listen for DTP requests.

The following describe the effect of each interface level configuration command for non-DTP and DTP modes:

switchport mode access = no trunking
switchport mode trunk = static (on) mode

switchport mode dynamic auto = listen for DTP requests
switchport mode dynamic desirable = listen for DTP requests
switchport mode nonegotiate = disable DTP

The following describes how each switch mode affects trunk setup between local and remote switches. Access mode is equivalent to a switch access port (no trunk). The **on** mode is configured manually at the switch (static trunk) and not a DTP mode.

auto - auto	= access mode (no trunk)
auto - desirable	= trunk
auto - on	= trunk
desirable - on	= trunk
desirable - desirable	= trunk
nonegotiate - nonegotiate	= access mode (no trunk)
nonegotiate - on	= trunk

The **nonegotiate** mode is configured on switches that don't support DTP mode. The Cisco neighbor switch is configured with **on** mode to enable trunk setup.

36. What are three primary advantages of VLANs?

A. broadcast domains minimize bandwidth usage and multicast traffic

B. enable routing on a layer 2 switch

C. increased scalability to support large multi-segment data center deployments

D. fewer collisions domains

E. VLANs assign all hosts to the same broadcast domain to prevent broadcast storms

F. improves network security with traffic segmentation

Correct Answers (A,C,F)
Subject Matter: VLANs

VLANs do not prevent broadcast storms, they minimize the size and effect of the broadcast storm on neighbor switches and hosts. The VLAN is a broadcast domain and as such broadcasts are not advertised outside of the VLAN.

Network security is optimized with VLANs by segmenting sensitive traffic and filter it from other network traffic. Bandwidth efficiency is accomplished through segmenting broadcast domains with VLANs. Unicasts, broadcasts and multicasts are not forwarded between VLANs minimizing bandwidth utilization. VLANs ease the adds, moves and deleting of hosts on the network. LANs control and filter user access to network services based on department for instance.

37. Refer to the exhibit. Select three statements that are correct?

```
switch-1# show spanning-tree vlan 10

VLAN 0010
Spanning tree enabled protocol rstp
Root ID Priority 28682
Address: 0000.abcd.aaaa
This bridge is the root
Hello Time 2 sec   Max Age 20 sec   Forward Delay 15 sec
Bridge ID priority 28682
Address 0000.abcd.aaaa
Hello Time 2 sec   Max Age 20 sec   Forward Delay 15 sec
Aging Time 300

Interface  Role    Sts    Cost  Prio.Nbr    Type
---------- ------- ------- ------ ----------- -------
Gi1/1      Desg    FWD     4     128.1       P2p
Gi1/1      Desg    FWD     4     128.1       P2p
Gi1/1      Desg    FWD     4     128.1       P2p
```

A. port states supported include discarding, learning and forwarding

B. switch-1 is the non-root bridge for VLAN 10

C. root bridge priority is lower than the default value for spanning tree

D. all designated ports are in a forwarding state

E. the same switch priority is assigned to all VLANs for switch-1

F. VLAN 10 is a trunk with three interfaces

Correct Answers (A,C,D)
Subject Matter: Spanning Tree Protocol (STP)

The IOS command **show spanning-tree vlan 10** provides per VLAN spanning tree status for VLAN 10. The **rstp** indicates 802.1w is enabled and port states are discarding, learning or forwarding. Switch-1 is assigned as the root bridge for VLAN 10. In addition the root bridge priority of 28682 is lower than the default 32768. The root bridge switch ports are always designated ports and they are in forwarding state.

38. What encapsulation type is required to configure trunking between a Cisco switch and a Juniper switch?

A. DTP

B. unsupported feature

C. ISL

D. 802.1q

E. PAgP

Correct Answer (D)
Subject Matter: Inter-Switch Connectivity

Encapsulation provides VLAN tagging at layer 2 across a switch trunk link. The open standard for multi-vendor switch connectivity is 802.1q encapsulation. It is the current Cisco default as well.

39. What switch will be elected as root bridge in the election process based on the following priority and MAC address values for the different switches?

A. 32769: 0000.000d.dddd

B. 32768: 0000.000e.eeee

C. 28673: 0000.000a.aaaa

D. 28673: 0000.0001.2345

Correct Answer (D)
Subject Matter: Spanning Tree Protocol (STP)

The root bridge elected for a spanning tree instance is the switch with the lowest bridge ID. STP calculates a unique numerical value for the bridge ID based on the switch priority setting and MAC address. The tie breaker is lower MAC address, when there are two switches with the same lowest priority.

The example has two switches (option C and option D) with the same lowest priority of 28673. The tie breaker is the switch with the lower MAC address. Counting from right to left, the **1** of option D is lower than **A** of option C. Hexidecimal **A** is equivalent to the number 10. The switch from option D is elected as root bridge.

28673: 0000.000**a**.aaaa
28673: 0000.000**1**.2345

40. What is a primary advantage of VLAN pruning?

    A. optimizes network security

    B. minimizes broadcast and multicast traffic

    C. decreases switch management traffic

    D. decreases the number of broadcast domains

Correct Answer (B)
Subject Matter: Inter-Switch Connectivity

The purpose of VLAN pruning is to filter VLANs across a switch trunk. It is a feature of VTP and disabled by default. The switch that has pruning enabled, won't forward specific VLANs across a switch trunk. The local switch alerts the neighbor switch of all local VLANs that are not active (configured). Those VLANs are pruned by the neighbor switch to minimize unicast, broadcast and multicast traffic across the trunk.

41. What is the purpose of Spanning Tree Protocol (STP)?

    A. prevent layer 2 loops

    B. switch redundancy

    C. port mirroring

    D. minimize network convergence

Correct Answer (A)
Subject Matter: Spanning Tree Protocol (STP)

The primary reason for deploying Spanning Tree is to prevent layer 2 loops. The result of layer 2 loops is broadcast storms where frames are forwarded in a loop between switches. There are a variety of Spanning Tree Protocols (STP) with the most current supporting VLANs. STP creates a loop free layer 2 topology by configuring some switch ports to forward traffic and some blocking traffic. That is based on electing a root bridge with the lowest bridge ID. The switch with the lowest priority and MAC address is elected root bridge. In addition STP calculates neighbor lowest cost path to the root bridge.

42. What IOS command will shutdown a switch access port when a managed switch is connected to that port?

    A. spanning-tree bpduguard on

    B. spanning-tree bpduguard enable

    C. switchport guard bpdu

    D. spanning-tree portfast

Correct Answer (B)
Subject Matter: Spanning Tree Protocol (STP)

The IOS command **spanning-tree bpduguard enable** is configured at the interface level to prevent network devices from affecting the STP topology. For instance connecting a network switch at your cubicle would trigger STP recalculation. The new switch is now connected to an access switch port causing layer 2 topology changes. The consequences could include a variety of network errors including a new root bridge. The purpose of BPDU guard is to errdisable (shutdown) the access switch port. That occurs when BPDUs are received from the new switch at the access switch interface. PortFast and BPDU guard are enabled on access edge switch ports where hosts connect.

43. What switching mode examines the first 14 bytes of the frame and makes a forwarding decision based on the switch MAC address table?

    A. CEF

    B. DTP

    C. cut-through

    D. store-and-forward

    E. process switching

Correct Answer (C)
Subject Matter: Switching Concepts

The cut-through switching technique optimizes performance by examining the first 14 bytes of the Ethernet frame. The first 14 bytes is comprised of MAC addressing used to make a forwarding decision. The switch does a MAC address table lookup for the destination MAC address and forwards the frame. The advantage is the forwarding decision is made before all of the frame arrives and thereby minimizing network latency.

44. Host-1 is connected to interface Gi1/1 of a switch with 802.1d spanning tree enabled. Select the order of states that spanning tree transitions the interface through before it starts forwarding traffic?

A. blocking, listening, learning, forwarding

B. blocking, forwarding, listening, learning

C. listening, learning, forwarding, blocking

D. listening, learning, blocking, forwarding

Correct Answer (A)
Subject Matter: Spanning Tree Protocol (STP)

The campus switching topology is comprised of multiple switches each connected with switch uplinks. The number of uplink ports and how they connect to neighbor switches defines the layer 2 topology.

Spanning Tree Protocol manages an election process for the root bridge (per VLAN where applicable). In addition the neighbor uplink switch ports are transitioned through multiple states. STP will assign a port type to each switch port uplink and an STP interface state for each port as well. The purpose is to create a loop free layer 2 topology.

All switches enabled with STP will transition all active switch ports through the STP port transition states. That includes access ports however PortFast transitions the access edge port immediately to forwarding state. The following describe the 802.1d original STP port states that occur when starting a switch or enabling a switch port.

- Blocking
- Listening
- Learning
- Forwarding

The newer 802.1w (RSTP) standard is comprised of only three states. They include discarding, learning and forwarding. RPVST+ is based on RSTP and would support only the 802.1w port states. The discarding state is equivalent to the blocking and listening states.

Learning = populating MAC address table

45. What is the purpose of Ethernet physical MAC addresses? (select two)

A. enable packet forwarding across multiple network segments

B. enable packet forwarding on a common network segment

C. enable spanning tree root bridge election

D. prevent collisions on a common segment

E. globally unique network device identifier

Correct Answer (B,E)
Subject Matter: Switching Concepts

Every network device is assigned a unique hardware address from the manufacturer called a MAC address. The purpose of a MAC address is to provide a unique layer 2 identifier. That enables communication between devices of the same network segment (VLAN) or different segments. The switch builds a MAC address table comprised of all MAC addresses. The VLAN is similar to a subnet with routing required to forward packets between segments. ARP is required in that situation to request the remote host MAC address.

46. What three statements best describe Cisco layer 2 switches?

A. switch ports have no VLAN assignment as a default

B. VLANs increase the number of broadcast domains

C. switches rewrite source MAC address in each frame based on the egress forwarding port selected

D. microsegmentation decreases the number of collisions on the network

E. VLAN based spanning tree for any switched network topology permits only one root bridge per VLAN

F. ARP requests are sent only when the destination MAC address is not in the switch ARP table

Correct Answers (B,D,E)
Subject Matter: Switching Concepts

The layer 2 switch provides some key features that optimize bandwidth and decrease network latency compared with hubs and bridges. The VLAN increases the number of broadcast domains (segments). That limits unicast, broadcast and multicast traffic across the switching infrastructure.

Microsegmentation is enabled with newer Ethernet Gigabit switch ports that support full-duplex operation. That eliminates collisions on the switch and dedicates all port bandwidth to the connected host.

Spanning Tree Protocol assigns only one root port to a switch where there are redundant links. The root port transitions to forwarding state and sends frames to the root bridge. The root port has the least cost to the root bridge. All switch uplinks for the root bridge are transitioned to forwarding state. In addition Per VLAN Spanning Tree (PVST) assigns a root bridge per VLAN segment.

Connectivity between VLANs require a routing process provided by a layer 3 network device. Switches make forwarding decisions based on destination MAC address (layer 2) only.

The switch will first flood the local VLAN segment (unicast MAC flooding) to determine if the host is local. The ARP broadcast is only sent for packet forwarding between local and remote hosts on different VLANs or subnets.

47. What does a layer 2 access switch do with a frame that arrives where the destination MAC address is unknown and multiple VLANs are configured?

   A. frame is forwarded out all active switch ports except the port for the same VLAN where the frame was learned

   B. frame is forwarded to all uplinks only

   C. frame is forwarded out all switch ports except the port where the frame was learned

   D. frame is dropped and switch advertises ICMP *unreachable* message to the host connected to the source port

Correct Answer (A)
Subject Matter: Switching Concepts

The layer 2 switch builds a MAC address table for each configured VLAN with all connected hosts. The **show mac-address table** command lists all MAC address tables as a single table for easy reference. Each entry includes MAC address, associated port and VLAN membership.

The switch first does a lookup in the local MAC address table associated with the port and VLAN where the frame was learned. If the destination MAC address isn't listed, the switch will flood the frame out all ports assigned to the VLAN except the port where the frame was learned. If the host isnt local then an ARP request is sent for the destination MAC address. Switches only flood the local broadcast domain and require ARP for hosts located in a different VLAN.

140

48. Select the IOS command that will configure 192.168.1.254 as the default gateway for a layer 2 access switch?

A. ip default-gateway 192.168.1.254

B. default gateway 192.168.1.254

C. ip default-network 192.168.1.254

D. ip route 0.0.0.0 0.0.0.0 192.168.1.254

Correct Answer (A)
Subject Matter: Switching Concepts

The following IOS command will configure a connected upstream layer 3 device as the default gateway for the switch. The switch default gateway is a router or multilayer switch. The router has an interface with the IP address of 192.168.1.1 on the same subnet as any management interface.

switch(config)# ip default-gateway 192.168.1.254

The switch forwards packets to a default gateway for layer 3 services. That could include ARP requests and Inter-VLAN routing.

49. The network administrator has connected a new access switch to a local Ethernet access jack at a cubicle for configuration. Select the most probable reason why the switch is not working?

A. wrong cabling caused errdisable state

B. BPDU guard shutdown the port

C. port security feature is not permitted between switches

D. connecting access switches requires trunk configuration

Correct Answer (B)
Subject Matter: Spanning Tree Protocol (STP)

The new switch starts sends BPDUs to the upstream access switch when connected to the Ethernet jack at a cubicle. The upstream access switch with BPDU guard enabled would errdisable its switch port. That prevents the new switch from joining the layer 2 topology. PortFast is designed to transition to forwarding state for an access port and doesn't shutdown or fix STP errors.

50. Define how a collision domain is created on a switch?

    A. The switch creates a collision domain per port

    B. The switch creates a collision domain per network

    C. The switch creates a collision domain per VLAN

    D. The switch creates a collision domain per device

Correct Answer (A)
Subject Matter: Switching Concepts

The newer Ethernet Gigabit switch port supports full-duplex operation. That eliminates collisions on each switch port and creates a single collision domain per port. In addition the Gigabit port provides dedicated bandwidth to the connected host.

51. What best describes the components of a MAC address table?

    A. MAC address, switch port and IP address

    B. switch port and VLAN assigned

    C. MAC address and switch port

    D. MAC address, switch port and VLAN

Correct Answer (D)
Subject Matter: Switching Concepts

The switch builds a MAC address table comprised of MAC address, switch port and VLAN membership for all active and connected hosts and network devices. The switch port must be enabled for a host to send packets to the switch. The switch adds the MAC address of the host when frames arrive along switch port where frames were learned and VLAN membership of the switch port.

52. What IOS command will list the MAC address table entries for a switch?

    A. switch# show cam table

    B. switch# show mac address-table

    C. switch# show mac-address-table

    D. switch(config)# show mac-address-table

Correct Answer (B)
Subject Matter: Switching Concepts

The following IOS show command will list the contents of the MAC address table for a switch. Where there are multiple VLANs configured, the switch will list all MAC address tables for all VLANs in a single table listing. The switch builds and maintains a separate MAC address table for each VLAN configured.

switch# show mac address-table

53. What statement best describes a VLAN?

    A. VLAN assigns one or more switch ports to the same collision domain

    B. multiple VLANs create a collision domain

    C. VLAN creates a broadcast domain from one or more switch ports

    D. VLAN assigns one or more router ports to the same collision domain

Correct Answer (C)
Subject Matter: VLANs

The primary purpose of a VLAN is to create a broadcast domain defined by assigning a single or multiple switch ports. All unicast, broadcast and multicast traffic is limited to the VLAN. That conserves bandwidth usage across the switching infrastructure.

54. Select three statement that correctly describe full-duplex operation?

    A. full-duplex is the default for Gigabit switch ports

    B. full-duplex supports simultaneous send and receive data

    C. full-duplex switch ports decrease collision domains

    D. full-duplex switch ports require CSMA/CD

    E. full-duplex switch ports create separate collision domains

Correct Answers (A,B,E)
Subject Matter: Switching Concepts

Gigabit Ethernet provide full-duplex traffic to the connected host. Traffic can be sent simultaneously in both directions between the host and network switch. That effectively doubles the bandwidth available from 1 Gbps to 2 Gbps.

There is a single collision domain created per port eliminating Ethernet collisions. That optimizes bandwidth (throughput) and network latency. The default setting for Ethernet Gigabit and higher is full-duplex mode.

55. What are the two components of a MAC address?

  A. 24-bit manufacturer OUI and 24-bit unique number

  B. 4-bit manufacturer OUI and a 48-bit unique number

  C. 4-bit manufacturer OUI and a 24-bit unique number

  D. 32-bit manufacturer OUI and a 24-bit unique number

Correct Answer (A)
Subject Matter: Switching Concepts

The MAC address is a unique 48-bit hardware identifier number assigned to the network interface card (NIC) of a host. In addition there is a unique MAC address assigned to switch and router Ethernet interfaces as well. It is used for layer 2 Ethernet addressing. The MAC address is used to add a source and destination MAC address to each frame header.

The MAC (physical) address is 48 bits of hexidecimal numbering. The first 24 bits is a manufacturer OUI and the last 24 bits (bold) is a unique serial number (SN). The source and destination MAC addresses are updated as frames are forwarded between routers. The source MAC address is the router egress interface and destination MAC address is the neighbor ingress interface.

  OUI | **SN**
  aaaa.bb**cc.dddd**

56. What is the layer 2 broadcast address in hexidecimal format?

  A. 0000.0000.0000

  B. f.f.f.f.f.f

  C. ffff.ffff.ffff

  D. 0xff

  E. 0000.0000.00ff

Correct Answer (C)
Subject Matter: Switching Concepts

The destination MAC address of a layer 2 broadcast is ffff.ffff.ffff used to flood a broadcast within a local network segment (VLAN). Not to be confused with MAC flooding (learning) that is unicast flooding with a specific destination MAC address. It is often used as part of an ARP request.

57. Refer to the results of the following IOS command. Switch-1 port Gi1/2 is connected to a neighbor switch and cabling is verified as correct. What is the reason why Gi1/2 trunking is not active?

    switch-1# show interface gigabitethernet 1/2 switchport

    Name: Gi1/2
    Switchport: Enabled
    Administrative Mode: static access
    Operational Mode: static access
    Administrative Trunking Encapsulation: dot1q
    Negotiation of Trunking: Disabled
    Access Mode VLAN: 10 (Data)
    Trunking Native Mode VLAN: 1 (default)
    Trunking VLANs Enabled: ALL
    Trunking VLANs Active: none

   A. default switch port operational status is shutdown

   B. wrong encapsulation type

   C. VLANs are not assigned to the access port

   D. native VLAN is not configured correctly

   E. switch port mode is configured incorrectly

Correct Answer (E)
Subject Matter: Inter-Switch Connectivity

The Cisco switch port supports access mode or trunk mode. The network administrator configures port **mode** when enabling the interface. The standard layer 2 switch port is referred to as an access port. There is only one VLAN that can be assigned to an access port. The exception is voice VLAN feature that allows a data and voice VLAN per port. Forwarding multiple VLANs across a switch link requires trunk mode for VLAN tagging feature.

    switch(config-if)# switchport mode trunk

The **administrative mode** (static access) is the switch port configuration and **operational mode** is the interface status. The switch won't setup a trunk unless the switch port mode is configured to trunk VLANs. The result is no network communication between switches that have common VLANs configured.

The default is to allow all VLANs across a trunk enabled switch link. Configure the following IOS command to allow only specific VLANs. Cisco switches permit assigning a range of VLANs as well.

switch(config-if)# switchport trunk allowed vlan add [vlan id, vlan id ...]

58. What spanning tree port state is new to Rapid-PVST (RPVST)?

    A. learning

    B. listening

    C. discarding

    D. forwarding

    E. dynamic

Correct Answer (C)
Subject Matter: Spanning Tree Protocol (STP)

The newer 802.1w (RSTP) standard is comprised of three port states. They include discarding, learning and forwarding. Rapid PVST (RPVST) is based on RSTP and would support only the 802.1w port states. The discarding state is new to RPVST and equivalent to the blocking and listening states of 802.1d.

59. The network switch has a default configuration. What is the result of issuing the following IOS commands on a Cisco switch?

    switch(config)# interface range gigabitethernet1/1-24
    switch(config-if)# switchport access vlan 10

   A. error message - vlan does not exist

   B. VLAN 10 is assigned to switch ports Gi1/1 through Gi1/24

   C. VLAN 10 cannot be assigned to an SVI

   D. switch ports transitions to spanning tree forwarding state immediately

   E. VLAN 10 is assigned to switch ports Gi1/1 and Gi1/24 only

Correct Answer (B)
Subject Matter: VLANs

The following IOS command creates and assigns VLAN 10 to switch ports Gi1/1 through Gi1/24 interfaces. There is no requirement to first create the VLAN in global configuration mode. The vlan.dat file is the VLAN database where the switch VLAN configuration is stored.

60. What setting or value is used by spanning tree to assign the root port on a non-root bridge (switch)?

   A. switch device MAC address

   B. network topology

   C. path cost

   D. port MAC address

   E. port priority

Correct Answer (C)
Subject Matter: Spanning Tree Protocol (STP)

There is only a single root bridge elected for any spanning tree instance. The neighbor switches are called non-root bridges (switches). Spanning Tree Protocol calculates the least cost path from a non-root switch link to the root bridge. The switch port for that link is assigned as root port to the root bridge.

61. What is the effect of issuing the following IOS command on a switch port interface?

    switch(config-if)# switchport trunk native vlan 999

    A. default management VLAN 1 is replaced with VLAN 999

    B. all traffic between switches is forwarded across VLAN 999

    C. all frames with a VLAN membership are forwarded across VLAN 999

    D. all frames with a VLAN membership are forwarded across VLAN 999

    E. all untagged frames are forwarded across VLAN 999

Correct Answer (D)
Subject Matter: Inter-Switch Connectivity

The IOS command changes the native VLAN from default VLAN 1 to VLAN 999. The native VLAN is used to forward untagged traffic such as DTP and STP messages across the switch trunk. Assigning the native VLAN from VLAN 1 to VLAN 999 is a Cisco security best practice. There are security vulnerabilities associated with the default VLAN 1. In addition STP issues are minimized by selecting an unused VLAN instead of VLAN 1. The default VLAN 1 forwards CDP, PAgP and VTP management traffic and cannot be deleted.

62. What best describes the result of creating a new VLAN and assigning ten switch ports to the VLAN?

    A. an additional broadcast domain is created

    B. fewer collision domains will exist

    C. an additional collision domain is created

    D. bandwidth is shared among switch ports assigned to the same VLAN

Correct Answer (A)
Subject Matter: Switching Concepts

Anytime a new VLAN is created a new broadcast domain is added to the network switch. Any assigned switch ports become members of that VLAN broadcast domain.

63. Refer to the network topology drawing. Switch-2 was recently installed however Telnet is not working correctly from Host-1. The network administrator has confirmed there are no issues with Telnet configuration at the layer 2 switch. In addition there is connectivity between Host-1 and Server-1. What IOS commands will enable network management access?

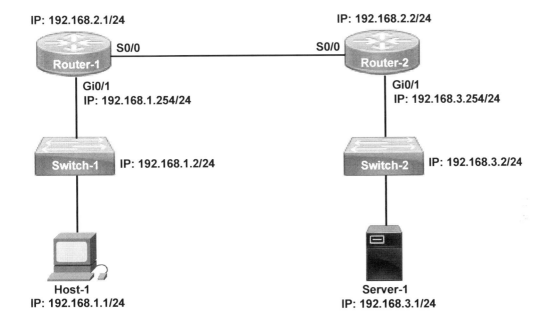

A. switch-2(config)# interface vlan 1
   switch-2(config-if)# ip address 192.168.2.1 255.255.255.0
   switch-2(config-if)# no shutdown

B. switch-2(config)# interface vlan 100
   switch-2(config-if)# ip address 192.168.2.1 255.255.255.0
   switch-2(config-if)# ip default-gateway 192.168.2.2 255.255.255.0
   switch-2(config-if)# no shutdown

C. switch-2(config)# ip default-gateway 192.168.3.254
   switch-2(config)# interface vlan 100
   switch-2(config-if)# ip address 192.168.3.2 255.255.255.0
   switch-2(config-if)# no shutdown

D. switch-2(config)# ip default-network 192.168.2.1
   switch-2(config)# interface vlan 100
   switch-2(config-if)# ip address 192.168.3.2 255.255.255.0
   switch-2(config-if)# no shutdown

E. switch-2(config)# ip route 192.168.1.254 255.255.255.0
switch-2(config)# interface vlan 100
switch-2(config-if)# ip address 192.168.1.1 255.255.255.0
switch-2(config-if)# no shutdown

Correct Answer (C)
Subject Matter: Switching Concepts

Switch-2 is a layer 2 device and has no routing (layer 3 forwarding) enabled. The switch makes forwarding decisions based on the destination MAC address.

Network management access to the switch with Telnet requires a default gateway. The purpose of a default gateway is for layer 3 connectivity between switch and upstream router. The switch is configured with a management IP address and VLAN called an SVI as well. The Telnet session connects to the IP address defined with the SVI (VLAN 100). Switch-2 forwards any packets that are not on the local subnet to the default gateway (Router-2). Host-1 for instance is on a remote subnet where Telnet is initiated from. Switch-2 and the default gateway configured must be on the same subnet (192.168.3.0) address.

switch-2(config)# ip default-gateway 192.168.3.254
switch-2(config)# interface vlan 100
switch-2(config-if)# ip address 192.168.3.2 255.255.255.0
switch-2(config-if)# no shutdown

64. What two spanning tree port states exist when RSTP has converged?

A. learning

B. forwarding

C. discarding

D. listening

E. disabled

Correct Answers (B,C)
Subject Matter: Spanning Tree Protocol (STP)

Spanning Tree Protocol creates a loop free layer 2 topology across a switching infrastructure. The loop free topology is based on switch uplinks in a blocking or forwarding state. Any topology change such as a link failure triggers STP to recalculate the topology and determine what switch ports to block and forward.

Layer 2 convergence occurs when STP has created the loop free topology.
RSTP discarding state is equivalent to blocking state of the older 802.1d.
Discarding and forwarding are the two states when convergence has occurred.

65. What two IOS commands can be used to verify trunk configuration status on
    a Cisco switch port interface?

    A. show interface detail

    B. show interface vlan

    C. show interface switchport

    D. show interface trunk

    E. show ip interface brief

Correct Answers (C,D)
Subject Matter: Inter-Switch Connectivity

The following IOS commands show switch trunk operation and configuration:

    switch# show interface switchport
    switch# show interface trunk

    • Trunk operational status
    • Switch port members
    • VLANs allowed
    • Native VLAN
    • Encapsulation type

66. Select the IOS command that will enable RSTP on a switch?

    A. spanning-tree rstp

    B. spanning-tree mode rstp

    C. spanning-tree mode rpvst

    D. spanning-tree mode rapid-pvst

Correct Answer (D)
Subject Matter: Spanning Tree Protocol (STP)

The following IOS global configuration command enables RSTP on a switch.

switch(config)# spanning-tree mode rapid-pvst

67. Refer to the results of the IOS command shown. What is the reason that switch port interface Gi1/1 was not elected root port for VLAN 12?

switch-3# show spanning-tree interface gigabitethernet1/1

Vlan	Role	Sts	Cost	Prio.Nbr	Type
VLAN0010	Root	FWD	4	128.1	P2p
VLAN0011	Root	FWD	4	128.2	P2p
VLAN0012	Altn	BLK	16	128.2	P2p

A. there are redundant links to the root bridge

B. GigabitEthernet1/1 has a lower MAC address

C. there is a switch port with a lower path cost to the root bridge

D. bridge ID for switch-3 is lower

Correct Answer (C)
Subject Matter: Spanning Tree Protocol (STP)

PVST+ and RPVST+ both support per VLAN spanning tree. There is a separate spanning tree instance calculated (defined) for each VLAN. As a result each VLAN is assigned a root bridge (switch). The switch ports for a root bridge are all assigned as designated ports. All neighbor switches become non-root bridges with a root port , designated port or alternate port (blocking). The assignment of root port is based on calculated link cost to the root bridge. Typically the switch port of the non-root bridge directly connected to the root bridge is lowest cost and assigned as root port.

The non-root switches are assigned a designated port as well. The designated port connects to a neighbor non-root bridge. The non-root switches compare link cost (bandwidth) for that switch link (network segment). The switch port with the lower cost (highest bandwidth) is the designated port for that link. Where the switch ports have an equal cost, the port of the non-root switch with the lower bridge ID is assigned as a designated port. The switch port on the neighbor switch is assigned as alternate (blocking) port type to prevent layer 2 loops.

The results of **show spanning-tree interface gigabitethernet1/1** indicate switch port Gi1/1 has a higher path cost (lower bandwidth) to the root bridge for VLAN 12. That is shown with the **Altn** (alternate/blocking) status. STP would calculate a new topology and transition the blocking port to forwarding when the link associated with the root port isn't available.

68. Why is it not possible for a switch to learn a broadcast address on an inbound frame?

    A. broadcast address is associated with the destination IP address of a packet

    B. broadcast frames are not supported by the MAC address table

    C. broadcasts frames are forwarded to router interfaces only

    D. MAC addresses are learned from MAC flooding events

    E. broadcast address is a destination MAC address forwarded from switch

Correct Answer (E)
Subject Matter: Switching Concepts

The layer 2 broadcast has a destination MAC address of ffff.ffff.ffff and sent from the switch to all hosts on a local VLAN (segment). The switch creates the broadcast packet and forwards it. As a result it isn't learned from a specific switch port.

69. Refer to the results of the IOS command issued on Switch-1 and determine why it was not elected as root bridge for VLAN 10?

        switch-1# show spanning-tree vlan 10

        VLAN010
        Spanning tree enabled protocol rstp
        Root ID priority 20490
          address 0000.000a.aaaa
          Cost 28
          Port 1 (GigabitEthernet1/2)
          Hello Time 2 sec max Age 20 sec Forward Delay 15 sec

        Bridge ID Priority 32769 (priority 32768 sys-id-ext 1)
          Address 0000.000b.bbbb
          Hello Time 2 sec max Age 20 sec Forward Delay 15 sec
          Aging Time 300 sec

Interface	Role	Sts	Cost	Prio.Nbr	Type
Gi1/1	Root	FWD	4	128.1	P2p
Gi1/2	Desg	FWD	28	128.1	P2p
Gi1/4	Desg	FWD	28	128.1	P2p
Gi1/3	Altn	BLK	54	128.1	P2p

A. It has a higher bridge ID than the elected root bridge

B. It has a lower MAC address than the elected root bridge

C. path cost to neighbor switches is higher

D. all switch port priorities were lower

Correct Answer (A)
Subject Matter: Spanning Tree Protocol (STP)

The results of the show spanning tree command list the elected root bridge for a particular VLAN and port types assigned for each interface. The root bridge for VLAN 100 is not Switch-1. The **Root-ID** section lists the priority and MAC address for the elected root bridge. The **Bridge-ID** section pertains to Switch-1 where the IOS command was issued. The priority is higher (32769) for Switch-1 than the priority (20490) of the switch that was elected root bridge. In addition the port types are not all designated ports. The root bridge assigns all switch ports as designated ports.

switch-1# show spanning-tree vlan 10

VLAN010
Spanning tree enabled protocol rstp
Root ID Priority **20490**
  Address 0000.000a.aaaa
  Cost 28
  Port 1 (GigabitEthernet1/2)
  Hello Time 2 sec max Age 20 sec Forward Delay 15 sec

Bridge ID Priority **32769** (priority 32768 sys-id-ext 1)
  Address 0000.000b.bbbb
  Hello Time 2 sec max Age 20 sec Forward Delay 15 sec
  Aging Time 300 sec

Interface	Role	Sts	Cost	Prio.Nbr	Type
Gi1/1	Root	FWD	4	128.1	P2p
Gi1/2	Desg	FWD	28	128.1	P2p
Gi1/4	Desg	FWD	28	128.1	P2p
Gi1/3	Altn	BLK	54	128.1	P2p

70. Based on the default Cisco switch configuration, select the VLAN range that can be added, modified or deleted?

A. 1-1001

B. 2-1001

C. 1-1002

D. 2-1005

Correct Answer (B)
Subject Matter: VLANs

All switch ports are assigned to VLAN 1 as a default configuration for Cisco Catalyst switches. In addition VLAN 1 is used for management traffic and can't be deleted. The normal range VLANs (2-1001) can be added, modified and deleted from the switch.

71. What statement is correct concerning VLAN operation on a layer 2 switch?

A. unicast frames are retransmitted to ports assigned to different VLANs

B. broadcast and multicast frames are not retransmitted across a trunk

C. unknown unicast frames are retransmitted only to ports that belong to the same VLAN

D. broadcast and multicast frames are retransmitted to ports assigned to different VLANs on the same switch

Correct Answer (C)
Subject Matter: Switching Concepts

The switch creates a separate MAC address table for each configured VLAN. Any unicast flooding of a frame to learn a MAC address is for the assigned VLAN only. Each VLAN defines a separate broadcast domain. The switch forwards unicasts, broadcasts and multicasts between the same VLANs only. That includes all VLANs assigned to a trunk. The VLAN ID (tag) is determined from the 802.1q field of the Ethernet frame. Ports between switches must be configured with trunk mode to forward multiple VLANs across a switch link.

72. Refer to the network drawing. What three switch ports will be assigned as designated ports by spanning tree when the link bandwidth is equal?

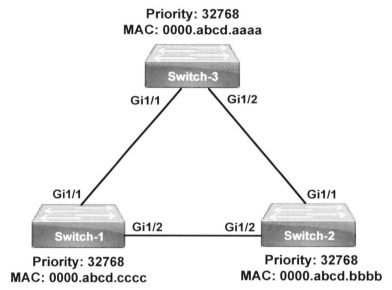

A. Switch-3 (Gi1/1)

B. Switch-3 (Gi1/2)

C. Switch-2 (Gi1/1)

D. Switch-2 (Gi1/2)

E. Switch-1 (Gi1/1)

F. Switch-1 (Gi1/2)

Correct Answers (A,B,D)
Subject Matter: Spanning Tree Protocol (STP)

The switch with the lowest bridge ID is elected as root bridge. In addition all switch ports of a root bridge are assigned as designated ports. The switch with the lowest priority is elected root bridge. All switches are assigned the same default priority so the tie breaker is the switch with the lowest MAC address.

The lowest MAC address is calculated from left to right per hexidecimal number. All numbers match until bit 9 where Switch-3 has the lower number (**a**) compared with Switch-2 (**b**) and Switch-1 (**c**). As a result, Switch-3 is elected as root bridge. The switch ports Gi1/1 and Gi1/2 on Switch-3 are designated ports.

Switch-1 = 0000.abcd.**c**ccc
Switch-2 = 0000.abcd.**b**bbb
Switch-3 = 0000.abcd.**a**aaa = **root bridge**

All neighbor switches become non-root bridges with a root port , designated port or alternate port (blocking). The switch port of the non-root bridge directly connected to the root bridge is lowest cost and assigned as root port. That would include Switch-2 port Gi1/1 and Switch-1 port Gi1/1.

The non-root switches are assigned a designated port as well. The designated port connects to a neighbor non-root bridge. The non-root switches compare link cost (bandwidth) for that switch link (network segment). The switch port with the lower cost (highest bandwidth) is the designated port for that link. Where the switch ports have an equal cost, the port of the non-root switch with the lower bridge ID is assigned as a designated port.

The topology has all equal Gigabit switch links connecting all non-root bridges. The tie breaker is the **non-root bridge (switch)** with the lowest MAC address. Switch-2 has a lower MAC address than Switch-1. From left to right the hexidecimal numbers match until bit 9. Switch-2 has a lower hexidecimal number (**b**) than Switch-1 with (**c**). The result is Switch-2 port Gi1/2 is the designated port for the switch link to the non-root neighbor.

Switch-1 = 0000.abcd.**c**ccc
Switch-2 = 0000.abcd.**b**bbb

73. Select three statements that accurately describe RSTP when compared with original 802.1d?

   A. compatible with 802.1d proposal-agreement sequence

   B. compatible with 802.1d timer-based process on point-to-point links

   C. lower convergence time than 802.1d

   D. port states are blocking, learning or forwarding

   E. alternate and backup port types were added

   F. faster transition to port forwarding state on point-to-point links

Correct Answers (C,E,F)
Subject Matter: Spanning Tree Protocol (STP)

The advantage of Rapid Spanning Tree Protocol (RSTP) is faster layer 2 convergence than the older 802.1 standard. The newer standard is 802.1w and includes the following features to minimize convergence time.

- BPDUs are now advertised from all switches instead of from the root bridge only.

- The amount of time is decreased to three hello packets (BPDUs) before detecting a root switch link failure.

- There are only three port states: discarding, learning and forwarding.

- There are two additional STP port types: alternate and backup.

Alternate Port:
Replaces the 802.1d blocking state. The alternate port as with all RSTP ports are actively forwarding or discarding. The discarding is equivalent to the older listening state. It transitions from discarding to forwarding immediately when the designated port fails so there is no waiting for convergence.

Backup Port:
Requires a hub with two switch links (single collision domain) to provide additional redundancy for faster convergence to the access layer.

- The RSTP proposal/agreement process is based on a handshake between point-to-point neighbor switch links. It provides current root bridge state information to all switches. It is not a timer-based proposal/agreement as with the original 802.1d (STP).

74. Refer to the network topology drawing. What switch port mode must be configured on a switch interface/s to enable proper forwarding of VLAN traffic between all network devices?

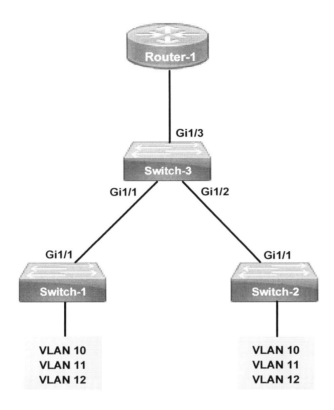

A. trunk mode for Switch-3 interfaces only

B. trunk mode for all switch interfaces

C. trunk mode for Switch-3 port Gi1/3 interface only

D. access mode for Switch-1 and Switch-2 interfaces

E. trunk mode for Switch-1 and Switch-2 interfaces only

Correct Answer (B)
Subject Matter: Inter-Switch Connectivity

Any switch with multiple VLANs will require an uplink to be configured as a trunk. Switch-1 and Switch-2 have multiple VLANs with uplinks to Switch-3. In addition switch port Gi1/1 and Gi1/2 for Switch-3 must be configured as trunks. The trunk enabled switch port tags the VLAN membership of each frame before forwarding to the neighbor switch. Configuring trunk mode on Switch-3 port Gi1/3 enables trunking to Router-1 as well.

75. Refer to the network topology drawing and output from the IOS commands. Ethernet frames from VLAN 10 of Switch-1 are arriving at VLAN 1 of Switch-2. What causes that forwarding behavior between switches?

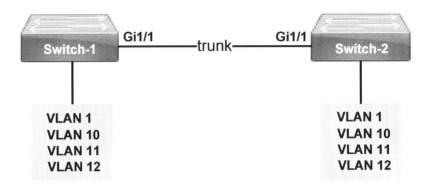

switch-1# show interfaces trunk

Port	Mode	Encapsulation	Status	Native vlan
Gi1/1	on	802.1q	trunking	1

Port	Vlans allowed on trunk
Gi1/1	10-12

Port	Vlans allowed and active in management domain
Gi1/1	1,10,11,12

Port	Vlans in spanning tree forwarding state and not pruned
Gi1/1	1,10,11,12

switch-2# show interfaces trunk

Port	Mode	Encapsulation	Status	Native vlan
Gi1/1	on	802.1q	trunking	2

Port	Vlans allowed on trunk
Gi1/1	10-12

Port	Vlans allowed and active in management domain
Gi1/1	1,10,11,12

Port	Vlans in spanning tree forwarding state and not pruned
Gi1/1	1,10,11,12

A. native VLAN mismatch

B. default gateway error

C. allowing VLAN 1 on the trunk

D. trunk mode mismatch

Correct Answer (A)
Subject Matter: Inter-Switch Connectivity

The native VLAN and the default management VLAN 1 both forward untagged traffic. The trunk tags all data VLANs for identification purposes. The untagged traffic is separated from data traffic as a result.

The native VLAN is reserved for DTP and STP control traffic across a trunk link. The default VLAN 1 forwards management traffic including CDP, PAgP and VTP between all switches and can't be deleted. That is true as well where the native VLAN for trunks is changed from VLAN 1. The native VLAN must match between any two neighbor switches.

The native VLAN was changed from VLAN 1 to VLAN 999 on Switch-1. It was not however changed on Switch-2. The native VLAN mismatch causes untagged management and control traffic from VLAN 999 on Switch-1 to get forwarded to VLAN 1 on Switch-2. It is sometimes referred to as VLAN hopping and well known as a security vulnerability.

76. What host command can be used to verify connectivity between a host and a server connected to different switches in the same VLAN?

A. traceroute

B. ARP

C. tracert

D. ping

Correct Answer (D)
Subject Matter: Inter-Switch Connectivity

The hosts are located in same VLAN (broadcast domain) so there is no routing required for reachability. The **ping [address]** command will verify connectivity from the source where it was issued. That is accomplished with a ping of the remote host IP address. The sending host encapsulates the layer 3 ping message/request in a frame that is forwarded to the switch. The frame is forwarded to the switch port where the remote host is connected.

77. What two statements are characteristics of the 802.1q protocol?

   A. It is a trunking protocol that can forward tagged and untagged frames

   B. It does not support class of service prioritization

   C. encapsulates the Ethernet frame header with VLAN ID

   D. enables network reconvergence

   E. CRC is unaffected by encapsulation

Correct Answers (A,C)
Subject Matter: Inter-Switch Connectivity

The 802.1q protocol is the current Cisco default encapsulation for switch trunks. It is an open standard that supports multi-vendor switch connectivity. The purpose of 802.1q is to enable forwarding of multiple VLANs across a trunk link. That is accomplished by tagging each frame with VLAN membership. The encapsulation and forwarding of frames starts after layer 2 convergence with STP and DTP has established the trunk. The Ethernet frame header is modified as a result of adding the VLAN tag. That requires recalculation of the FCS value used for CRC.

78. Based on the network topology drawing what protocol must be enabled on all switches to prevent network errors?

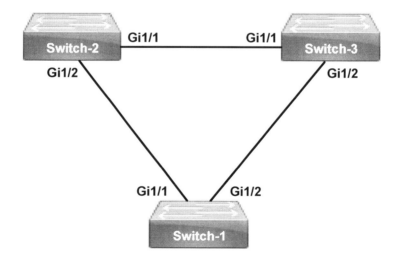

A. RSTP

B. Split Horizon

C. VTP

D. 802.1q

E. CSMA/CD

Correct Answer (A)
Subject Matter: Spanning Tree Protocol (STP)

The switching topology creates a layer 2 loop that can cause broadcast storms. The purpose of Rapid Spanning Tree Protocol (RSTP) is to create a loop free topology. That requires blocking a switch port so that frames are not forwarded in a loop between switches.

Split Horizon = prevents layer 3 loops

VTP = VLAN management protocol

802.1q = trunking encapsulation

CSMA/CD = older Ethernet collision detection

79. Select three Dynamic Trunking Protocol (DTP) modes that are available for a switch port used as a VLAN trunk?

A. transparent

B. auto

C. on

D. desirable

E. blocking

Correct Answers (B,C,D)
Subject Matter: Inter-Switch Connectivity

The switch port is configured as a trunk to enable trunking. The trunk is setup with a neighbor switch using static or dynamic negotiation. The static trunk is a manual configuration that isn't based on any negotiation protocol.

The switches on both sides of the link are configured with the command **switchport mode trunk**. It is equivalent to the **on** keyword for dynamic trunking. DTP provides dynamic negotiation based on the **switchport mode dynamic auto** or **switchport mode dynamic desirable** commands.

80. Refer to the network topology drawing. The switches are configured with RSTP and all links are equal bandwidth. Select the correct RSTP port type assigned to the noted switch ports based on the information provided?

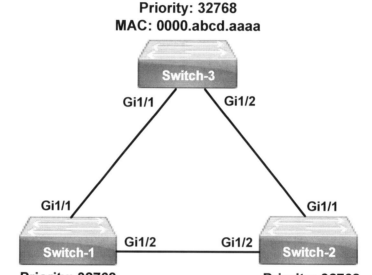

A. Switch-1 (Gi1/1) = root port
   Switch-2 (Gi1/2) = designated port
   Switch-3 (Gi1/1) = designated port

B. Switch-1 (Gi1/1) = root port
   Switch-2 (Gi1/2) = designated port
   Switch-3 (Gi1/1) = root port

C. Switch-1 (Gi1/1) = designated port
   Switch-2 (Gi1/2) = alternate port
   Switch-3 (Gi1/1) = root port

D. all root ports

E. all designated ports

Correct Answer (A)
Subject Matter: Spanning Tree Protocol (STP)

The first step is to identify the root bridge (switch). The switch with the lowest priority is elected root bridge. All switches have equal priorities (default) so the switch with the lowest MAC address is elected root bridge. The priority and MAC address of a switch comprise the bridge ID. As a result the switch with the lowest bridge ID is elected root bridge. Switch-3 has the lowest MAC address based on numbering from left to right.

All spanning tree ports of the root bridge are assigned as designated ports. The directly connected switch port of each neighbor switch is assigned as root port. That is the default when all switch links are equal bandwidth. Switch-1 (Gi1/1) and Switch-2 (Gi1/1) are root ports as a result.

All RSTP switch ports are assigned as a root port, designated port or alternate port. Switch-1 (Gi1/1) and Switch-2 (Gi1/1) are assigned as root ports already.

The network segment between Switch-1 and Switch-2 must elect a designated port. The bridge ID for Switch-2 is lower than Switch-1. That is based on the lower MAC address where priority values are equal. As a result Switch-2 (Gi1/2) is the designated port for the network segment. The connected neighbor switch port on Switch-1 (Gi1/2) is assigned as an alternate (discarding) port.

- Switch-1 (Gi1/1) = root port
- Switch-2 (Gi1/2) = designated port
- Switch-3 (Gi1/1) = designated port

81. What is required for a host to establish an SSH session with a switch?

    A. remote host must have DNS enabled

    B. configure a default gateway on the switch to the upstream router

    C. enable ip routing on the switch

    D. configure a static route on the upstream router

    E. configure an SVI on the router in the same subnet as the switch

Correct Answer (B)
Subject Matter: Switching Concepts

The default gateway is required by the layer 2 switch to establish connectivity between different VLANs or subnets. The default gateway is the directly connected (upstream) router where the switch forwards packets for routing purposes. ARP requests are forwarded from the layer 2 switch as well.

82. Refer to the network topology drawing and select the number of broadcast domains and collision domains that are enabled?

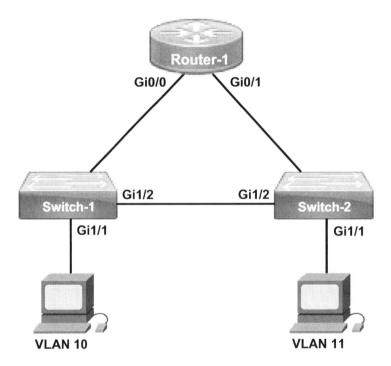

A. 5 broadcast domains, 5 collisions domains

B. 2 broadcast domains, 2 collisions domains

C. 3 broadcast domains, 2 collisions domains

D. 1 broadcast domain, 3 collisions domains

Correct Answer (A)
Subject Matter: Switching Concepts

The default setting assigns all switch ports to VLAN 1 unless assigned to a different VLAN. The default VLAN 1 cannot be deleted. Each additional VLAN configured is a separate broadcast domain. As a result there is a broadcast domain for each VLAN (1,10,12). In addition Router-1 creates a separate broadcast domain for each of its two interfaces. That is five broadcast domains for the network topology.

Each Gigabit Ethernet interface whether on a switch or a router is a single collision domain. There are five **active** (enabled) switch interface links making it five collision domains for the topology.

83. Select the network state where multiple connected switches with spanning tree enabled has all switch ports in either blocking or forwarding state?

   A. redundant

   B. converged

   C. spanned

   D. provisioned

Correct Answer (B)
Subject Matter: Spanning Tree Protocol (STP)

The older 802.1d (STP) standard supports blocking or forwarding port states when the network is layer 2 converged.

84. Refer to the network topology drawing. Switch-1 and Switch-2 were assigned as non-root bridges (switches) by spanning tree protocol (STP). What switch and switch port interface is assigned discarding port state?

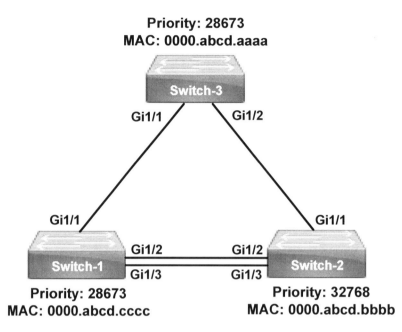

A. Switch-1, Gi1/1

B. Switch-1, Gi1/2

C. Switch-2, Gi1/3

D. Switch-2, Gi1/2

E. Switch-3, Gi1/1

Correct Answer (D)
Subject Matter: Spanning Tree Protocol (STP)

RSTP is based on the original 802.1d however there are enhancements that lower convergence time. The port states were reassigned with RSTP so there is discarding, learning and forwarding. The discarding state includes the original disabled, blocking and listening states of 802.1d. The switching topology is converged when all ports are either discarding or forwarding. The discarding state is assigned to the alternate port type where traffic blocking is enabled to prevent layer 2 loops. STP must assign a designated port for the network segment connecting Switch-1 and Switch-2. That is based on the switch link with the lower bandwidth. Switch-1 and Switch-2 have two equal bandwidth switch links connecting them.

The tie breaker is the switch with the lower bridge ID. Switch-1 has a lower priority so switch ports Gi1/2 and Gi1/3 of Switch-1 are assigned as designated ports. STP transitions designated ports to forwarding state.

Switch-2 must assign a switch port to alternate port type to prevent a layer 2 loop. The alternate port type is transitioned to discarding (blocking) state. Where there are multiple switch links, the lower switch port number is the tie breaker. Switch-1 has switch ports Gi1/2 and Gi1/3. Switch-2 considers the lower Gi1/2 as preferred and forwards traffic from Gi1/2 that is directly connected. The result is that Switch-2 (Gi1/2) is the alternate port in discarding state. Traffic between Switch-1 and Switch-2 is forwarded across the Gi1/2 link between switches.

85. Select two statements that correctly describe RSTP?

  A. RSTP defines new port roles

  B. RSTP defines no new port states

  C. RSTP is compatible with the original IEEE 802.1d STP

  D. RSTP cannot operate with PVST+

  E. RSTP is a proprietary implementation of IEEE 802.1d STP

Correct Answers (A,C)
Subject Matter: Spanning Tree Protocol (STP)

RSTP adds alternate and backup port types for optimizing layer 2 convergence. It can support 802.1d enabled neighbor switches for compatibility as well.

86. Refer to the results of the following IOS command on Switch-1. What two of the following statements are correct?

    switch-1# show mac address-table

       MAC Address Table

Vlan	MAC Address	Type	Ports
1	000a.0aaa.aaaa	Dynamic	Gi1/1
10	000a.0aaa.bbbb	Dynamic	Gi1/2
10	000a.0aaa.cccc	Dynamic	Gi1/3
10	000a.0aaa.dddd	Dynamic	Gi1/4
11	000a.0aaa.dddd	Dynamic	Gi1/2
12	000a.0aaa.ffff	Dynamic	Gi1/2

A. MAC address of switch port Gi1/3 was statically assigned

B. VLAN 1 is not the current default management VLAN

C. switch port Gi1/2 is configured as a trunk

D. traffic on VLAN 1 is untagged

E. VLAN 10 is the native VLAN

Correct Answers (C,D)
Subject Matter: Inter-Switch Connectivity

The output from IOS command **show mac address-table** lists all active host connections to Switch-1. That includes VLAN membership, MAC address, type and switch port assigned.

Switch-1 port Gi1/2 is receiving traffic from multiple VLANs (10, 11 and 12) indicating it is assigned as a trunk. In addition VLAN 1 is always the default management VLAN and cannot be deleted. The traffic as a result is untagged. All entries are dynamically learned instead of statically assigned MAC addresses.

87. Based on a default switch configuration, what switch is elected as the root bridge for the spanning tree instance of VLAN 10?

A. switch with the highest IP address

B. switch with the lowest IP address

C. switch with the highest MAC address

D. switch with the lowest MAC address

Correct Answer (D)
Subject Matter: Spanning Tree Protocol (STP)

The default priority of a Cisco switch is 32768. STP selects the root bridge (switch) with the lowest priority. The switch with the lowest bridge ID is selected when all switches have the same priority. The bridge ID is calculated from the priority setting and MAC address. The switch with the lowest MAC address would become the root bridge as a result.

88. The network administrator assigns VLAN 10 as the native VLAN to Switch-1 trunk interface. What will occur when frames are sent to Switch-2 that has a default configuration?

A. VLAN 10 will send tagged frames

B. native VLAN mismatch error message will appear

C. frames are dropped

D. layer 2 broadcast storm

Correct Answer (B)
Subject Matter: Inter-Switch Connectivity

The native VLAN is enabled as a default on a switch trunk. In addition the native VLAN is assigned to VLAN 1. The native VLAN for Switch-1 is assigned to VLAN 10 and Switch-2 is assigned the default VLAN 1. The result is there is a VLAN mismatch between the switches.

89. Select the statement that correctly describes the OSI layer for interface status and line protocol status when running **show interfaces** command?

A. Interface = Layer 1, Line protocol = Layer 2

B. Interface = Layer 2, Line protocol = Layer 1

C. Interface = Layer 3, Line protocol = Layer 2

D. Interface = Layer 2, Line protocol = Layer 3

Correct Answer (A)
Subject Matter: Troubleshooting Interface and Cable Issues

The **show interfaces** command provides layer 1 and layer 2 status information for all or individual network interfaces (ethernet, serial etc).

Interface = Layer 1, Line protocol = Layer 2

The possible interface states for interface and line protocol include **up, down** or **administratively down**. The normal status of an Ethernet interface is up/up. The **shutdown** command would change interface status to admin down. (i.e **down/down**)

90. There is a host that cannot connect to the network. What two IOS commands can verify the operational status of a switch port interface?

A. show port status

B. show protocols

C. show interfaces

D. show interface protocol

E. show running-config

Correct Answers (B,C)
Subject Matter: Troubleshooting Interface and Cable Issues

The following IOS commands can verify interface and line protocol status for a switch interface:

switch# show interfaces

switch# show protocols

Example:

The Interface status is the Layer 1 signaling while line protocol is the data link Layer 2 for switch interface GigabitEthernet1/1.

switch# show interfaces gigabitethernet 1/1

GigabitEthernet 1/1 **up***, line protocol* **up** *(normal state)*

Typical Causes:

Layer 1 = cabling, switch configuration mismatches (speed/duplex) errors.

Layer 2 = encapsulation mismatch, spanning tree, clocking errors.

91. Select the correct IOS commands required to configure a switch access port and assign VLAN 10?

A. switch(config-if)# switchport access
switch(config-if)# vlan 10

B. switch(config-if)# switchport access mode
switch(config-if)# vlan 10

C. switch(config-if)# vlan 10
switch(config-if)# access mode

D. switch(config-if)# switchport mode access
switch(config-if)# switchport access vlan 10

Correct Answer (D)
Subject Matter: VLANs

The switch access port is assigned to a single VLAN to provide connectivity for access devices such as a desktops and access points. The exception is connecting an IP phone where a data VLAN and voice VLAN is permitted on an access port. The first interface command configures the mode as an access port. The second command creates and assigns VLAN 10 to the switch port.

switch(config-if)# switchport mode access
switch(config-if)# switchport access vlan 10

92. What two IOS commands will list all VLANs configured on a switch?

A. switch# show vlan

B. switch# show all vlan

C. switch# show vlan brief

D. switch# show interface vlan

E. switch# show vlan interface

Correct Answers (A,C)
Subject Matter: VLANs

The following IOS commands list all layer 2 VLANs (access) configured on a switch. That includes VLAN number, VLAN name, status and port assigned.

switch# show vlan
switch# show vlan brief

93. How do you configure trunking on a Cisco switch port interface?

A. switch(config)# interface [interface]
   switch(config-if)# switchport mode trunk
   switch(config-if)# encapsulation dot1q

B. switch(config)# interface [interface]
   switch(config-if)# switchport trunk on
   switch(config-if)# encapsulation dot1q

C. switch(config)# interface [interface]
   switch(config-if)# trunk mode on
   switch(config-if)# encapsulation dot1q

D. switch(config)# interface [interface]
   switch(config-if)# switchport dot1q

Correct Answer (A)
Subject Matter: Inter-Switch Connectivity

Configuring a switch port as a trunk requires enabling trunk mode and 802.1q encapsulation. The trunk is configured as static where there is no dynamic trunk setup negotiation (DTP).

    switch(config)# interface [interface]
    switch(config-if)# switchport mode trunk
    switch(config-if)# encapsulation dot1q
    switch(config-if)# end

94. What three modes are available with VLAN Trunk Protocol (VTP)?

A. client, server, transparent

B. client, server, none

C. client, server, switch

D. switch, server, transparent

Correct Answer (A)
Subject Matter: Inter-Switch Connectivity

The three VTP modes assignable to a Cisco switch are client, server and transparent. The default when enabling VTP is server mode.

95. What three statements correctly describe Dynamic Trunking Protocol (DTP) operation?

A. open standard

B. Cisco default setting is DTP enabled with auto negotiation

C. negotiate dynamic trunk between two switches

D. Cisco default setting is DTP disabled

E. **switchport nonegotiate** command disables DTP

Correct Answers (B,C,E)
Subject Matter: Inter-Switch Connectivity

DTP enables dynamic trunk negotiation between two connected switches. The Cisco switch enables DTP as a default setting with auto mode. The DTP protocol is disabled with the interface level IOS command **switchport nonegotiate**.

96. What represents the Spanning Tree Protocol (STP) bridge ID?

A. switch priority

B. switch priority + MAC address

C. highest MAC address

D. device serial number

Correct Answer (B)
Subject Matter: Spanning Tree Protocol (STP)

The bridge ID is a numerical value for a switch based on the priority setting and MAC address. The bridge ID is calculated by STP to assign the root bridge for a VLAN. The switch with the lowest bridge ID is elected as root bridge. The lowest MAC address becomes the tie breaker when none of the switches have the lowest priority.

97. What is the default priority setting assigned to a Cisco switch?

    A. 65565

    B. 0

    C. 1

    D. 32768

Correct Answer (D)
Subject Matter: Spanning Tree Protocol (STP)

The default priority setting for a Cisco switch is 32768. The switch with the lowest priority number is elected by STP as root bridge. The MAC address is the tie breaker where switch priorities are equal or no lowest exist. The network administrator can configure a lower switch priority as well to assign it as root bridge.

98. How is spanning tree information communicated between switches?

    A. ICMP

    B. BPDU

    C. PortFast

    D. RSTP

    E. DTP

Correct Answer (B)
Subject Matter: Spanning Tree Protocol (STP)

The BPDU is a Spanning Tree Protocol message that is sent between switches. The hello timer setting is the interval between BPDU advertisements. The BPDU messages contains STP information from the sending switch. That includes STP timers, root bridge ID, sender bridge ID and port (path) cost.

99. What three statements are correct concerning PortFast BPDU guard?

A. STP enhancement supported with RSTP and RPVST+

B. recommended for access switch ports only

C. errdisables the switch port to prevent STP issues

D. improves layer 2 convergence time

E. transitions switch port to forwarding state

Correct Answers (A,B,C)
Subject Matter: Spanning Tree Protocol (STP)

PortFast BPDU guard is an enhancement available with the newer RSTP and RPVST+ Spanning Tree Protocols. The feature errdisables any switch access port with PortFast enabled that receives a BPDU. The switch access ports have desktops and servers connected that don't send or receive BPDUs. PortFast allows them to transition to forwarding state immediately. As a host, they should never receive a BPDU from the switch. When connecting a switch instead of a desktop for instance, BPDUs are sent between switches It prevents connecting any network devices that could affect the STP topology and cause layer 2 loops.

100. What IOS command will list the root bridge and spanning tree port states for switch-1 and VLAN 10?

A. switch-1# show spanning tree vlan 10

B. switch-1# show spanning-tree vlan 10

C. switch-1# show spanning-tree 10 pvst

D. switch-1# show spanning tree vlan 10 pvst

Correct Answer (B)
Subject Matter: Spanning Tree Protocol (STP)

The IOS command **show spanning-tree vlan** [number] is used to list the local bridge ID and STP port states for the local switch. In addition it lists the root bridge for the VLAN. The root bridge is identified by the MAC address. The **show cdp neighbor detail** command lists the MAC address for each connected switch making it easier to identify the root bridge (switch).

101. The network administrator must add 70 new employees to the network in a single broadcast domain. The hosts each require their own collision domain and the company would like to repurpose some Cisco 3850 access switches. What network switch hardware that will enable scalability for company growth? (select two)

A. switch stacking

B. management SVI

C. enable ip routing

D. Gigabit Ethernet

E. single router

F. virtual switching system (VSS)

Correct Answers (A,D)
Subject Matter: Switch Stacking

Connecting 70 new users to the same VLAN (broadcast domain) on a single switch requires 70 switch ports. Stacking (chassis aggregation) of 2 - 3850 switches with 48 ports per switch is the preferred solution. It creates a single logical switch with 96 access ports. The network administrator can dynamically add switches to the stack for scalability. The Gigabit Ethernet switch port enables a separate collision domain per port.

102. Refer to the network topology drawing. CDP is enabled by default and STP is blocking the link between Switch-2 and Switch-1. What neighbors of Switch-2 are detected when the following IOS command is issued from Switch-2? (select two).

switch-2# show cdp neighbors

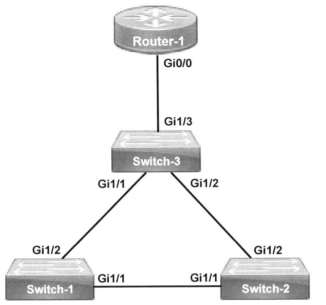

switch-2# **show cdp neighbors**

A. Router-1

B. Switch-3

C. Switch-1

D. Switch-1, Switch-3 and Router-1

E. Switch-3 and Router-1

Correct Answers (B,C)
Subject Matter: Layer 2 Protocols

The output from the IOS command **show cdp neighbor** lists connectivity information for directly connected neighbors only. In addition any switch ports assigned as blocking by STP are unaffected by CDP. The link between Switch-2 and Switch-1 can forward CDP packets and detect neighbors. The following are the neighbor switches detected by CDP.

- Switch-1
- Switch-3

103. Host-1 has established a session with Server-1. What is the source MAC address of frames arriving at Host-1 from Server-1?

A. MAC address of Server-1

B. MAC address of Host-1

C. MAC address of upstream Ethernet router interface

D. MAC address of upstream connected switch

E. MAC address of upstream router serial interface

Correct Answer (C)
Subject Matter: Switching Concepts

As packets are forwarded between Host-1 and Server-1, the MAC addressing changes (rewritten) per router hop by routers only. The switches do not rewrite any source or destination MAC addressing. The IP addressing does not change between source and destination. The router will do a routing table lookup then rewrite the source and destination MAC address in the frame header. The source MAC address is the router Ethernet interface used to egress the packet to the Host. The destination MAC address is the switch port Ethernet interface where the host is connected.

104. Select the statement that best describes Ethernet interface MTU setting?

A. TCP maximum window size

B. minimum TCP segment size

C. maximum payload size

D. maximum Ethernet frame length

E. minimum Ethernet frame length

F. maximum Ethernet packet length

Correct Answer (D)
Subject Matter: Ethernet Frame Format

The MTU refers to the maximum size (bytes) of an Ethernet frame. The default Ethernet MTU is 1500 bytes. The frame is comprised of a header and payload (data). The header is a fixed size with fields for control and MAC addressing.

Decreasing the MTU size would decrease the payload amount (bytes) that can be transmitted. The MTU setting configured on an Ethernet interface can be verified with the following IOS command.

switch# show interfaces [interface] [slot/port]

105. Select three correct statements concerning LLDP?

    A. vendor-neutral auto discovery

    B. Cisco switches support IEEE 802.1AB LLDP for multivendor support

    C. LLDP enable network devices to share identity and functionality

    D. OSI network layer

    E. Cisco default setting is enabled

Correct Answers (A,B,C)
Subject Matter: Layer 2 Protocols

LLDP is the open standard counterpart to Cisco CDP for network discovery in a multi-vendor environment. Cisco supports LLDP (IEEE 802.1ab) and thereby optimizing auto-discovery and network management. The network devices share identity and feature support functionality via LLDP and with neighbors.

106. What is the LLDP update timer interval?

    A. 60 second update timer

    B. 30 second update timer

    C. 10 second update timer

    D. 120 second update timer

Correct Answer (B)
Subject Matter: Layer 2 Protocols

The default packet update interval for LLDP is 30 seconds.

107. What is the IEEE standard for LLDP?

    A. IEEE 802.1ae

    B. IEEE 802.1ac

    C. IEEE 802.1X

    D. IEEE 802.1ab

Correct Answer (D)
Subject Matter: Layer 2 Protocols

LLDP is an open standard network discovery protocol specified with IEEE 802.1ab standard.

108. What IOS command enables LLDP globally on a Cisco switch?

    A. switch(config)# lldp enable

    B. switch(config)# lldp run

    C. switch(config)# enable lldp

    D. switch(config)# lldp service

Correct Answer (B)
Subject Matter: Layer 2 Protocols

The following enables LLDP globally on a Cisco switch.

    switch(config)# lldp run

109. What IOS command enables a Cisco switch to receive LLDP packets on an interface?

    A. switch(config-if)# lldp receive

    B. switch(config-if)# lldp enable rx

    C. switch(config-if)# lldp rx

    D. switch(config-if)# lldp receive enable

    E. none of the above (default setting)

Correct Answer (A)
Subject Matter: Layer 2 Protocols

The following IOS interface level command enables a Cisco switch to receive LLDP packets on an interface.

    switch(config-if)# lldp receive

110. Match the IOS show command with the correct description?

show lldp	list Ethernet media and interface description
show lldp neighbors detail	verify LLDP is enabled and global timers
show lldp interface	list the LLDP interfaces enabled

Correct Answers.
Subject Matter: Layer 2 Protocols

The following describe the information provided with each IOS command for LLDP operational status and configuration.

show lldp	**verify LLDP is enabled and global timers**
show lldp neighbors detail	**list Ethernet media, interface description**
show lldp interface	**list the LLDP interfaces enabled**

111. What is required to enable LLDP for Cisco IP phone discovery?

    A. IP phone sends LLDP-MED packets first

    B. IP phone sends LLDP packets first

    C. enable LLDP-MED TLVs

    D. configure voice VLAN

    E. proxy ARP enabled

Correct Answer (B)
Subject Matter: Layer 2 Protocols

Cisco IP phones are enabled for LLDP when LLDP packets are first sent from the phone to the switch.

112. What are three primary advantages of stacking Cisco access switches?

    A. ease of management

    B. faster convergence

    C. switch redundancy

    D. routing features

    E. power over ethernet (PoE)

    F. wireless support

Correct Answers (A,B,C)
Subject Matter: Switch Stacking

Switch Stacking creates a single logical switch from up to nine Catalyst switches where supported. The advantages include easier management of a single switch instead of multiple switches. In addition there is faster convergence with fewer switch uplinks. The spanning tree topology is less complex minimizing STP issues. The Stack elects a stack master switch and a standby master switch for processor redundancy. The Stacking cable provides redundant data paths between stack neighbors. Link redundancy is enabled with Cross-stack EtherChannel between different switch stacks.

113. Refer to the network topology drawing. How many collision domains and broadcast domains are available based on a default switch configuration?

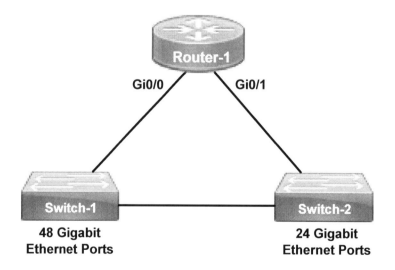

A. 3 broadcast domains, 3 collision domains

B. 2 broadcast domains, 72 collision domains

C. 3 broadcast domains, 72 collision domains

D. 1 broadcast domain, 3 collision domains

Correct Answer (C)
Subject Matter: Switching Concepts

Each Gigabit switch port is a single collision domain. There are 72 Gigabit Ethernet switch ports that create a maximum 72 available collision domains when all are active. There is a default VLAN 1 on each switch that defines a single broadcast domain between switches. In addition there is a separate broadcast domain for each router interface. The network topology defines 3 broadcast domains and 72 collision domains.

114. Refer to the output from the IOS command shown. What interface on Router-1 connects to Switch-3?

   switch-3# show cdp neighbors

   Capability Codes: R - Router, T - Trans Bridge, B - Source Route Bridge
                     S - Switch, H - Host, I - IGMP, r - Repeater

Device ID	Local Interface	Holdtime	Capability	Platform	Port ID
Switch-1	Gi1/1	127	S	3750	Gi1/1
Switch-2	Gi1/2	112	S	3750	Gi1/2
Router-1	Gi1/3	177	R	2900	Gi0/0

A. Gi0/0

B. Gi1/3

C. Gi1/2

D. unknown

Correct Answer (A)
Subject Matter: Layer 2 Protocols

The Local Interface is the local switch port of Switch-3 where the IOS command was issued. The neighbor switch interface is Port ID. As a result Router-1 interface Gi0/0 is connected to Switch-3 local interface Gi1/3.

115. Refer to the network drawing where the following IOS command was issued on Switch-2. There are a high number of input errors and CRC errors. What are the two most probable causes?

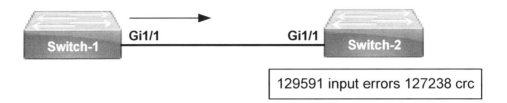

switch-2# show interfaces gigabitethernet 1/1

A. crossover cable type deployed between switches

B. native VLAN mismatch between switches

C. defective cabling

D. speed/duplex mismatch between switches

E. collisions

F. network interface card (NIC) error

Correct Answers (C,D)
Subject Matter: Troubleshooting Interface and Cable Issues

The high number of input errors and CRC errors indicate a layer 1 issue between the switches. Switch-1 is sending frames that are corrupt when they arrive at Switch-2. The most probable cause is duplex mismatch between the switch interfaces or cabling errors. The switch ports must agree on the duplex setting. Gigabit Ethernet ports do not use half-duplex at all. The Cisco switch default setting is **duplex auto** (for full-duplex mode. There is however the option to hard code with the interface command **duplex full**. In addition the speed setting must match between switches. That is configured with the interface command **speed auto** or hard code with the command **speed 1000.** Since the frames were arriving at Switch-2, verify the duplex setting on Switch-1 to start with. Cabling defects, where the correct cable type is currently used, requires replacement to fix layer 1 issues.

116. Refer to the network topology drawing. Host-1 from VLAN 10 cannot communicate with Server-1 assigned to VLAN 10. Identify issues based on the information provided? (select three)

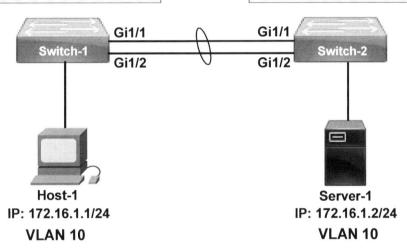

```
interface gigabitethernet1/1
switchport mode access
switchport access vlan 10
duplex full
speed auto
channel-group 1 mode auto

interface gigabitethernet1/2
switchport mode access
switchport access vlan 10
duplex full
speed 100
channel-group 1 mode auto
```

```
interface gigabitethernet1/1
switchport mode access
switchport access vlan 10
duplex full
speed auto
channel-group 1 mode on

interface gigabitethernet1/2
switchport mode access
switchport access vlan 10
duplex half
speed 1000
channel-group 1 mode desirable
```

Switch-1 Gi1/1 Gi1/1 **Switch-2**
Gi1/2 Gi1/2

Host-1
IP: 172.16.1.1/24
VLAN 10

Server-1
IP: 172.16.1.2/24
VLAN 10

A. port channel not configured to bundle link

B. duplex settings not correct on an interface

C. EtherChannel mode incorrect on an interface

D. layer 3 interface required for VLAN spanning across switches

E. switchport mode incorrect on an interface

F. port speed incorrect on an interface

Correct Answers (B,C,F)
Subject Matter: Troubleshooting Interface and Cable Issues

The network topology drawing is an EtherChannel between two switches connecting Host-1 to Server-1. In addition Host-1 and Server-1 are on the same subnet and same VLAN. It is a layer 2 configuration similar to any data center design. The access ports are forwarding a single VLAN (no trunk required).

All switch ports assigned to an EtherChannel must be configured with matching settings. That includes speed, duplex, EtherChannel mode, switchport mode, STP and VLAN membership for each port.

Switch-1 (Gi1/1) to Switch-2 (Gi1/1) have a PAgP mode mismatch between switch ports. EtherChannel requires desirable mode on at least one switch port to enable it.

Switch-1 (Gi1/2) to Switch-2 (Gi1/2) have a duplex and speed mismatch between switch ports. The correct settings for Gigabit speed or higher is 1000 or auto. The supported duplex setting is half, full or auto however full-duplex is the Cisco default.

EtherChannel across a trunk link requires the native VLAN, allowed VLANs and encapsulation type to match as well.

117. What three options correctly describe VLAN configuration on a switch?

   A. normal range VLANs include 1-1005

   B. extended range VLANs include 1006-4005

   C. VLAN 1, 1002-1005 cannot be deleted

   D. VLAN 1, 1006-4094 cannot be deleted

   E. VLAN 1006-4094 cannot be pruned from a trunk

Correct Answers (A,C,E)
Subject Matter: VLANs

The following are the guidelines for deploying VLANs to a Cisco switch.

   • Normal Range VLANs = 1-1005
   • Extended Range VLANs = 1006-4094
   • VLAN 1, 1002-1005 are automatically created and cannot be deleted
   • VLAN 1006-4094 cannot be pruned from a trunk

118. The network administrator has configured a trunk between two switches. The configuration must prune VLANs to allow only VLAN 10, 11 and 12 across the trunk. What is the correct IOS command to accomplish that?

A. switch(config-if)# switchport trunk allowed vlans 10-12

B. switch(config-if)# switchport trunk vlan allowed 10-12

C. switch(config-if)# switchport trunk allowed vlan add 10-12

D. switch(config-if)# switchport trunk allowed vlan 10-12

Correct Answer (D)
Subject Matter: Inter-Switch Connectivity

The default trunk configuration allows all VLANs from the range 1-4094 across the trunk link. The following IOS command will **allow only** VLAN 10, VLAN 11 and VLAN 12 across the trunk. The network administrator can add or remove VLANs after that IOS command is issued based on requirements.

switch(config-if)# switchport trunk allowed vlan 10-12

119. What IOS interface level command will remove VLAN 10 from a trunk where pruning is allowing VLAN 10, VLAN 11 and VLAN 12?

A. switch(config-if)# switchport trunk allowed remove 10

B. switch(config-if)# switchport trunk vlan remove 10

C. switch(config-if)# switchport trunk allowed vlan remove 10

D. switch(config-if)# switchport trunk remove vlan 10

E. switch(config-if)# switchport trunk allowed vlan 10-11

Correct Answer (C)
Subject Matter: Inter-Switch Connectivity

The following IOS command will remove VLAN 10 from the trunk. That will filter all traffic from that VLAN so it cannot traverse the trunk link between switches. To remove a range of consecutive VLANs such as from VLAN 1 to VLAN 100 inclusive, use a hyphen (1-100). For a non-consecutive list such as VLAN 1 and VLAN 10,11,12 use commas and hyphens (1,10-12).

switch(config-if)# switchport trunk allowed vlan remove 10

120. What IOS interface level command will add VLAN 12 to a trunk interface where pruning is only allowing VLAN 10 and VLAN 11?

A. switch(config-if)# switchport trunk allowed vlan add 12

B. switch(config-if)# switchport trunk allowed vlan 12

C. switch(config-if)# switchport trunk vlan add 12

D. switch(config-if)# switchport trunk add vlan 12

Correct Answer (A)
Subject Matter: Inter-Switch Connectivity

The following IOS interface command will add VLAN 12 to the trunk interface. That will permit all traffic from that VLAN so it can traverse the trunk link between switches. To add a range of consecutive VLANs such as from VLAN 1 to VLAN 100 inclusive, use a hyphen (1-100). For the example where there is a non-consecutive list such as VLAN 1 and VLAN 10,11,12 use commas and hyphens (1,10-12).

switch(config-if)# switchport trunk allowed vlan add 12

The add/remove keyword only applies after pruning has already occurred on the trunk interface to limit the number of VLANs allowed from the default (1-4094). That IOS interface level command is **switchport trunk allowed vlan** [list].

121. What VTP version 2 feature enhancements are not available with VTP version 1? (select three)

A. Token Ring VLANs

B. 40 Gigabit Ethernet (40 Gbps)

C. VLAN consistency check

D. transparent mode switch forwards VTP advertisements without version check

E. transparent mode switch forwards VTP advertisements with version check

F. increase VLAN database size (vlan.dat) to 200 VLANs

G. extended range VLAN support

Correct Answers (A,C,D)
Subject Matter: Inter-Switch Connectivity

The primary feature enhancements available with VTP v2 include the following:

- Token Ring VLANs
- VLAN consistency check
- Transparent mode switch forwards VTP advertisements without any version check

122. Select two statements that accurately describe full-duplex Ethernet?

    A. host network interface card and switch port must support full-duplex

    B. full-duplex still requires CSMA/CD for media access

    C. default switch port setting for Gigabit is half-duplex

    D. switch port full-duplex mode creates multiple VLANs

    E. there are no collisions in full-duplex mode

Correct Answers (A,E)
Subject Matter: Switching Concepts

Full-duplex eliminates collisions per switch port and the need for CSMA/CD. The host network interface card and switch port must support full-duplex. The default for Gigabit switch ports is full-duplex mode. Single VLANs are created per switch port except where there is a voice VLAN.

123. Select the network design feature that provides maximum dedicated bandwidth?

    A. connect each host to a separate switch port

    B. connect each host to separate wireless access points

    C. connect each host to a separate switch port and configure half-duplex

    D. connect each host to a separate switch port with a crossover cable

Correct Answer (A)
Subject Matter: Switching Concepts

Only Gigabit switch ports support full-duplex dedicated bandwidth (microsegmentation) per switch port. Wireless access points are half-duplex only. The full-duplex uplink to the router is shared by all connected desktops and network servers. The bridge is half-duplex as well.

124. Match the network message types on the left with the correct description on the right?

layer 2 broadcast	255.255.255.255
DHCP client broadcast	ffff.ffff.ffff
layer 2 broadcast domain	local subnet only
layer 3 broadcast	VLAN (network segment)

Correct Answers.
Subject Matter: Switching Concepts

Broadcast messages are a key component of network connectivity particularly for layer 2 and layer 3.

Layer 2 broadcast = ffff.ffff.ffff
The layer 2 broadcast is forwarded to all devices on a single broadcast (segment) domain. It uses ffff.ffff.ffff as the destination MAC address. ARP is an example of a layer 2 broadcast.

DHCP client broadcast = 255.255.255.255
The layer 3 broadcast is sent from a DHCP client requesting an IP address. They are sent to all network devices on a local subnet

Layer 2 broadcast domain = VLAN (network segment)

Layer 3 broadcast = local subnet only

125. What layer 2 interface errors are caused by collisions? (select two)

A. CRC

B. giants

C. runts

D. TTL

E. UDLD

Correct Answers (A,C)
Subject Matter: Troubleshooting Interface and Cable Issues

The output of **show interfaces** list various layer 2 errors including runts, giants, collisions and CRC errors. The most common cause of CRC and runts is collisions. Gigabit Ethernet switch ports have eliminated collisions unless there is a configuration error or hardware issue. Collisions can occur when there is a misconfiguration of speed and duplex settings between host and switch. In addition collisions can occur when there is a bad network interface card (NIC) or cabling error. Giants result from either a bad NIC card or an MTU configuration error.

Module 3: Routing Technologies

1. Select the network addressing that comprise an ARP table?

    A. IP address and VLAN

    B. IP address and MAC address

    C. MAC address

    D. route prefixes

Correct Answer (B)
Subject Matter: Routing Concepts

The ARP table is comprised of IP address to MAC address bindings (mappings).

2. What protocol will a host use to determine the MAC address of a server?

    A. HTTP

    B. DNS

    C. DHCP

    D. ARP

    E. NTP

Correct Answer (D)
Subject Matter: Routing Concepts

ARP is a layer 3 network protocol that resolves a known IP address to an unknown MAC address. The local host must know the IP address and MAC address of the remote host before packets can be sent. That enables switches and routers to forward packets between local and remote host (server). The host checks it's local ARP cache for an entry with the IP address and MAC address of a server. The host sends an ARP request to the default gateway if there is no local ARP entry. The default gateway (router) sends an ARP broadcast and returns the MAC address for a server to the host In addition all routers between source and destination update their ARP table bindings (mappings). The switches note the server MAC address as well and update their MAC address table.

3. Refer to the network drawing. Host-1 would like to initiate a new session with Server-1 on a remote subnet. What two statements are correct?

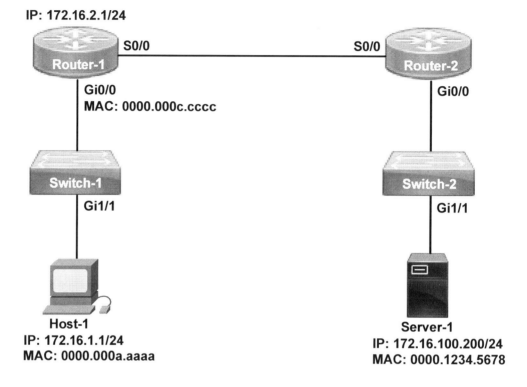

IP: 172.16.2.1/24

Router-1 — S0/0 .... S0/0 — Router-2

Gi0/0
MAC: 0000.000c.cccc

Gi0/0

Switch-1

Switch-2

Gi1/1

Gi1/1

Host-1
IP: 172.16.1.1/24
MAC: 0000.000a.aaaa

Server-1
IP: 172.16.100.200/24
MAC: 0000.1234.5678

A. Host-1 verifies there is no local ARP cache entry for Server-1

B. Host-1 sends an ARP request to the default gateway

C. Switch-1 sends the ARP request to Server-1

D. Host-1 sends an ARP request to Router-2

E. Host-1 requests the MAC address of Switch-1

Correct Answers (A,B)
Subject Matter: Routing Concepts

When a host initiates a session with a remote server (different subnet) the IP address is resolved first. Host-1 then checks the local ARP cache to verify there isn't an entry for Server-1. The ARP entry would list MAC addresses associated with the server IP address. The IP address is on a remote subnet so Host-1 sends an ARP request for the MAC address of the default gateway (Router-1).

Switch-1 as a layer 2 device forwards the ARP request to Router-1. The MAC address of Router-1 (0000.000c.cccc) is sent to Host-1 and added to the local ARP cache. Host-1 sends a second ARP request to the default gateway requesting the MAC address of Server-1. Router-1 does a routing table lookup and forwards the ARP request to Router-2.

The default gateway IP address is often configured with TCP/IP settings for the host. In addition when there are previous sessions with a server, the default gateway MAC address is already known.

4. Refer to the network topology drawing. What is the source and destination MAC address of the packet at P1 when it is forwarded to Router-2?

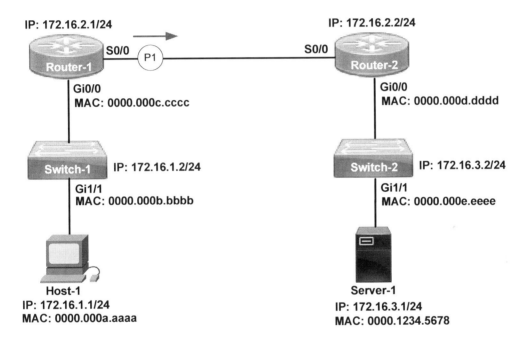

A. source MAC address = 0000.000a.aaaa
   destination MAC address = 0000.000e.eeee

B. source MAC address = 0000.000c.cccc
   destination MAC address = 0000.000d.dddd

C. source MAC address = 0000.000a.aaaa
   destination MAC address = 0000.1234.5678

D. source MAC address = 0000.000c.cccc
   destination MAC address = 0000.1234.5678

Correct Answer (B)
Subject Matter: Routing Concepts

The router is the only network device that rewrites source and destination MAC address. The source MAC address is derived from the local router (Router-1) egress interface. The destination MAC address is derived from the remote router (Router-2) ingress interface. WAN serial interfaces do not have an assigned MAC address. As a result, Router-1 assigns the MAC address of the Ethernet interface (Gi0/0) where the packet was learned as source MAC address. In addition, Router-1 assigns the MAC address of Router-2 Ethernet interface Gi0/0 as destination MAC address. The MAC address of Router-2 is obtained from the router ARP table.

- source MAC address = 0000.000c.cccc
- destination MAC address = 0000.000d.dddd

5. Refer to the network topology drawing where Host-1 is sending a packet to Server-1. Select the correct source and destination MAC address at P1. In addition select the correct source and destination IP address at P2?

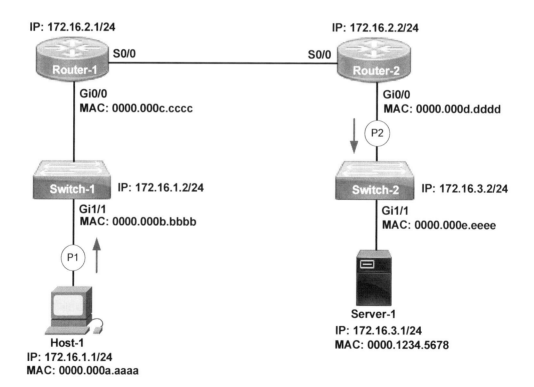

A. P1: source MAC address = 0000.000a.aaaa
   P1: destination MAC address = 0000.000b.bbbb
   P2: source IP address = 172.16.2.2
   P2: destination IP address = 172.16.3.2

B. P1: source MAC address = 0000.000a.aaaa
   P1: destination MAC address = 0000.000c.cccc
   P2: source IP address = 172.16.1.1
   P2: destination IP address = 172.16.3.1

C. P1: source MAC address = 0000.000a.aaaa
   P1: destination MAC address = ffff.ffff.ffff
   P2: source IP address = 172.16.3.2
   P2: destination IP address = 172.16.3.1

D. P1: source MAC address = 0000.000a.aaaa
   P1: destination MAC address = 0000.1234.5678
   P2: source IP address = 172.16.2.1
   P2: destination IP address = 172.16.3.1

Correct Answer (B)
Subject Matter: Routing Concepts

The source and destination MAC address are rewritten at each router hop. The switch only examines the source and destination MAC address. Host-1 sends a packet at P1 with it's local (NIC) MAC address as source MAC address (0000.000a.aaaa). The destination MAC address at P1 is Router-1 Ethernet interface Gi0/0 (0000.000c.cccc). Switch-1 is only forwarding the packet and must know the destination MAC address.

The source and destination IP address do not change as packets traverse the network. The packet direction is forwarded from Host-1 to Server-1. The source IP address is 172.16.1.1 for the host and destination IP address is 172.16.3.1 for the server.

P1: source MAC address = 0000.000a.aaaa
P1: destination MAC address = 0000.000c.cccc

P2: source IP address = 172.16.1.1 (Host-1)
P2: destination IP address = 172.16.3.1 (Server-1)

6. Select the correct statement concerning stub routing?

    A. configured with a static route

    B. assigned to data center routers

    C. configured with a default route

    D. not supported with EIGRP

Correct Answer (C)
Subject Matter: IPv4/IPv6 Static Routing

The stub router is configured with a default route to the data center. It is designed to minimize routing traffic and provide security to a branch office. In addition no external traffic is permitted to transit through a stub router.

7. What network device is responsible for best path selection and branch office connectivity?

    A. wireless LAN controller (WLC)

    B. router

    C. firewall

    D. switch

Correct Answer (B)
Subject Matter: Routing Concepts

Routers are primarily responsible for network interconnection and best path selection. They forward packets between different subnets, VLANs and across the WAN. They build the routing table with routes comprised of network prefix, metric and next hop address. The router selects the route based on destination IP address and forwards packets to the next hop router (neighbor). There is support for load balancing, flow control and error recovery as well.

8. Refer to the network topology drawing. What ARP cache entry is added to Host-1 when it pings Server-1?

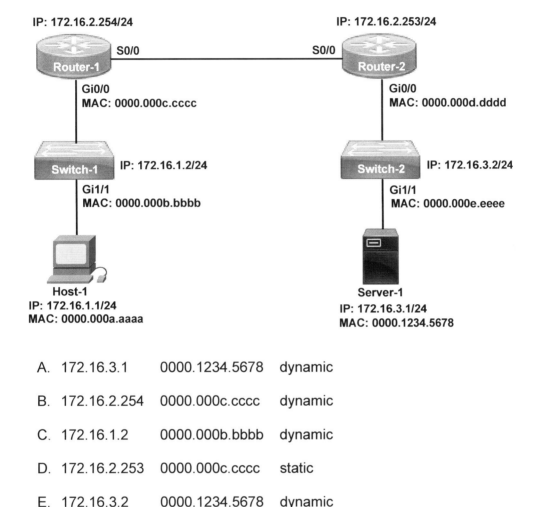

IP: 172.16.2.254/24
S0/0
Router-1
Gi0/0
MAC: 0000.000c.cccc

IP: 172.16.2.253/24
S0/0
Router-2
Gi0/0
MAC: 0000.000d.dddd

Switch-1   IP: 172.16.1.2/24
Gi1/1
MAC: 0000.000b.bbbb

Switch-2   IP: 172.16.3.2/24
Gi1/1
MAC: 0000.000e.eeee

Host-1
IP: 172.16.1.1/24
MAC: 0000.000a.aaaa

Server-1
IP: 172.16.3.1/24
MAC: 0000.1234.5678

A. 172.16.3.1   0000.1234.5678   dynamic

B. 172.16.2.254   0000.000c.cccc   dynamic

C. 172.16.1.2   0000.000b.bbbb   dynamic

D. 172.16.2.253   0000.000c.cccc   static

E. 172.16.3.2   0000.1234.5678   dynamic

Correct Answer (B)
Subject Matter: Routing Concepts

Host-1 first checks its local ARP cache for Server-1 when sending packets including a ping. When there is no entry for Server-1 in the ARP cache, it sends an ARP request to the default gateway (Router-1). The default gateway responds with the IP address and MAC address assigned to Gi0/0 interface. That is the LAN interface nearest to Host-1. The host adds the IP address (172.16.2.254/24) and MAC address 0000.000c.cccc to its local ARP cache.

9. Refer to the network topology drawing. The network administrator attempts to ping from Host-1 to Router-2 and receives the ICMP **destination host unreachable** error message. What is the most probable cause for the error?

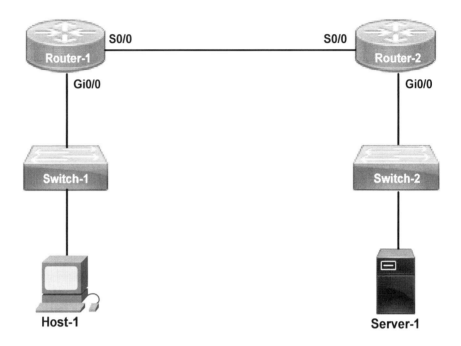

A. Ethernet link between Router-2 and Server-1 is down

B. WAN serial link between routers is down

C. Router-1 interface Serial0/0 is admin shutdown

D. ACL on Router-1 filtering packets

E. Switch-1 uplink is down

F. no default gateway on Host-1

Correct Answer (B)
Subject Matter: Troubleshooting Layer 3 Connectivity

The ICMP **destination host unreachable** message is returned by Router-1 to Host-1 The message indicates that Router-1 can't forward packets to Router-2. The most reasonable explanation is a link failure between routers. The cause of a link failure could include routing issues, WAN circuit down or serial interface error. Consider where the WAN link is available and it is Router-2 LAN interface that was shutdown. Router-2 would have returned the destination unreachable error confirming it is the LAN segment that isn't available.

10. Refer to the network topology drawing. Host-1 cannot send packets to Server-1. Select two possible causes based on the results of the following IOS command?

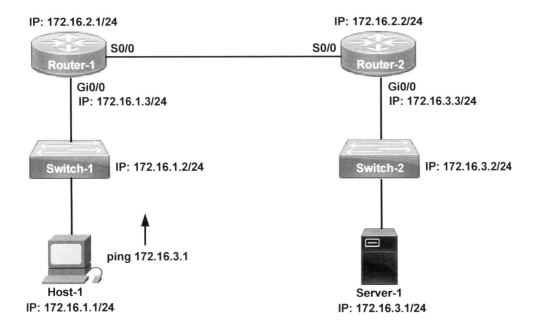

router-1# show ip interface brief

Interface	IP address	OK	Method	Status	Protocol
GigabitEthernet0/0	172.16.1.3	YES	NVRAM	up	up
GigabitEthernet0/1	Unassigned	YES	Manual	administratively down	down
Serial0/0	172.16.2.1	YES	Unset	up	down
Serial0/1	Unassigned	YES	Manual	administratively down	down

A. clocking error between routers

B. cabling issue

C. serial line encapsulation mismatch between routers

D. Router-2 interface Serial0/0 (S0/0) is administratively down

E. Router-1 is configured with the wrong subnet mask

F. Router-2 loopback is assigned the wrong subnet mask

Correct Answers (A,C)
Subject Matter: Troubleshooting Layer 3 Connectivity

The IOS command **show ip interface brief** provides interface and line protocol status. That include all network interfaces with an assigned IP address. The **Status** column is layer 1 Ethernet signaling while the **Protocol** column is layer 2 data link connectivity.

Router-1 interface S0/0 (172.16.2.1) is **up/down** confirming the problem is with line protocol (layer 2). Typical layer 2 causes include clocking errors and encapsulation mismatch between routers. There are sometimes device misconfiguration errors caused by layer 2 or higher errors.

11. Host-1 with IP address 192.168.1.1/24 needs to establish a session with a Server-1 that has IP address 172.33.1.1/27. The default gateway has IP address 192.168.1.254/24. How is the unknown MAC address for Server-1 obtained?

    A. Host-1 sends a layer 3 broadcast to the local segment first

    B. Host-1 sends an ARP request for the MAC address of upstream switch

    C. The router sends an ARP request for the MAC address of Server-1

    D. Host-1 (192.168.1.1) sends an ARP request for the MAC address of the default gateway

Correct Answer (D)
Subject Matter: Routing Concepts

Host-1 must first request the MAC address of the default gateway before sending packets to an unknown server on a different subnet. The default gateway would respond with the MAC address of its LAN Ethernet interface. Host-1 updates its local ARP cache and sends a new ARP request for Server-1.

12. Select the IOS command used to configure a static ARP entry with a MAC address of 0000.dddd.eeee and IP address of 172.16.1.1?

    A. arp 172.16.1.1 0000.dddd.eeee arpa

    B. arp 172.16.1.1 0000.dddd.eeee dynamic

    C. arp 172.16.1.1 0000.dddd.eeee sap

    D. arp 172.16.1.1 0000.dddd.eeee snap

Correct Answer (A)

Subject Matter: Routing Concepts

The following IOS command will add a static ARP entry to the ARP table.

    router(config)# arp 172.16.1.1 0000.dddd.eeee arpa

13. What is the administrative distance for the route to the destination network 192.168.3.0/24?

    router# show ip route

    Codes: C - connected, S - static, R - RIP, M - mobile, B - BGP
        D - EIGRP, EX - EIGRP external, O - OSPF, IA - OSPF inter area
        N1 - OSPF NSSA external type 1, N2 - OSPF NSSA external type 2
        E1 - OSPF external type 1, E2 - OSPF external type 2
        o - ODR, P - periodic downloaded static route

    Gateway of last resort is 172.33.0.1 to network 0.0.0.0

        10.1.0.0/24 is subnetted, 4 subnets
    C   10.1.0.0 is directly connected, Serial0/0
    C   10.1.5.0 is directly connected, GigabitEthernet0/1
    C   10.1.6.0 is directly connected, GigabitEthernet0/0
    C   10.1.7.0 is directly connected, Serial0/1
    C   10.1.254.0 is directly connected, Loopback0
    R   192.168.3.0/24 [120/6] via 192.168.1.1

A. 126

B. 150

C. 120

D. 6

Correct Answer (C)
Subject Matter: Administrative Distance

The **show ip route** command lists the network prefixes to subnet destinations. The router would select the following route to destination 192.168.3.0/24

    R   192.168.3.0/24 [**120**/6] via 192.168.1.1

It is a RIPv2 route with next hop 192.168.1.1 that has an administrative distance of 120 and hop count (metric) of 6.

14. The static route with an administrative distance of 255 is not installed in the routing table?

   A. True

   B. False

Correct Answer (True)
Subject Matter: Administrative Distance

Any route assigned an administrative distance of 255 won't be installed into the routing table. The router doesn't trust the source of the route and considers it untrustworthy.

15. What routing protocol is not an Interior Gateway Protocol (IGP)?

   A. RIPv2

   B. BGP

   C. OSPF

   D. EIGRP

Correct Answer (B)
Subject Matter: Interior and Exterior Routing Protocols

Interior gateway routing protocols (IGP) advertise routes between routing domains that are privately managed. The IGP routing protocols include RIPv2, OSPF and EIGRP. BGP enables access to external routing domains managed by service providers (ISP) and enterprise companies. That allows routing advertisements across the service provider network. The enterprise network can connect to external partners, customers and cloud services.

16. Based on the routing table shown below, when the router receives a packet destined to 192.168.1.65 where will the router forward the traffic?

    router# show ip route

    Codes: C - connected, S - static, R - RIP, M - mobile, B - BGP
        D - EIGRP, EX - EIGRP external, O - OSPF, IA - OSPF inter area
        N1 - OSPF NSSA external type 1, N2 - OSPF NSSA external type 2
        E1 - OSPF external type 1, E2 - OSPF external type 2
        o - ODR, * - candidate default

    Gateway of last resort is 172.33.1.1 to network 0.0.0.0

        192.168.1.0/24 is variably subnetted, 4 subnets, 4 masks
    C   192.168.1.1/24 is directly connected, GigabitEthernet0/0
    S   192.168.1.128/25 [1/0] via 192.168.2.1
    S   192.168.1.64/26 [1/0] via 192.168.2.2
    S   192.168.1.32/27 [1/0] via 192.168.2.3
    S   10.254.254.254/32 [1/0] via 192.168.2.4
    S*   0.0.0.0/0 [1/0] via 172.33.1.1

    A. 192.168.2.2

    B. 192.168.2.3

    C. 192.168.2.1

    D. 192.168.2.4

    E. 172.33.1.1

Correct Answer (A)
Subject Matter: Routing Concepts

The longest match is in effect when there are multiple routes to the same destination (192.168.1.65). The 192.168.1.64/26 is the correct prefix with the longest match subnet prefix (/26). It is a static route (S) with 192.168.2.2 as the next hop address. The destination route 192.168.1.65 is within the subnet 192.168.1.128/25 range as well. The /26 prefix is longer than the /25 route.

    S   192.168.1.64/26 [1/0] via 192.168.2.2

17. Select the true distance vector routing protocol?

    A. EIGRP

    B. Static

    C. OSPF

    D. RIPv2

Correct Answer (D)
Subject Matter: Distance Vector and Link-State Routing Protocols

Routing protocols are either link-state, distance vector or hybrid. The distance vector protocol assigns metric based on hop count. The best path selected has the least number of hops. OSPF is a link-state protocol that uses a cost metric that is based on link bandwidth. EIGRP is a hybrid routing protocol that calculates a composite metric. The default EIGRP metric is the composite of bandwidth and delay. The distance vector routing protocol is RIPv2.

18. What is the administrative distance (AD) of an external EIGRP route?

    A. 110

    B. 90

    C. 170

    D. 120

Correct Answer (C)
Subject Matter: Administrative Distance

The administrative distance of an external EIGRP route is 170. The router assigns a lower (preferred) administrative distance to internal EIGRP. The external EIGRP route is a route that was redistributed into EIGRP.

19. What field in the IP header prevents routing loops by limiting the maximum number of hops possible?

   A. TTL

   B. CRC

   C. ICMP

   D. MTU

   E. ToS

Correct Answer (A)
Subject Matter: Routing Concepts

The IP header has a field called Time-to-Live (TTL) that has a default value of 255. The purpose of TTL is to prevent packets from infinitely looping as a result of a routing loop. The TTL field is decremented by one with each router hop. That guarantees the packet will be discarded after 255 hops.

20. Based on the output of debug ip packet as shown, what type of packet is this and where is it destined?

   IP: s=172.16.2.1 (GigabitEthernet 0/1), d=224.0.0.5, len 83, rcvd 0, Proto=89

   A. OSPF multicast packet destined to all BDR routers on the network segment where GigabitEthernet 0/1 is attached.

   B. OSPF multicast packet destined to all OSPF routers on the multi-access network segment where GigabitEthernet0/1 is attached.

   C. EIGRP multicast packet destined to all member routers with interfaces assigned to the same autonomous system.

   D. RIPv2 multicast packet destined to IP address 172.16.2.1

   E. EIGRP unicast packet destined to GigabitEthernet0/1

Correct Answer (B)
Subject Matter: OSPFv2 for IPv4

The output of **debug ip packet** command includes source and destination IP address. In addition there is the network interface that received the packet and IP protocol number. Any destination IP address that starts with 224.0.0.5 is an OSPF multicast. In addition the IP protocol 89 indicates it is OSPF.

The output is from an OSPF multicast packet sent to all OSPF enabled routers on a network segment (subnet). It is sent from a designated router (DR) to advertise a route to multiple OSPF routers.

21. What is the maximum hop count for RIPv2 routes?

    A. 255

    B. 256

    C. 16

    D. 15

Correct Answer (D)
Subject Matter: RIPv2 for IPv4

The maximum hop count (metric) for the distance vector routing protocol RIPv2 is 15. That is the same maximum hop count as RIPv1. The packet is discarded at router hop 15.

22. What routing feature enables propagation of routing information between different routing protocols?

    A. route redistribution

    B. administrative distance

    C. access control list (ACL)

    D. route summarization

    E. policy-based routing

Correct Answer (A)
Subject Matter: Routing Concepts

Routers can advertise routes to different routing protocols such as between OSPF and EIGRP. The feature called redistribution enables specific routes and assigned metrics to be advertised between routing protocols. The metrics are configurable to prefer specific routes for instance.

23. What is cause for the interface operational status - administratively down, line protocol down?

> router# show interfaces serial 1/0
>
> *Serial 1/0 is administratively down, line protocol is down*

    A. interface Serial1/0 was manually shutdown

    B. line protocol error caused interface to shutdown

    C. wrong cable connected to the interface

    D. duplex setting mismatch between router interfaces

    E. clock signal from ISP not received

Correct Answer (A)
Subject Matter: Troubleshooting Layer 3 Connectivity

The network interface status becomes "administratively down" when the network engineer configures the **shutdown** command. It is an interface level IOS command that manually changes the interface to down. The interface status from show interface command lists the Ethernet interface (layer 1) first and line protocol (layer 2) second. It is not possible to have line protocol in **up** state when the interface is **down** (down/up).

24. There is a Metro Ethernet WAN interface on a router that isn't forwarding packets. What can you conclude based on the results of the following IOS command?

> router# show ip interface gigabitethernet 1/2
>
> *GigabitEthernet1/2 is up, line protocol is down*

A. **shutdown** command was issued on interface

B. there is a cabling issue

C. router cannot send route updates to the peering neighbor

D. router can only send (not receive) routing updates from the neighbor

E. IP address was configured correctly

Correct Answer (C)
Subject Matter: Troubleshooting Layer 3 Connectivity

The output from **show ip interface** will list the interface status. The normal operational status for any network interface is **up/up.** The example has the interface (layer 1) as **up** and line protocol (layer 2) as **down**. The Ethernet signaling is working and no issues exist with cabling. The problem is at the data link layer or higher. It is possible there is a routing or IP addressing issue at layer 3 however that is unknown.

25. The network route 172.16.1.0/24 is advertised from multiple sources. What route is considered the most reliable for 172.16.1.0/24?

A. EIGRP route to the same destination

B. OSPF route to the same destination

C. static route to the same destination

D. default route with a next hop address of 172.16.0.1

E. directly connected interface with an IP address of 172.16.1.254/24

F. the router will discard the route advertisement

Correct Answer (E)
Subject Matter: Administrative Distance

The administrative distance (AD) is a value based on the routing protocol and used by the router to select what route is installed in the global routing table. The route with the lowest AD is considered the most reliable (trustworthy). Directly connected routes have the lowest administrative distance (0) and are most reliable. The route is the interface of a connected neighbor router. Longest match rule selects the route with the longest network prefix. AD is the tie breaker for routes with the same prefix length to same destination. The metric is used for best path selection where there are multiple routes for the same routing protocol.

26. What is the next hop selected by Router-1 to forward packets from Host-1 to 192.168.2.0/24 subnet based on the routing table?

   router-1# show ip route

   Codes: C - connected, S - static, R - RIP, M - mobile, B - BGP
   D - EIGRP, EX - EIGRP external, O - OSPF, IA - OSPF inter area
   N1 - OSPF NSSA external type 1, N2 - OSPF NSSA external type 2
   E1 - OSPF external type 1, E2 - OSPF external type 2
   o - ODR, P - periodic downloaded static route

   Gateway of last resort is 172.16.0.1 to network 0.0.0.0

        172.16.0.0/24 is subnetted, 3 subnets, 2 masks
   C   172.16.1.0/24 is directly connected, Serial0/0
   C   172.16.2.0/24 is directly connected, Serial0/1
   C   172.16.3.128/27 is directly connected, GigabitEthernet0/0
        192.168.25.0/30 is subnetted, 2 subnets
   D   192.168.25.1 [90/2681856] via 192.168.25.2, 00:00:10, GigabitEthernet0/1
   D   192.168.25.4 [90/1823638] via 192.168.25.5, 00:00:50, GigabitEthernet0/2
        192.168.1.0/24 is variably subnetted, 3 subnets, 2 masks
   O   192.168.1.1/24 [110/8] via 192.168.1.254, GigabitEthernet0/3
   O   192.168.2.1/24 [110/11] via 192.168.2.2, Serial0/2
   O   192.168.3.64/30 [110/15] via 192.168.1.65, Serial0/3
   S*   0.0.0.0/0 [1/0] via 172.16.0.1

A. 192.168.2.2

B. 192.168.1.254

C. 192.168.1.0

D. 192.168.1.65

E. 172.16.0.1

F. 192.168.25.1

Correct Answer (A)
Subject Matter: Routing Concepts

The longest match rule would select the following OSPF route with next hop 192.168.2.2 IP address.

O 192.168.2.1/24 [110/11] via 192.168.2.2, Serial0/2

27. What IOS command is used to show the operational status of an interface?

A. show interfaces [type] [module/slot/port]

B. show run interfaces

C. show ip protocols

D. show interfaces hardware

Correct Answer (A)
Subject Matter: Troubleshooting Layer 3 Connectivity

The following is correct IOS command syntax for showing the status of a specific network interface:

router# show interfaces [type] [module/slot/port]

The type is Ethernet and module/slot/port is based on the interface hardware such as **show interfaces gigabitethernet 1/0/0** for example.

28. Select the correct IOS command to manually assign an IPv6 address to a router interface?

A. ipv6 auto ::1/64

B. ipv6 address 2001:43AD:21AF:4F32::32/64

C. ipv6 autoconfig 2001:43AD:21AF:2D71::32 /64

D. ipv6 autoconfig

Correct Answer (B)
Subject Matter: IPv6 Addressing

The following interface level IOS command assigns a static IPv6 address to a router interface.

router(config-if)# ipv6 address 2001:43AD:21AF:4F32::32/64

The IPv6 address is manually assigned to an interface. There is dynamic IP address Stateless Autoconfiguration with SLAAC and DHCPv6 server as well.

29. Match the routing protocol on the left with the correct administrative distance on the right?

RIPv2	1
OSPF	0
External EIGRP	170
Internal BGP (iBGP)	110
Internal EIGRP	90
Directly Connected	200
Static Route	120

Correct Answers.
Subject Matter: Administrative Distance

The following are the default administrative distances for each routing protocol and/or route type. Each routing entry in the routing table includes the administrative distance and metric in brackets.

RIPv2	**120**
OSPF	**110**
External EIGRP	**170**
Internal BGP (iBGP)	**200**
Internal EIGRP	**90**
Directly Connected	**0**
Static Route	**1**

30. Refer to the network topology drawing. How will Router-1 forward packets from 172.16.3.0/24 to 172.16.2.0/24 with EIGRP enabled on all routers and default settings? (select two)

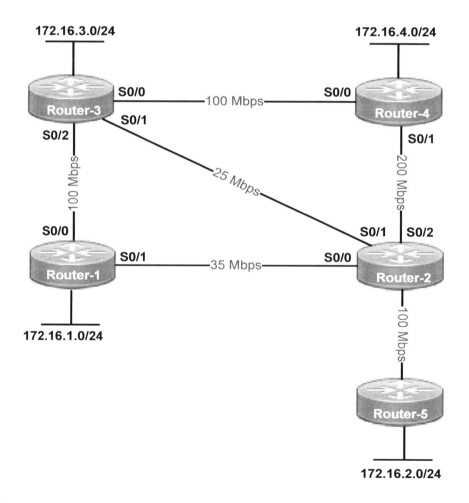

A. Router-3 - Router-4 - Router-2 - Router-5

B. Router-3 - Router-1 - Router-2 - Router-5

C. Router-3 - Router-2 - Router-5

D. Path 1: Router-3 - Router-4 - Router-2 - Router-5
   Path 2: Router-3 - Router-1 - Router-2 - Router-5

E. lowest metric

F. highest metric

Correct Answers (A,E)
Subject Matter: EIGRP for IPv4

EIGRP selects the path between source and destination based on lowest metric when there are multiple routes to the same destination. The bandwidth and delay are the defaults used to calculate metric value. The delay is a fixed value based on interface speed. The link bandwidth isn't cumulative with EIGRP. There are multiple paths from 172.16.3.0 (source) to 172.16.2.0 (destination). Each path between source and destination is comprised of multiple individual links. EIGRP examines the links and determines the lowest bandwidth link for each path. The path that has the highest bandwidth (lowest metric) from among all lowest bandwidth links is selected (bolded path).

Router-3 -> Router-4 -> Router-2 -> Router-5 = 100 Mbps

Router-3 -> Router-1 -> Router-2 -> Router-5 = 35 Mbps

Router-3 -> Router-2 -> Router-5 = 25 Mbps

EIGRP does support load balancing across unequal links to the same destination with the variance feature. The default for EIGRP is equal-cost (metric) load balancing.

31. EIGRP, OSPF and RIPv2 are advertising routes to the same destination. What route is selected based on the following routing table information?

    EIGRP = [90/1252335]

    OSPF = [110/10]

    RIPv2 = [120/3]

A. OSPF route

B. EIGRP route

C. RIPv2 route

D. all three routes are installed

E. OSPF and RIPv2 routes

Correct Answer (B)
Subject Matter: Administrative Distance

The route with the lowest administrative distance will be installed in the routing table. Internal EIGRP (90) has a lower administrative distance than OSPF (110) or RIPv2 (120). The result is the EIGRP route is selected for the global routing table. The metric is only considered for best path calculation when multiple routes exist to the same destination.

32. Refer to the network topology drawing. What route when configured on Router-1 will forward all internet traffic to Router-2?

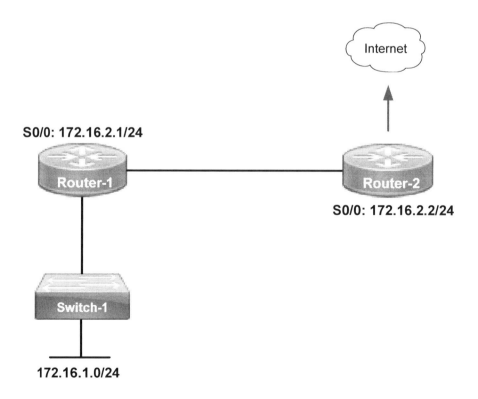

A. ip route 0.0.0.0 0.0.0.0 172.16.2.2

B. ip route 0.0.0.0 255.255.255.0 172.16.2.2

C. ip route 0.0.0.0 0.0.0.0 172.16.2.1

D. ip route 172.16.2.1 255.255.0.0 172.16.2.2

Correct Answer (A)
Subject Matter: IPv4 Static Routing

The default route will forward all traffic to the configured next hop IP address (172.16.2.2). Packets arriving at Router-1 will use the default route when there is no route in the routing table . It is typically configured as a gateway of last resort on a router. Router-1 will forward packets with an unknown destination to the serial interface of Router-2.

router-1(config)# ip route 0.0.0.0 0.0.0.0 172.16.2.2

33. Refer to the network topology drawing. There are no dynamic routing protocols currently running on any of the routers. The network administrator must allow traffic between hosts on subnet 172.16.10.0/24 and hosts on 10.64.1.0/24. What two solutions are preferred that is easiest to manage?

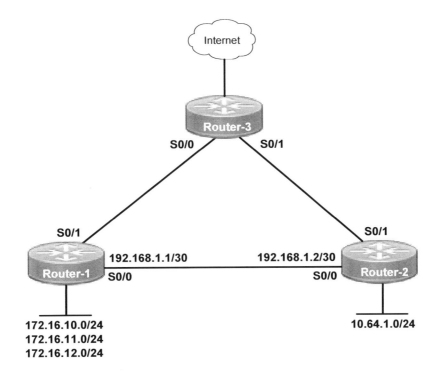

A. enable link-state routing on all routers

B. default routes on Router-1 and Router-2

C. static route on Router-1 with next hop 192.168.1.2/30 to Router-2

D. static route on Router-1 with higher administrative distance to 192.168.1.2/30

E. static route on Router-2 with next hop of 192.168.1.1/30 to Router-1

F. enable distance vector routing protocol on all routers

Correct Answers (C,E)
Subject Matter: IPv4 Static Routing

The static route is more specific than a default route. The static route says - *to reach this destination subnet forward packets to this next hop address.* The default route says - *forward all traffic to this next hop when no route to the destination exists in the routing table.*

The specific subnet would use the next hop as neighbor network interface IP address or local router interface. Static routes are required at both routers as well to route (forward) in both directions.

34. Select two advantages of static routing compared with dynamic routing?

A. increased security with managed route advertisements and routing table changes

B. configuration complexity decreases as network size increases

C. routing updates dynamically advertised to neighbors

D. bandwidth utilization is reduced with static routes

E. route summarization

F. routing table is updated with topology changes

Correct Answers (A,D)
Subject Matter: Compare Static and Dynamic Routing

The deployment of static routes is preferable where security is of the utmost concern. That would include for instance links between internet routers and firewalls. In addition there is the advantage of less bandwidth utilization. The static route is added to the routing table and doesn't require updating unless there is a link failure. Dynamic routing protocols send messages between router links to advertise routes and for state information. That requires additional bandwidth that increases with multipoint links.

35. Refer to the network drawing. Select two IOS commands that when configured on Router-1 provide a static route to network 172.16.12.0/24 on Router-3?

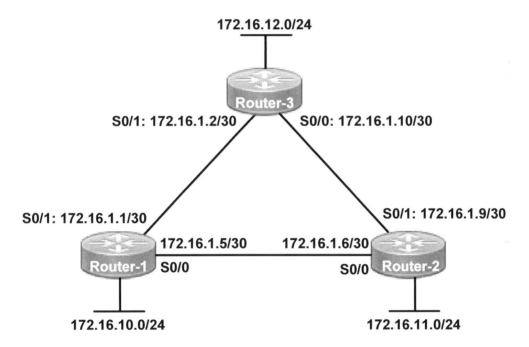

A. router-1(config)# ip route 172.16.12.0 0.0.0.255 S0/0

B. router-1(config)# ip route 172.16.12.0 255.255.255.0 172.16.1.2

C. router-1(config)# ip route 172.16.12.0 0.0.0.255 172.16.1.1

D. router-1(config)# ip route 172.16.12.0 255.255.255.0 S0/1

E. router-1(config)# ip route 172.16.12.1 0.0.0.255 172.16.1.1

F. router-1(config)# ip route 0.0.0.0 255.255.255.255 172.16.1.2

Correct Answers (B,D)
Subject Matter: IPv4 Static Routing

The following are two options for configuring a static route on Router-1 to network 172.16.12.0/24

    router-1(config)# ip route 172.16.12.0 255.255.255.0 172.16.1.2
    router-1(config)# ip route 172.16.12.0 255.255.255.0 Serial0/1

The first static route command configures the next hop as the IP address of a neighbor router interface (172.16.1.2). The second static route command configures the next hop as an exit interface (Serial0/1) on Router-1.

Wildcard masks are not used when configuring static routes. The correct format for a static route configured on a router is the following:

ip route [destination IP address] [subnet mask] [next hop IP address] [interface]

36. What two message types are used by OSPF to build and maintain its topology database?

    A. link-state ACK

    B. routing tables update

    C. SPF packets

    D. hello packets

    E. route flooding packet

    F. link-state advertisements

Correct Answers (D,F)
Subject Matter: OSPFv2 for IPv4

The OSPF link-state routing protocol builds and maintains a topology database. The hello packets and LSAs are used for that purpose. The hello packets discover neighbors and establish neighbor adjacencies first. The LSAs are exchanged between all OSPF routers to build the topology database. That is used for best path selection.

37. Select three characteristics of a link-state routing protocol?

A. utilizes frequent periodic updates

B. provides global view of enterprise network topology

C. hop count = 15

D. exchange routing table with neighbors at fixed intervals

E. utilizes event-triggered routing updates

F. calculates shortest path (lowest cost)

Correct Answers (B,E,F)
Subject Matter: Distance Vector and Link-State Routing Protocols

OSPF is a link-state routing protocol that builds an enterprise level topology database with link-state information. The link types along with path cost are used for selecting the shortest path. They are the routes installed in the routing table and designated as best path routes. There is no exchange of routing tables at specific intervals as with distance vector protocols (RIPv2). OSPF sends event-triggered updates only such as when a link failure occurs to conserve bandwidth.

38. Refer to the routing table. According to the routing table entries, where will Router-1 send a packet destined for 172.16.1.128/27?

    router-1# show ip route

    Codes: C - connected, S - static, R - RIP, M - mobile, B - BGP
        D - EIGRP, EX - EIGRP external, O - OSPF, IA - OSPF inter area
        N1 - OSPF NSSA external type 1, N2 - OSPF NSSA external type 2
        E1 - OSPF external type 1, E2 - OSPF external type 2
        o - ODR, P - periodic downloaded static route

    Gateway of last resort is 172.16.0.1 to network 0.0.0.0

        172.16.0.0/24 is subnetted, 3 subnets, 3 masks
    C   172.16.1.128/25 is directly connected, Serial0/1
    C   172.16.1.128/26 is directly connected, Serial0/1
    C   172.16.1.128/27 is directly connected, GigabitEthernet0/0
        172.16.254.0/24 is subnetted, 1 subnet

A. 172.16.1.128/25

B. 172.16.1.128/27

C. 172.16.1.128/26

D. 172.16.0.0/24

Correct Answer (B)
Subject Matter: Routing Concepts

The administrative distance (AD) is a value based on the routing protocol and used by the router to **select what route is installed in the routing table.** The route with the lowest administrative is preferred. AD is the tie breaker for routes with the same subnet (prefix) mask length to the same destination.

The longest match rule is used to **select a route already installed in the routing table** as a forwarding decision. Each route to a destination has a specific prefix (subnet) length. The route with the longest prefix is selected from multiple routes to the same destination. For instance 172.16.1.128/27 has a longer prefix than 172.16.1.128/26 and 172.16.1.128/25. As a result it is used to forward packets to that network destination. The lowest metric is used for best path selection where there are multiple routes to the same destination for the same routing protocol.

39. Based on the source of the advertised routes, what route to 192.168.10.0/24 is considered most reliable?

A. static route to network 192.168.10.0/24

B. OSPF route to 192.168.0.0/16

C. directly connected interface with IP address 192.168.10.254/24

D. default route with a next hop address of 192.168.10.1

E. static router to network 192.168.10.0/24 with a local serial interface configured as the next hop

F. RIPv2 update for network 192.168.10.0/24

Correct Answer (C)
Subject Matter: Administrative Distance

All routing sources are advertising a route to the same destination subnet. The route with the lowest administrative distance (AD) is installed in the routing table. The directly connected route, with an administrative distance of zero (0) is considered the most reliable among routes to the same destination. The subnet length is only considered when selecting from multiple routes to the same destination already installed in the routing table. It is commonly referred to as the longest match rule.

40. What two primary activities are performed by a router when forwarding a packet?

    A. updates the source and destination IP address of IP header

    B. forwards packet out the required egress interface

    C. forwards ARP requests

    D. updates the destination IP address of IP header

    E. determines the next hop IP address to forward packet

Correct Answers (B,E)
Subject Matter: Routing Concepts

The router does a routing table lookup of an ingress packet based on the destination IP address. The next hop IP address is obtained from the routing table and the packet is forwarded out the proper local interface. In addition source and destination MAC addressing is updated in the frame header.

41. Refer to the network topology drawing. What is the easiest and fastest technique available to enable routing between the branch office and the corporate data center?

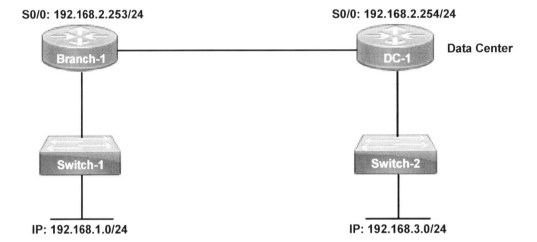

S0/0: 192.168.2.253/24   **S0/0: 192.168.2.254/24**

IP: 192.168.1.0/24   **IP: 192.168.3.0/24**

A. branch-1(config)# ip route 192.168.1.0 255.255.255.0 S0/0

B. branch-1(config)# ip route 192.168.2.253 255.255.255.0 192.168.1.0

C. branch-1(config)# ip route 192.168.2.253 255.255.255.0 192.168.2.254

D. branch-1(config)# ip route 0.0.0.0 0.0.0.0 192.168.2.254

Correct Answer (D)
Subject Matter: IPv4/IPv6 Static Routing

The easiest and most popular solution for connecting a branch office to a data center is with a default route. In the context of routing protocols it is referred to as a stub router. The branch office router (Branch-1) is sometimes called a stub router. All packets with an external destination is forwarded to the data center and there is no transit routing permitted.

The following is the IOS global command syntax for configuring a default route. All traffic is forwarded to the next hop ip address. That is the IP address of the data center router (DC-1) S0/0 interface.

branch-1(config)# ip route 0.0.0.0 0.0.0.0 192.168.2.254

All other options provided are static routes that point to a specific destination route or router interface. The packet is forwarded only when there is a match on the destination IP address. The default route will forward all packets arriving for any destination IP address to the next hop IP address.

226

42. Refer to the network topology drawing. Select the correct IOS command to configure a floating (backup) static route on router Branch-1 to network address 192.168.3.1/24?

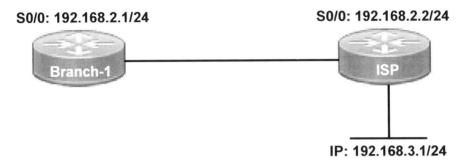

S0/0: 192.168.2.1/24   **S0/0: 192.168.2.2/24**

IP: 192.168.3.1/24

A. branch-1(config)# ip address 192.168.3.1 255.255.255.0 192.168.2.1

B. branch-1(config)# ip route 192.168.3.1 255.255.255.0 192.168.2.2 200

C. branch-1(config)# ip route 192.168.3.1 255.255.255.255 192.168.2.2 1

D. branch-1(config)# ip route 0.0.0.0/0 192.168.3.1

Correct Answer (B)
Subject Matter: IPv4 Static Routing

The following IOS command will configure a backup static route (floating) on Branch-1 to subnet 192.168.3.1/24 with an administrative distance of 200.

router-1(config)# ip route 192.168.3.1 255.255.255.0 192.168.2.2 200

- destination IP address (route) = 192.168.3.1
- subnet mask = 255.255.255.0 (/24)
- next hop IP address = 192.168.2.2
- administrative distance = 200

Traffic destined for subnet 192.168.3.1 is forwarded to next hop 192.168.2.2. The administrative distance is a local value and affects route selection. The default administrative distance for a static route is 1. Assigning a value of 200 to the static route makes it a floating static route. That is often used as a backup route when a primary link fails.

43. Select the statement that best describes the effect of this IOS command?

router-1(config)# ip route 172.33.64.1 255.255.255.224 172.33.1.2

A. IP address 172.33.64.1 is local to router-1

B. configures a gateway of last resort for router-1

C. packets with destination IP address 172.33.64.1 are forwarded to next hop IP address 172.33.1.2

D. default route for packets with destination IP address 172.33.1.2 are forwarded to next hop IP address 172.33.64.1

E. packets with destination IP address 172.33.1.2 are forwarded to next hop IP address 172.33.64.1

Correct Answer (C)
Subject Matter: IPv4 Static Routing

The IOS command is a static route. All packets with destination IP address 172.33.64.1 are forwarded to next hop 172.33.1.2

router-1(config)# ip route 172.33.64.1 255.255.255.224 172.33.1.2

44. What two activities do routers perform on packets?

A. examines the Layer 3 IP header and select the complete path for packet routing to the endpoint destination

B. updates the Layer 3 IP header of outbound packets to forward packets to the valid next hop

C. updates the Layer 3 IP header of outbound packets so they are forwarded to the endpoint destination

D. updates the Layer 2 headers of outbound packets with the MAC address of the next hop

E. examines the Layer 3 IP header address field and use that to determine the next hop forwarding

F. examines the Layer 2 frame header of inbound packets and use that to select the next hop

Correct Answers (D,E)
Subject Matter: Routing Concepts

The primary purpose of the router is to forward packets based on best path selection. The router does a routing table lookup based on destination IP address from the IP header. The packet is then forwarded to the next hop address associated with the selected best route. In addition the source and destination MAC addresses are updated (rewritten). The source MAC address is the local outbound router interface. The destination MAC address is the MAC address of the next hop (neighbor) router interface.

45. Select two IOS commands that have the correct syntax for a default route?

    A. router(config)# ip route 0.0.0.0/0 192.168.1.2

    B. router(config)# ip route 0.0.0.0 0.0.0.0 Serial0/0

    C. router(config-router)# ip route 0.0.0.0 0.0.0.0 Serial0/0

    D. router(config)# ip route 0.0.0.0 255.255.255.0 192.168.1.2

Correct Answers (A,B)
Subject Matter: IPv4 Default Routing

There are three standard formats allowed when configuring a default route. The correct answers are option A and option B.

    router(config)# ip route 0.0.0.0 0.0.0.0 [next hop ip address]

The match any IP address and subnet mask of 0.0.0.0 0.0.0.0 can be summarized to 0.0.0.0/0 for option A. The next hop IP address can be specified as an IP address or router local interface (Serial0/0) for option B.

    router(config)# ip route 0.0.0.0/0 192.168.1.2
    router(config)# ip route 0.0.0.0 0.0.0.0 Serial0/0

46. What two IOS commands provide basic layer 1 and layer 2 interface status including IP address?

A. router# show protocols

B. router# show controllers

C. router# show version

D. router# show running-config

E. router# show interfaces

Correct Answers (A,E)
Subject Matter: Troubleshooting Layer 3 Connectivity

The following IOS commands can verify interface and line protocol status for a router interface:

router# show interfaces
router# show protocols

Example:

The interface (ethernet, serial etc.) status is the layer 1 signaling and line protocol is the data link (layer 2) for router interface GigabitEthernet1/1.

router# show interfaces gigabitethernet 1/1

GigabitEthernet 1/1 **up**, *line protocol* **up** *(normal state)*

Typical Causes:

Layer 1 = cabling issues
Layer 2 = encapsulation mismatch, clocking errors

47. Refer to the network topology drawing. Host-1 and Server-1 are assigned to the same VLAN. Select two correct statements from the following?

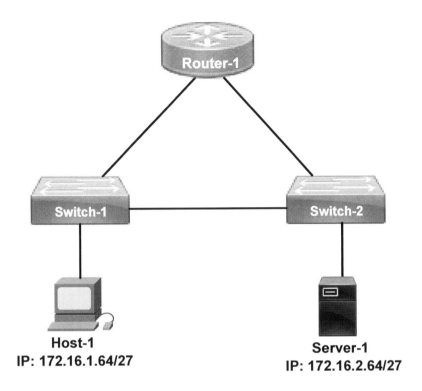

Host-1
IP: 172.16.1.64/27

Server-1
IP: 172.16.2.64/27

A. Router-1 is required for Host-1 to communicate with Server-1

B. trunk between switches allows Host-1 to communicate with Server-1

C. Router-1 is not required for Host-1 to communicate with Server-1

D. Host-1 and Server-1 must be assigned to the same VLAN

E. multiple VLANs require trunks between each switch and Router-1

Correct Answers (A,E)
Subject Matter: Inter-VLAN Routing

Host-1 and Server-1 are on different subnets. As a result routing is required to forward packets between subnets. The layer 2 switches do not provide routing services including ARP requests. Switch-1 with no default gateway configured (router) would drop any packet that is not on the switch subnet. Assigning Host-1 and Server-1 to the same or different VLANs would not enable communication between them.

48. What two IOS commands will verify the operational status of all router interfaces?

A. router# show ip protocols

B. router# show ip interface brief

C. router# show interfaces

D. router# show run interfaces

E. router# debug interface

Correct Answers (B,C)
Subject Matter: Troubleshooting Layer 3 Connectivity

The operational status of router interfaces can be verified with the following IOS commands:

    router# show interfaces
    router# show ip interface brief

The **show ip interface brief** lists unconfigured interfaces as an unassigned IP address with status of down/down. The normal status is an assigned IP address with status of up/up. The **show interfaces** command lists the interface status and configuration settings.

49. What IOS command will configure an interface with the IP address 172.16.1.1/19?

A. router(config-if)# ip address 172.16.1.1/19

B. router(config-if)# ip address 172.16.1.1 255.255.0.0

C. router(config-if)# ip address 172.16.1.1 255.255.255.0

D. router(config-if)# ip address 172.16.1.1 255.255.192.0

E. router(config-if)# ip address 172.16.1.1 255.255.224.0

F. router(config-if)# ip address 172.16.1.1 255.255.255.224

Correct Answer (E)
Subject Matter: IPv4 Addressing

The IP address and subnet mask is assigned to a router interface. The following is standard IOS syntax for assigning 172.16.1.1/19 to an Ethernet interface.

```
router# conf t
router(config)# interface gigabitethernet0/0
router(config-if)# ip address 172.16.1.1 255.255.224.0
router(config-if)# end
```

50. Refer to the routing table output for router-1. How will router-1 forward a packet with source IP address 172.16.3.1 and destination IP address 172.16.200.1?

    router-1# show ip route

    Codes: C - connected, S - static, R - RIP, M - mobile, B - BGP
        D - EIGRP, EX - EIGRP external, O - OSPF, IA - OSPF inter area
        N1 - OSPF NSSA external type 1, N2 - OSPF NSSA external type 2
        E1 - OSPF external type 1, E2 - OSPF external type 2
        o - ODR, P - periodic downloaded static route

    Gateway of last resort is not set

        172.16.0.0/24 is subnetted, 4 subnets
    C   172.16.1.0 is directly connected, Serial0/0
    C   172.16.2.0 is directly connected, Serial0/1
    C   172.16.3.0 is directly connected, GigabitEthernet0/0
    C   172.16.4.0 is directly connected, GigabitEthernet0/1
    S   172.16.100.0/24 [1/0] via 172.16.2.1
    R   172.31.1.0/24 [120/3] via 172.16.1.2

    A. send routing update request to neighbor router

    B. forward packet using the default route

    C. send ARP request for MAC address of remote host

    D. discard packet and send ICMP *destination unreachable* error message

    E. forward packet to upstream default gateway

Correct Answer (D)
Subject Matter: Routing Concepts

The router makes a forwarding decision based on the destination IP address. There is currently no route advertised for 172.16.200.1 in the routing table of router-1. In addition there is no default route (gateway of last resort) configured either. The router will discard the packet and send an ICMP *destination unreachable* error message.

51. What route type is assigned to the IP address of a router interface?

    A. default route

    B. dynamic route

    C. null route

    D. directly connected

    E. static routing

Correct Answer (D)
Subject Matter: Routing Table Components

The directly connected route refers to the network interface of a directly connected neighbor. The next hop is the IP address assigned to that interface.

52. What are two common characteristics of a distance vector routing protocol?

    A. algorithm based on least cost is used for selecting best path

    B. routing table updates are based on routing advertisements from neighbors

    C. full routing table updates are sent at fixed intervals to neighbor routers

    D. send only routing table changes to connected neighbors

    E. send only routing table changes to all routers on the same network segment

Correct Answers (B,C)
Subject Matter: Distance Vector Routing Protocols

The router running a distance vector routing protocol such as RIPv2 will send routing table updates at regular intervals to neighbors. In addition the routing table is updated based on route advertisements from neighbors.

53. The network administrator has enabled IP routing. What two IOS commands are required to set the gateway of last resort to the default gateway?

A. ip default-network 0.0.0.0

B. ip default-route 0.0.0.0 0.0.0.0 172.16.2.1

C. ip default-gateway 0.0.0.0

D. ip route 0.0.0.0 0.0.0.0 172.16.2.1

E. ip route 172.16.2.1 0.0.0.0 0.0.0.0

Correct Answers (A,D)
Subject Matter: Routing Table Components

The network engineer would enable routing on a router or layer 3 switch. The IOS command **ip default-network** assigns a gateway of last resort for a classful subnet when routing is enabled. The dynamic routing protocol advertises the network address as a default route to neighbor routers. For instance the IOS command **ip default-network 192.168.64.0** would advertise routes to 192.168.64.0 subnet as the gateway of last resort for the router.

The default route is configured with **ip route 0.0.0.0 0.0.0.0 192.168.64.1** to forward all packets to that next hop IP address. As a result, the packets that do not match any route are forwarded to next hop 192.168.64.1 (gateway of last resort). The standard default route applies to all routing protocols and has a default administrative distance of 1.

The **ip default-gateway** command is assigned with layer 2 switches. It assigns an upstream router as default gateway based on a network address. The network address assigned is typically the Ethernet interface connected to the switch. The default gateway IP address must be in the same subnet as the assigned hosts and management SVI unless Inter-VLAN routing is configured.

54. What is the easiest method to enable routing between four VLANs where there are two switches and a single router?

A. router-on-a-stick configuration

B. enable routing on a layer 2 switch

C. configure SVIs on the switches

D. configure a default gateway on each switch

E. configure trunking between the switches and allow all VLANs

Correct Answer (A)
Subject Matter: Inter-VLAN Routing

There are four VLANs defines on a switch with a requirement to extend them to the router for Inter-VLAN routing. Router-on-a-stick is a solution for enabling Inter-VLAN routing.

1. Configure a routed interface and define four subinterfaces on a router physical Ethernet interface.

2. Assign a VLAN to each subinterface on the router Ethernet interface.

3. Create a trunk on the switch and allow the four VLANs.

55. Refer to the network topology drawing. What is the TTL value at points 1,2,3 and 4 when Host-1 pings Server-1?

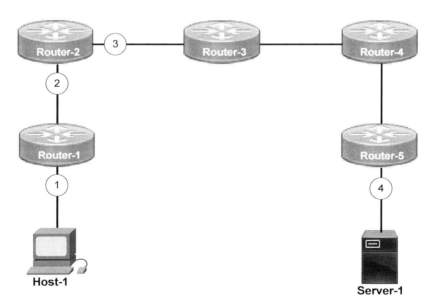

A. P1 = 255
   P2 = 254
   P3 = 253
   P4 = 250

B. P1 = 254
   P2 = 253
   P3 = 252
   P4 = 251

C. P1 = 255
   P2 = 255
   P3 = 254
   P4 = 252

D. P1 = 255
   P2 = 254
   P3 = 254
   P4 = 251

Correct Answer (A)
Subject Matter: Routing Concepts

The TTL value of an IP packet when it arrives at Router-1 is the default 255. The TTL is decremented by one only when it is forwarded (egress). As a result the TTL is decremented by Router-1 to 254 when it is forwarded to Router-2. The TTL is 253 when it arrives at Router-3. The TTL is 250 when it arrives at the egress interface connected to Server-1

P1 = 255

P2 = 254

P3 = 253

P4 = 250

56. Refer to the network topology drawing and output of the following IOS command. There is no dynamic routing configured on the routers. Host-1 cannot communicate with Server-1. The network administrator can ping from Server-2 to Host-1. Identify the cause of the problem based on the information provided?

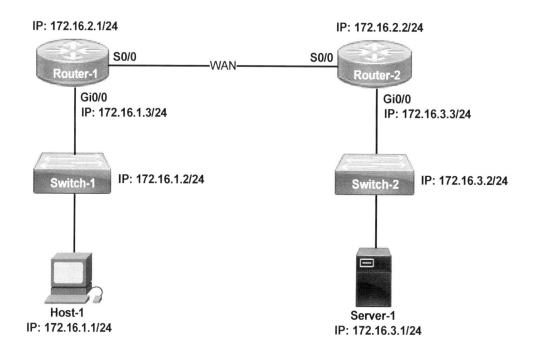

router-1# show ip route

Codes: C - connected, S - static, R - RIP, M - mobile, B - BGP
    D - EIGRP, EX - EIGRP external, O - OSPF, IA - OSPF inter area
    N1 - OSPF NSSA external type 1, N2 - OSPF NSSA external type 2
    E1 - OSPF external type 1, E2 - OSPF external type 2
    o - ODR, P - periodic downloaded static route

Gateway of last resort is 172.33.0.1 to network 0.0.0.0

        172.16.0.0/24 is subnetted, 1 subnet
C   172.16.1.0/24 is directly connected, GigabitEthernet0/0
        172.16.254.0/32 is subnetted, 1 subnet
C   172.16.254.1 is directly connected, Loopback0
S   172.16.3.0/24 [1/0] via GigabitEthernet0/0
S*   0.0.0.0/0 [1/0] via 172.33.0.1

A. incorrect IP address on Router-1

B. static route configuration error

C. default route configuration error

D. interface Serial0/0 is administratively shutdown

E. no route to Host-1

Correct Answer (B)
Subject Matter: Troubleshooting Layer 3 Connectivity

There is no dynamic routing configured on the routers however the network administrator can ping from Server-1 to Host-1. There is either a default route or a static route configured on Router-2 enabling connectivity to Router-1. There is a static route configured on Router-1 noted from the output of **show ip route.** The gateway of last resort (172.33.0.1) forwards packets to any unknown destination. There is a static route listed in the routing table to 172.16.3.0 however it is incorrect. The static route incorrectly forwards packets destined for Server-1 subnet (172.16.3.0) to Switch-1 via Gi0/0 interface.

S   172.16.3.0/24 [1/0] via GigabitEthernet0/0

57. What three statements correctly describe a static route?

A. administrative distance = 1

B. static route is added to global routing table

C. next hop is local interface or IP address

D. administrative distance = 0

E. static route is never part of the longest match rule

Correct Answers (A,B,C)
Subject Matter: IPv4 Static Routing

The static route is a manually configured route added to the global routing table. It has an administrative distance of 1 making it a preferred route over dynamically learned routes. The static route is configured from global configuration mode. The next hop to a destination subnet is configured as an IP address or local exit interface.

58. What three statements correctly describe default routing?

    A. gateway of last resort for packets with an unknown destination

    B. typically used to forward packets to the internet or from a stub router

    C. administrative distance = 1

    D. administrative distance = 0

    E. administrative distance = 255

Correct Answers (A,B,C)
Subject Matter: IPv4/IPv6 Static Routing

The default route is referred to as gateway of last resort packet forwarding. Any route, where no match exists, is forwarded to the default route next hop address. In the context of a router, the default route is often configured to forward packets to the internet. The administrative distance of a default route is 1 (the same as a static route).

59. Select four statements that accurately describe routing and path selection?

    A. administrative distance is configurable to influence routing

    B. route 192.168.24.0/24 is preferable to 192.168.24.0/27

    C. longest match rule determines what route is selected in the routing table when there are multiple routes to the same destination

    D. summarization increases the size of a routing table

    E. administrative distance determines the route installed in the routing table

    F. administrative distance is a value based on the routing protocol

Correct Answer (A,C,E,F)
Subject Matter: Routing Concepts

The router builds a routing table with multiple routes (prefixes). The routes are assigned an administrative distance and metric cost.

Route Selection:
The administrative distance is based on dynamic routing protocol. Metric is a path cost assigned to a specific route. The administrative distance and metric assigned to a route will determine **what route is installed in the routing table.**

The router installs the route with the lowest administrative distance. The route with the lowest metric is installed when there are multiple routes from the same routing protocol to the same destination. Administrative distance is configurable to influence route selection.

Packet Forwarding:

The longest match rule is used to **select a route installed in the routing table as a forwarding decision.** Each route to a destination has a specific prefix (subnet) length. The route with the longest prefix is selected from multiple routes to the same destination. For instance 172.16.0.0/22 has a longer prefix than 172.16.0.0/18 and used to forward packets to that network destination.

60. What is the primary difference between RIPv1 and RIPv2 routing protocols?

    A. RIPv2 supports CIDR (slash notation) for a subnet prefix

    B. RIPv2 supports hop count of 15

    C. RIPv2 has administrative distance of 120

    D. RIPv2 sends routing table updates at 30 second intervals to 224.0.0.9

    E. none of the above

Correct Answer (A)
Subject Matter: RIPv2 for IPv4

The primary enhancement to RIPv2 is support for VLSM's referred to as classless subnets (CIDR). That enables advertisement of subnet mask length with routing advertisements. In addition there is MD5 authentication of RIPv2 routes between routers for optimized security. RIPv2 sends routing table updates as a multicast to 224.0.0.9 instead of a broadcast used with RIPv1.

61. What three statements accurately describe the TTL field of an IP header?

    A. IP header field decrements each time a packet traverses a router

    B. support for layer 2 switches

    C. default value for the TTL count in the IP header = 1

    D. prevents routing loops as packet is dropped after TTL value decrements to zero

    E. default value for the TTL count in the IP header = 255

Correct Answers (A,D,E)
Subject Matter: Routing Concepts

The purpose of Time-to-Live (TTL) is to limit the number of hops an IP packet can traverse. The TTL field of the IP header is decremented by one for each router hop. The packet is discarded after 255 hops to prevent a routing loop.

62. Select three correct statements concerning split horizon feature?

    A. prevents routing loops

    B. enabled by default for RIPv2 and EIGRP

    C. routes learned from an interface cannot be advertised to that same interface

    D. prevents route redistribution between RIPv2 and OSPF

    E. prevents layer 2 and layer 3 routing loops

    F. routes can be advertised to subinterfaces

Correct Answers (A,B,C)
Subject Matter: Distance Vector Routing Protocols

The purpose of split horizon is to prevent routing loops. It is enabled as a feature of distance vector routing protocols. It prevents routes from being advertised on the same interface where they were learned.

63. What two statements accurately describe route poisoning operation?

    A. increases hop count of a route so it is larger than the maximum hop count and advertises route to neighbor as unreachable

    B. prevents routing loops

    C. decreases the hop count to zero

    D. decreases route convergence

    E. supported by link-state routing protocols only

Correct Answers (A,B)
Subject Matter: Distance Vector Routing Protocols

The purpose of route poisoning is to prevent routing loops. The hop count for a route is increased so it is larger than the maximum supported. The router advertises the route to a neighbor as unreachable. It is a feature of distance vector routing protocols.

64. Select the three statements that contrast link-state and distance vector routing protocols?

   A. distance vector protocols are preferred where there are less router hops while link-state protocols are more scalable with unlimited hop count

   B. distance vector protocols have a higher convergence time

   C. distance vector protocols advertise full routing table updates while link-state protocols advertise only new route changes

   D. load balancing isn't supported with distance vector protocols

   E. link-state protocols use split horizon, route poisoning and holddown timer to prevent routing loops

   F. distance vector protocols have a lower convergence time

Correct Answers (A,B,C)
Subject Matter: Distance Vector and Link-State Routing Protocols

The following describe the differences between distance vector and link-state routing protocols.

Distance Vector Routing Protocols
- RIPv2
- Metric = hop count
- Regular routing table updates to neighbors
- Slower network convergence
- Small network
- Not scalable

Link-State Routing Protocols
- OSPF, IS-IS
- Metric = path cost (bandwidth)
- Event-triggered routing updates
- Enterprise network
- Scalable

65. Select two statements that describe EIGRP holddown timer operation?

   A. holddown timer is the wait time interval before adverting the same route to the EIGRP neighbor

   B. default setting is when three hello packets are not sent from an EIGRP neighbor

   C. holddown timer is the time interval that EIGRP router waits before declaring the neighbor unreachable

   D. amount of time equal to five hello packets the EIGRP router waits before declaring the neighbor unreachable

   E. hello timer and holddown timer must match between EIGRP neighbors

Correct Answers (B,C)
Subject Matter: EIGRP

EIGRP holddown timer affects how fast the network converges when there is a link failure. Each router interface enabled with EIGRP sends hello packets to its EIGRP neighbors. The default holddown timer value is equivalent to three hello packets not sent from a neighbor. That is the time interval that EIGRP waits before declaring the neighbor unreachable.

66. What IOS commands enable OSPF for IPv4 routing and assign a network subnet address (prefix) to advertise?

   A. R1(config)# router ospf [process id]
      R1(config-router)# network [ip address] [wildcard mask] area [number]

   B. R1(config)# router ospf [process id]
      R1(config-router)# network [ip address] [subnet mask] area [number]

   C. R1(config)# router ospf
      R1(config-router)# network area [ip address] [wildcard mask]

   D. R1(config)# ospf [process id]
      R1(config-router)# network [ip address] [wildcard mask] area [number]

Correct Answer (A)
Subject Matter: OSPFv2 for IPv4

The following IOS global commands will enable OSPF IPv4 on a router and assign a network subnet address (prefix) to advertise.

R1(config)# router ospf [process id]
R1(config-router)# network [ip address] [wildcard mask] area [number]

67. The following static routes are configured on router-1. Match the destination route on the left with next hop address on the right?

router-1(config)# ip route 0.0.0.0 0.0.0.0 192.168.1.1
router-1(config)# ip route 10.1.0.0 255.255.255.0 192.168.2.2
router-1(config)# ip route 10.1.0.0 255.255.0.0 192.168.3.3

10.1.1.10	192.168.3.3
10.1.0.14	192.168.3.3
10.5.8.4	192.168.1.1
10.1.4.6	192.168.2.2
10.2.1.3	192.168.2.2
10.1.0.123	192.168.1.1

Correct Answers.
Subject Matter: IPv4 Static Routing

The static route is comprised of a destination subnet (prefix), subnet mask and next hop address for packet forwarding. The subnet mask length determines the static route selected based on longest match rule.

10.1.1.10   192.168.3.3 (longest match rule **10.1**.0.0/16)

10.1.0.14   192.168.2.2 (longest match rule selects **10.1.0**.0/24)

10.2.1.3   192.168.1.1 (no matching route rule selects default route)

10.1.4.6   192.168.3.3 (longest match rule **10.1**.0.0/16)

10.1.0.12   192.168.2.2 (longest match rule selects **10.1.0**.0/24)

10.5.8.4   192.168.1.1 (no matching route rule selects default route)

68. What network performance metric/s are used to calculate OSPF cost?

A. bandwidth, MTU, reliability, delay and load

B. bandwidth, delay and MTU

C. bandwidth and delay

D. bandwidth

Correct Answer (D)
Subject Matter: OSPF

Each routing protocol has a unique method for calculating route metrics (cost). OSPF calculates cost based on link bandwidth. The default cost of an OSPF enabled Fast Ethernet link = 1 (100 Mbps/100 Mbps).

The lowest link cost assignable to a link is 1 even though the calculation could arrive at a lower number. The reference bandwidth is configurable for OSPF with the following IOS commands.

router(config)# router ospf 1
router(config-router)# auto-cost reference-bandwidth 1000

The reference bandwidth must match for all routers in the same OSPF routing domain. Route redistribution advertises routes between different routing domains (OSPF, BGP etc).

69. What are three advantages of OSPF hierarchical design?

A. confine network instability to a single area

B. decrease latency by increasing bandwidth

C. reduce the complexity of router configuration

D. lower costs by replacing routers with switches

E. speed up network convergence

F. reduce routing overhead

Correct Answers (A,E,F)
Subject Matter: OSPF

The hierarchical design is characterized by well-defined layers that optimize performance and routing. The advantage of a hierarchical design is less routing overhead, faster network convergence. In addition routing issues such as flapping or routing loops are limited to an OSPF area.

The OSPF areas provide a hierarchy that allows route summarization and smaller routing tables per router. The routing updates are minimized when there are link failures enabling faster convergence.

70. What are two advantages of static routing when compared with dynamic routing?

    A. static routes provide optimized network convergence

    B. static routes are not affected by administrative distance

    C. static routes minimize router CPU utilization

    D. static routes provide scalability and ease of management

    E. route summarization is easier with static routes

    F. static routes optimize network security

    G. static routes provide easier best path selection

Correct Answers (C,F)
Subject Matter: Static and Dynamic Routing

The two advantages of static routes are security and minimal router CPU processing. The static routes are manually configured, enabled and managed by the network administrator. Route selection and forwarding packets to the destination subnets is less complex.

Dynamic routing protocols have security vulnerabilities that make them less desirable when connecting firewalls for instance. In addition dynamic routing protocols require more processing for hello packets, route calculation, convergence and routing updates.

71. Refer to the network topology drawing. Router-1 cannot establish an OSPFv2 neighbor adjacency with Router-2.

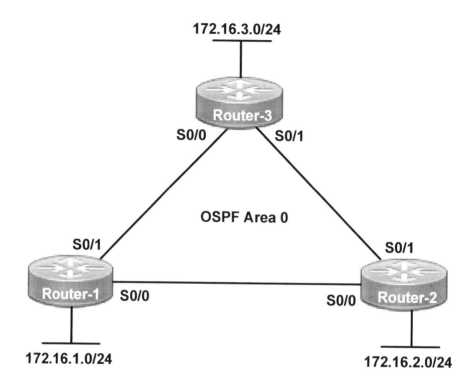

What is the most probable cause?

A. router ID is not in the same subnet for routers

B. hello timer mismatch between routers

C. loopback IP addresses are not assigned the same subnet mask

D. process ID mismatch between neighbor routers

E. serial interfaces are directly assigned to area 0

F. both routers are configured as stub router area type

Correct Answer (B)
Subject Matter: OSPF

OSPF enabled routers establish adjacencies with neighbors for communicating operational status and routing updates. The routing messages use timers that must match between directly connected neighbors. OSPF neighbor adjacencies are not formed when there is a mismatch of hello or dead timers.

The following describe some additional reasons why a neighbor adjacency would not occur between OSPF enabled neighbors.

- Network type mismatch
- Interface MTU mismatch
- Area ID mismatch
- Stub area when deployed is not configured on both routers
- OSPF neighbor physical interfaces are not in the same subnet

72. Router-1 must select a route to forward packets to 172.16.4.0/28 network. Select the routing method, next hop ip address and router interface based on the routing table exhibit?

    router-1# show ip route

    Codes: C - connected, S - static, R - RIP, M - mobile, B - BGP
        D - EIGRP, EX - EIGRP external, O - OSPF, IA - OSPF inter area
        N1 - OSPF NSSA external type 1, N2 - OSPF NSSA external type 2
        E1 - OSPF external type 1, E2 - OSPF external type 2
        o - ODR, P - periodic downloaded static route

    Gateway of last resort is not set

        172.16.0.0/24 is variably subnetted, 4 subnets, 2 masks
    C   172.16.1.0/24 is directly connected, GigabitEthernet0/0
    C   172.16.200.0/30 is directly connected, Serial0/0
    C   172.16.200.16/30 is directly connected, Serial0/1
    D   172.16.200.32/30 [90/1234567] via 172.16.200.2, Serial0/0
                             [90/1234567] via 172.16.200.18, Serial0/1
    D   172.16.2.0/27 [90/1234567] via 172.16.200.18, Serial0/1
    D   172.16.4.0/27 [90/1463212] via 172.16.200.2, Serial0/0
    R   172.16.4.0/26 [120/3] via 172.16.200.17, Serial0/2

A. EIGRP, 172.16.200.32/30, Serial0/0

B. Connected, 172.16.200.16/30, Serial0/1

C. Connected, 172.16.1.0/24, GigabitEthernet0/0

D. EIGRP, 172.16.4.0/27, Serial0/0

E. RIPv2, 172.16.4.0/26, Serial0/2

Correct Answer (D)
Subject Matter: Routing Concepts

The router selects the route with the longest prefix (subnet) where there are multiple routes to the same destination. It is referred to as the longest match rule. The following EIGRP route has the longest prefix (/27) to the destination 172.16.4.0 subnet. The next hop address to forward packets destined for 172.16.4.0 is 172.16.200.2 via S0/0 local interface.

D   172.16.4.0/27 [90/1463212] via 172.16.200.2, Serial0/0

The routes 172.16.4.0/26 (RIPv2) and 172.16.4.0/27 (EIGRP) have different prefix lengths so they are considered different destinations by router. The router will install multiple routes from different routing protocols as a result. The administrative distance only applies to routes with the same subnet and prefix length (same destination).

73. A network administrator is troubleshooting an EIGRP problem. What IOS troubleshooting command will list all EIGRP neighbor adjacencies and associated link performance issues?

A. router# show ip eigrp neighbors

B. router# show ip eigrp interfaces

C. router# show ip eigrp topology

D. router# show ip eigrp adjacency

Correct Answer (A)
Subject Matter: EIGRP

The IOS command **show ip eigrp neighbors** lists the active EIGRP neighbor adjacencies along with IP address and operational status. The smooth round trip time (SRTT), retransmit timeout setting (RTO) and queue count are included.

Smooth Round-Trip Time (SRTT) - amount of time (msec) required for the local router to send an EIGRP packet to the neighbor and receive an acknowledgment.

Retransmission Timeout (RTO) - amount of time EIGRP waits before retransmitting packets from the retransmission queue to a neighbor.

Queue Count - number of update, query and reply packets in the EIGRP queue waiting to be sent to the neighbor.

74. Refer to the network topology drawing. Router-1 has an OSPFv2 adjacency with Router-2 however cannot establish OSPFv2 adjacency with Router-3. What are two possible causes and/or effects?

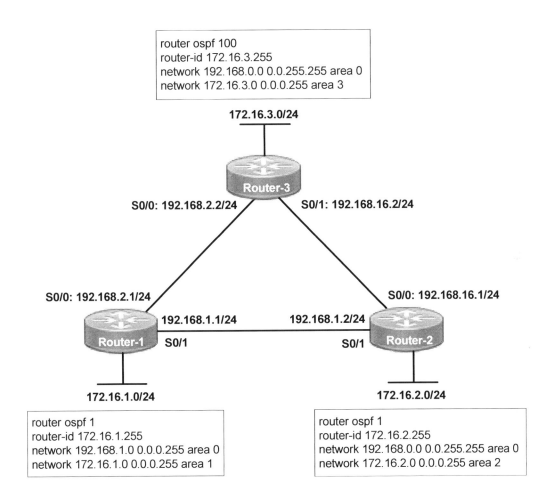

```
router ospf 100
router-id 172.16.3.255
network 192.168.0.0 0.0.255.255 area 0
network 172.16.3.0 0.0.0.255 area 3
```

172.16.3.0/24

Router-3

S0/0: 192.168.2.2/24   **S0/1: 192.168.16.2/24**

S0/0: 192.168.2.1/24   **S0/0: 192.168.16.1/24**

192.168.1.1/24   **192.168.1.2/24**

Router-1 **S0/1**   **S0/1** **Router-2**

172.16.1.0/24   **172.16.2.0/24**

```
router ospf 1
router-id 172.16.1.255
network 192.168.1.0 0.0.0.255 area 0
network 172.16.1.0 0.0.0.255 area 1
```

```
router ospf 1
router-id 172.16.2.255
network 192.168.0.0 0.0.255.255 area 0
network 172.16.2.0 0.0.0.255 area 2
```

A. Router-3 has an incorrect wildcard mask

B. Router-1 has an incorrect router ID

C. Router-3 interface Serial0/0 is not enabled for area 0

D. Router-1 interface Serial0/0 is not enabled for area 0

E. OSPF process identifiers do not match between Router-1 and Router-3

F. Router-1 has an incorrect wildcard mask

Correct Answers (D,F)
Subject Matter: OSPFv2

Interface Serial0/0 of Router-1 is assigned IP address 192.168.2.1/24 and that is in the same subnet as 192.168.2.2/24 neighbor subnet. The wildcard mask however excludes 192.168.2.1/24 from advertising OSPFv2 routes to area 0.

The wildcard mask **0.0.0.255** only enables 192.168.1.1/24 on interface Serial0/0 of Router-1. As a result it is out of range and not enabled for OSPFv2. Modifying the IP address to **192.168.0.0** and wildcard mask to **0.0.255.255** would fix the problem. That enables all routes for IP range 192.168.0.0 - 192.168.255.255 range. Modifying the IP address to 192.168.2.0 and wildcard mask to 0.0.0.255 would enable OSPF advertisements for that subnet as well.

    router-1(config)# router ospf 1
    router-1(config-router)# router-id 172.16.1.255
    router-1(config-router)# network 192.168.0.0 0.0.255.255 area 0
    router-1(config-router)# network 172.16.1.0 0.0.0.255 area 1

75. Refer to the network topology drawing. What network design change would enable EIGRP route advertisements between all routers?

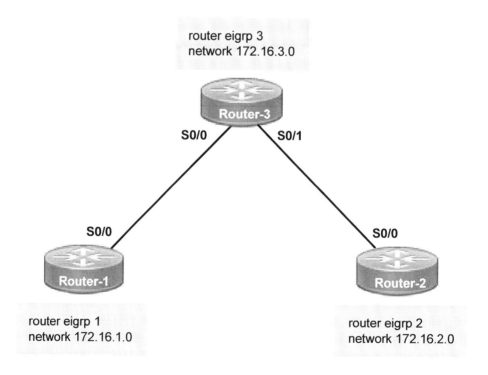

router eigrp 3
network 172.16.3.0

S0/0   S0/1

Router-3

S0/0   S0/0

Router-1   Router-2

router eigrp 1   router eigrp 2
network 172.16.1.0   network 172.16.2.0

A. migrate to a single EIGRP autonomous system (AS)

B. configure stub routing

C. enable **no auto-summary** on all routers

D. configure all classful network addresses to all routers

Correct Answer (A)
Subject Matter: EIGRP

EIGRP enabled routers can only advertises routes within the same autonomous system (AS). As a result the AS number assigned to each router must match.

76. There is a new application on a network server assigned to VLAN 12 on a switch. Hosts on VLAN 10 of the same switch cannot start the application on the server. What is the easiest solution to enable communication between hosts and server?

A. configure trunk mode on the server connected switch port

B. configure access mode on all switch ports

C. connect a router with a port channel link to the switch

D. configure a router with subinterfaces for the VLANs (10,12) and enable trunking between the router and switch.

Correct Answer (D)
Subject Matter: Inter-VLAN Routing

Router-on a-stick (Inter-VLAN routing) is required when multiple VLANs are configured at the switches. Each VLAN requires a subinterface at the router physical interface. The switches trunk VLANs to the router for packet forwarding between VLANs.

77. What IOS command is used to display the collection of OSPF link-states?

A. show ip ospf neighbors

B. show ip ospf database

C. show ip ospf link-state

D. show ip ospf lsa database

Correct Answer (B)
Subject Matter: OSPF

The IOS command **show ip ospf database** provides a list of all known link states for an OSPF enabled network. It creates a network topology used to calculate best path (shortest) to a destination. The network topology and path cost for each link is considered as part of the calculation. The routing table is updated with the destination subnet and preferred next hop address.

78. What feature or setting can influence the selection of a static route as a backup when a dynamic routing protocol is enabled for the same router?

   A. link bandwidth

   B. hop count

   C. link delay

   D. link cost

   E. administrative distance

Correct Answer (E)
Subject Matter: Administrative Distance

The static route configured with a higher administrative distance than a dynamic routing protocol is a floating static route. It is installed in the routing table only when a dynamically learned route isn't available. That could result from a link failure for instance. The static route has a lower administrative distance compared with the unavailable route and becomes active. The floating static route is often used to route traffic across a backup link. Sometimes two static routes are configured where one static route has a higher administrative distance. The static route with the higher administrative distance becomes active when the primary static route isn't available.

79. The network administrator has configured OSPF on a router with the following IOS command to permit only specific route advertisements.

   router(config-router)# network 192.168.12.64 0.0.0.63 area 0

   Refer to the results of **show ip interface brief** command and select two network interfaces that will be advertised by the OSPF process?

router# show ip interface brief

Interface	IP address	OK	Method	Status	Protocol
GigabitEthernet0/0	192.168.12.0	YES	NVRAM	up	down
GigabitEthernet0/1	192.168.12.129	YES	Manual	up	up
Serial0/0	192.168.12.121	YES	Manual	up	up
Serial0/1	192.168.12.128	YES	Manual	up	up
Serial0/2	192.168.12.125	YES	Manual	up	up

A. Serial0/0

B. Serial0/1

C. Serial0/2

D. GigabitEthernet0/0

E. GigabitEthernet0/1

Correct Answers (A,C)
Subject Matter: OSPFv2 for IPv4

The IOS command **show ip interface brief** lists the status of all router interfaces and IP address. The normal status for a network interfaces is **up/up** confirming layer 1 and layer 2 connectivity.

The following IOS command creates a filter for what subnets are advertised by OSPF to neighbors. Any network interfaces assigned an IP address that is outside of that range won't be advertised by OSPFv2.

   router(config-router)# network 192.168.12.64 0.0.0.63 area 0

The wildcard mask allows the address range included by all zeros and masks off everything else. The address range with the wildcard mask starts from 192.168.12.64 to 192.168.12.127 for the 4th octet (host portion).

```
    192.      168.      12.      64
11000000.10101000.00001100.01 000000
00000000.00000000.00000000.00 111111
    0.        0.        0.      63
```

The following interfaces with IP addresses are assigned within the range 192.168.12.64 -192.168.12.127 (subinterfaces)

   Serial0/0 - 192.168.12.121
   Serial0/2 - 192.168.12.125

80. What three statements describe the routing protocol OSPF?

    A. OSPF increases CPU utilization significantly

    B. OSPF limits network issues to an area

    C. OSFP supports unequal-cost load balancing

    D. OSPF supports classless subnet masks (VLSM)

    E. OSPF routing is less complex and easier to manage

    F. OSPF is scalable

Correct Answers (B,D,F)
Subject Matter: OSPF

Link-state routing protocols such as OSPF support VLSMs (advertising classless subnets/CIDR). In addition the hierarchical area design limits any network instability to an area. There is complex policy-based routing available for granular control of routing updates as well.

81. What three characteristics are representative of link-state routing protocols?

    A. exchange routing table with neighbors at fixed intervals

    B. enables event-triggered routing updates

    C. provides global topology of links for routing purposes

    D. LSAs are sent between neighbors at fixed intervals

    E. algorithm for calculating route metric is based on cumulative link cost

Correct Answers (B,C,E)
Subject Matter: Link-State Routing Protocols

Link-state routing protocols discover the routing topology for enabled links and calculate the shortest (best) path. In addition they only send event-triggered routing updates. For instance a link failure on a router would trigger a routing reconvergence.

82. Refer to the network drawing. The layer 2 switch is connected to a router where Inter-VLAN routing is configured. There are three hosts connected to the switch with the following VLAN and IP address assignments.

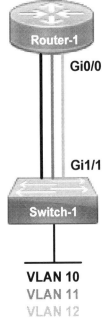

```
router-1(config)# interface gigabitethernet0/0
router-1(config-if)# no ip address
router-1(config-if)# speed auto
router-1(config-if)# duplex auto
!
router-1(config)# interface gigabitethernet0/0.10
router-1(config-sub)# ip address 192.168.10.254 255.255.255.0
!
router-1(config)# interface gigabitethernet0/0.11
router-1(config-sub)# ip address 192.168.11.254 255.255.255.0
!
router-1(config)# interface gigabitethernet0/0.12
router-1(config-sub)# ip address 192.168.12.254 255.255.255.0
```

Gi0/0

Gi1/1

VLAN 10
VLAN 11
VLAN 12

```
switch-1(config)# interface gigabitethernet1/1
switch-1(config-if)# description trunk uplink to router-1
switch-1(config-if)# switchport trunk encapsulation dot1q
switch-1(config-if)# switchport mode trunk
switch-1(config-if)# switchport trunk allowed vlan 10-12
switch-1(config-if)# switchport trunk native vlan 999
!
switch-1(config)# interface gigabitethernet1/2
switch-1(config-if)# switchport mode access
switch-1(config-if)# switchport access vlan 10
!
switch-1(config)# interface gigabitethernet1/3
switch-1(config-if)# switchport mode access
switch-1(config-if)# switchport access vlan 11
!
switch-1(config)# interface gigabitethernet1/4
switch-1(config-if)# switchport mode access
switch-1(config-if)# switchport access vlan 12
```

- Host-1 = Gi1/2, VLAN 10, 192.168.10.1/24
- Host-2 = Gi1/3, VLAN 11, 192.168.11.1/24
- Host-3 = Gi1/4, VLAN 12, 192.168.12.1/24

What configuration error will prevent routing between VLANs?

A. no encapsulation type is configured on router interface Gi0/0

B. no routing protocol is enabled on router interface Gi0/0

C. router subinterfaces have no VLAN assigned

D. SVI for each VLAN is not configured on the switch

E. there is no IP address configured on router interface Gi0/0

F. static routes are required for 192.168.0.0 subnet

Correct Answer (C)
Subject Matter: Inter-VLAN Routing

The only configuration error is not assigning each VLAN to a subinterface on the router trunk link. Each VLAN requires a subinterface on the router with the matching VLAN number configured on the switch. The router physical interface does not require an IP address or trunk mode command. It is enabled with **no shutdown** command and any interface settings for speed and duplex. Layer 2 switches do not require an SVI for each VLAN. The VLANs are created and assigned to an access port. The host subnets are configured on the subinterfaces of the router.

Note: bold text highlights the required IOS commands

Router-1:

```
router-1(config)# interface gigabitethernet0/0
router-1(config-if)# no ip address
router-1(config-if)# speed auto
router-1(config-if)# duplex auto

router-1(config)# interface gigabitethernet0/0.10
router-1(config-subif)# encapsulation dot1q 10
router-1(config-subif)# ip address 192.168.10.254 255.255.255.0

router-1(config-subif)# interface gigabitethernet0/0.11
router-1(config-subif)# encapsulation dot1q 11
router-1(config-subif)# ip address 192.168.11.254 255.255.255.0
```

router-1(config-subif)# interface gigabitethernet0/0.12
router-1(config-subif)# encapsulation dot1q 12
router-1(config-subif)# ip address 192.168.12.254 255.255.255.0

Switch-1:

switch-1(config)# interface gigabitethernet1/1
switch-1(config-if)# description trunk uplink to router-1
switch-1(config-if)# switchport trunk encapsulation dot1q
switch-1(config-if)# switchport mode trunk
switch-1(config-if)# switchport trunk allowed vlan 10-12
switch-1(config-if)# switchport trunk native vlan 999

switch-1(config)# interface gigabitethernet1/2
switch-1(config-if)# switchport mode access
switch-1(config-if)# switchport access vlan 10

switch-1(config)# interface gigabitethernet1/3
switch-1(config-if)# switchport mode access
switch-1(config-if)# switchport access vlan 11

switch-1(config)# interface gigabitethernet1/4
switch-1(config-if)# switchport mode access
switch-1(config-if)# switchport access vlan 12

83. Refer to the network topology drawing. What is the reason why Router-1 cannot establish an EIGRP neighbor adjacency with Router-2?

router eigrp 1 network 192.168.0.0 network 172.16.2.0 interface Serial0/0 ip address 192.168.1.1 255.255.255.252 interface Loopback 0 ip address 192.168.1.254 255.255.255.255	router eigrp 1 network 192.168.0.0 network 172.16.3.0 interface Serial0/0 ip address 192.168.1.4 255.255.255.252 interface Loopback 0 ip address 192.168.1.253 255.255.255.255

A. incorrect subnet mask on both serial interfaces

B. loopback interfaces are not in the same subnet

C. serial interfaces are not in the same subnet

D. **network** command incorrect for Router-1

E. **network** command incorrect for Router-2

F. hello timer mismatch between neighbors

Correct Answer (C)
Subject Matter: EIGRP for IPv4

The IP addresses assigned to the WAN (serial) network interfaces are not in the same subnet as required by EIGRP. As a result the point-to-point link won't establish neighbor adjacency. The physical interface of Router-1 is assigned 192.168.1.1/30 and Router-2 is assigned 192.168.1.4/30. Loopback interfaces do not have to be assigned to the same subnet. In addition the timers for EIGRP do not have to match.

192.168.1.1/30 = 192.168.1.1 - 192.168.1.3
192.168.1.4/30 = 192.168.1.4 - 192.168.1.7

84. What is the maximum hop count allowed with OSPF before a route is marked as unreachable?

A. 255

B. unlimited

C. 16

D. 15

Correct Answer (B)
Subject Matter: OSPF

There is no maximum hop count for OSPF so it is unlimited.

85. What is the common backbone area for OSPF?

    A. area 0

    B. area 1

    C. area 100

    D. none of the above

Correct Answer (A)
Subject Matter: OSPF

OSPF is based on defining areas that create a hierarchical traffic flow for routing packets. There is a mandatory common backbone **area 0** that all other areas must connect to. That is required to advertise LSAs between areas.

86. What is the purpose of an OSPF designated router (DR)?

    A. OSPF DR is used for deploying OSPF to a multi-access network type such as Ethernet

    B. OSPF DR is the hub for advertising routes to multiple OSPF neighbor routers (spokes)

    C. OSPF DR minimizes routing advertisements

    D. OSPF DR sends routing updates to multicast 224.0.0.6 address

    E. OSPF enabled router with highest priority and router ID is elected DR

    F. all of the above

Correct Answer (F)
Subject Matter: OSPFv2 for IPv4

The OSPF designated router (DR) advertises routing updates to connected spokes on a shared network segment (Ethernet etc). The primary advantage is to minimize the number of route updates. The DR is a hub and advertises route updates to 224.0.0.6 multicast address. Any connected spoke routers on the local segment will receive multicasts of the route updates. The OSPF router with the highest priority is elected as DR for the local network segment (subnet). The router priority is configurable as well to influence the DR election. Where there are equal priorities, the OSPF router with higher router ID is elected, then higher loopback address, then higher physical interface number.

87. Based on the partial output from the running configuration, router-1 will become the OSPF designated router for all routers connected to that network segment (Gi0/1)?

```
router-1# show running-config

interface gigabitethernet0/1
ip address 172.16.22.1 255.255.255.0
ip ospf priority 0
speed 100
full-duplex
!
router ospf 1
log-adjacency-changes
network 172.16.22.1 0.0.0.0 area 0
!
end
```

    A. True

    B. False

Correct Answer (False)
Subject Matter: OSPFv2 for IPv4

Any OSPF enabled router with a priority of zero (0) cannot be elected as the designated router (DR) or BDR. The following IOS command assigns a priority of zero (0) to a router:

```
router(config-if)# ip ospf priority 0
```

88. Using the default auto-cost reference-bandwidth for OSPF, what is the link cost assigned to a standard Gigabit Ethernet link (1000 Mbps)?

    A. 1000

    B. 1

    C. 100

    D. 10

The default reference bandwidth used by OSPF to calculate link cost is 100 Mbps. The link cost (metric) is based on the following calculation:

cost = reference bandwidth / link bandwidth

The link cost for Fast Ethernet (100 Mbps) and any higher speed (Gigabit etc) is equal to 1. There is no calculation of link cost that is ever less than 1. It is recommended to change reference bandwidth to the fastest switch link. That allows OSPF to distinguish between 1 Gbps, 10 Gbps and 100 Gbps links.

89. What OSPF area type blocks Type 3, 4, 5 and 7 LSAs with the exception of a default route?

   A. stub area

   B. not-so-stubby-area (NSSA)

   C. non-stub area

   D. totally stubby area

The totally stubby area provides the most filtering of LSAs of any class. They only allow routing (LSA Type 1) and network links (LSA Type 2) within an OSPF area. There is a default route injected from the ABR into the area as a summary (LSA Type 3). All additional summary LSAs, summary ASBR (Type 4 LSA) and external (LSA Type 5 and 7) are filtered. Area 10 for instance is configured as a totally stubby area with **no-summary** added to stub command:

router(config-router)# area 10 stub no-summary

90. What OSPF packet type provides reliable transport and exchange of routing information?

   A. link-state request

   B. database descriptor

   C. link-state update

   D. link-state acknowledgement

Correct Answer (D)
Subject Matter: OSPF

The purpose of an OSPF link-state acknowledgement (LSack) is to provide reliability to the transport of flooded LSAs. The receiving OSPF router sends an LSA acknowledgement to the sender when the LSA arrives. In addition multiple LSAs can be acknowledged with a single LSA ACK.

OSPF packet types:

- **Hello** - neighbor discovery/adjacencies

- **Database Descriptor** - summarizes database topology

- **Link-State Request** - LSA request from neighbors

- **Link-State Update** - flooding LSAs to neighbors

- **Link-State ACK** - acknowledges LSA updates

91. What are two potential causes of OSPF neighbor connectivity issues?

    A. line protocol operational status is not *established* state

    B. incorrect wildcard mask on OSPF interface

    C. OSPF area mismatch

    D. OSPF subnet mask does not match between local and remote router interfaces

Correct Answers (B,C)
Subject Matter: OSPF

Some typical causes of OSPF errors occur with the interface configuration. They include wrong area assignment and OSPF not enabled on the interface. For instance OSPF Interfaces on the same link must be assigned to the same area number. OSPF must be enabled globally first and then assign an interface to an area. In addition all OSPF timers must match between connected neighbors to establish neighbor adjacencies.

92. Refer to the results of the following IOS command. What router ID will OSPF select based on the currently configured IP addresses?

router# show ip interface brief

Interface	IP Address	OK	Method	Status	Protocol
GigabitEthernet0/0	10.10.1.254	YES	NVRAM	up	up
GigabitEthernet0/1	10.1.1.1	YES	Manual	up	up
Serial0/0	192.168.254.254	YES	NVRAM	up	up
Serial0/1	172.16.3.254	YES	Manual	up	up
Loopback0	192.168.1.1	YES	Manual	up	up

A. 10.1.1.1

B. 192.168.254.254

C. 172.16.3.254

D. 192.168.1.1

E. 10.10.1.254

Correct Answer (D)
Subject Matter: OSPFv2 for IPv4

OSPF assigns the highest IP address of any existing loopback address for the router ID (192.168.1.1). That occurs only when there isn't any manual configuration. The highest IP address of any active physical interface is assigned if no Loopback interface exists. The router ID is advertised with Type 1 (Router) LSAs.

93. What two IOS commands are required to properly configure a router to run OSPF and advertise network 92.168.16.0/24 to OSPF area 0?

A. router(config-router)# network 192.168.16.0 0.0.0.255 0

B. router(config-router)# network 192.168.16.0 255.255.255.0 area 0

C. router(config-router)# network 192.168.16.0 0.0.0.255 area 0

D. router(config)# router ospf area 0

E. router(config)# router ospf 1

F. router(config)# router ospf 0

Correct Answers (C,E)
Subject Matter: OSPFv2 for IPv4

OSPF configuration starts with enabling it globally on the router and assigning a network address to advertise. The following IOS commands enable OSPF with process ID 1 and advertise network 192.168.16.0 in area 0.

```
router(config)# router ospf 1
router(config-router)# network 192.168.16.0  0.0.0.255 area 0
```

94. What is the default maximum number of equal-cost paths that can be installed into the routing table of a router enabled with OSPF?

   A. 4

   B. 2

   C. 16

   D. unlimited

Correct Answer (A)
Subject Matter: OSPF

OSPF running on a Cisco router supports a maximum of 4 equal-cost paths for load balancing.

95. A network administrator is trying to add a new router into an established OSPF network. The network addresses attached to router-1 are not installed in the routing tables of OSPF neighbors. Consider the recent configuration and determine the cause?

```
router-1(config)# router ospf 1
router-1(config-router)# network 10.0.0.0 255.0.0.0 area 0
```

   A. process ID does not match for connected OSPF interfaces

   B. OSPF area ID is incorrect

   C. new router does not have a license for OSPF

   D. existing routers must be restarted to enable network convergence

   E. **network** command wildcard mask is incorrect

Correct Answer (E)
Subject Matter: OSPFv2 for IPv4

OSPF uses wildcard masks to advertise network prefixes to OSPF neighbors. The zeros are used to select the network portion bits. The configured network statement is using a traditional subnet mask instead of a wildcard mask.

96. What are two enhancements that OSPFv3 supports over OSPFv2?

   A. OSPFv3 forwards routes per link instead of per subnet

   B. OSPFv3 permits multiple DR routers per network segment

   C. OSPFv3 supports multiple IPv6 addresses per interface

   D. OSPFv3 supports hop count and path cost as metrics

   E. OSPFv3 sends fewer routing updates

Correct Answers (A,C)
Subject Matter: OSPF

OSPFv3 supports multiple IPv6 addresses per interface. In addition routing is per link instead of per subnet with multiple instances per link available.

97. What is the purpose of **ip ospf cost** command?

   A. globally configured cost assigned to all OSPF enabled interfaces

   B. enables unequal load balancing across OSPF links

   C. replaces OSPF reference bandwidth

   D. manually assigns a link cost to an OSPF interface

Correct Answer (D)
Subject Matter: OSPF

OSPF derives the path cost metric from the actual interface bandwidth. It is calculated using a reference bandwidth. Changing the default reference bandwidth would affect how OSPF calculates link cost.

The **ip ospf cost** command is an alternative to reference bandwidth method. It allows the network engineer to configure the cost on an interface. The third option is to manually change the interface speed with the interface **bandwidth** command.

98. Refer to the network topology drawing. After network convergence has occurred, what standard OSPF packets are sent at regular intervals between Router-3 and Router-1?

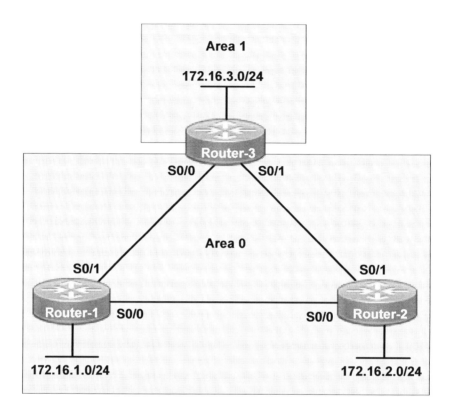

A. link-state update

B. topology database descriptor

C. none

D. link-state request

E. hello packet

Correct Answer (E)
Subject Matter: OSPF

OSPF hello packets are sent at fixed intervals based on the hello timer setting. Router-1 and Router-3 (ABR) would both send hello packets. The purpose of hello packets are to discover neighbors and establish neighbor adjacencies. In addition hello packets are sent as keepalives to confirm the connected neighbor is active. The neighbor is declared unreachable when hello packets are not received for the interval of the dead timer.

99. The following routes include classful and classless subnet masks. What network prefixes are installed in the OSPF routing table?

- 10.10.10.1/8
- 172.16.1.1/16
- 192.168.1.1/24
- 10.10.10.1/17
- 172.16.1.129/26
- 192.168.1.64/30

A. 10.10.10.1/17, 172.16.1.129/26, 192.168.1.64/30

B. 172.16.1.1/16, 172.16.1.129/26

C. 192.168.1.1/24

D. none

E. 10.10.10.1/8, 172.16.1.1/16, 192.168.1.1/24

F. all routes

Correct Answer (F)
Subject Matter: OSPFv2 for IPv4

OSPF is a link-state routing protocol that supports advertising classful and classless routes. The subnet mask is advertised with the route. Any routing protocol that supports variable length subnet masks (VLSM) can advertise classful and classless subnets.

Classful subnet masks are based on the default mask length for each IP class. That includes Class A = /8 , Class B = /16 and Class C = /24. Any routing protocol that only supports classful subnet masks must use the default for the routing domain and class deployed.

Class A = 255.0.0.0 (1.0.0.0 - 126.255.255.255)

Class B = 255.255.0.0 (128.0.0.0 - 191.255.255.255)

Class C = 255.255.255.0 (192.0.0.0 - 223.255.255.255)

The following are some examples of IP addresses with classful subnet masks.

- 10.10.10.1/8
- 172.16.1.1/16
- 192.168.1.1/24

269

Classless subnets masks can use the default or variable length subnet masks for any class IP address. Each class defines the default subnet mask length as well. The following are some examples of classless subnet masks:

- 10.10.10.1/17
- 172.16.1.129/26
- 192.168.1.64/30

100. Refer to the network topology drawing. All routers are configured with the default OSPF priority. What router will be elected designated router (DR) for Router-1?

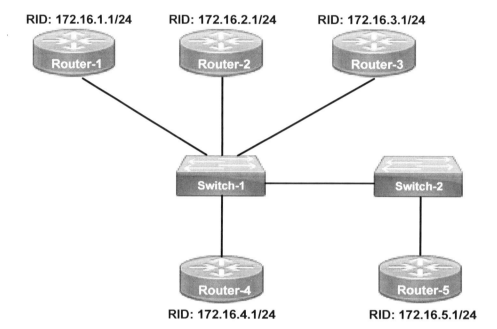

A. 172.16.5.1

B. 172.16.4.1

C. 172.16.3.1

D. 172.16.2.1

E. 172.16.1.1

Correct Answer (B)
Subject Matter: OSPFv2 for IPv4

The default OSPF configuration has no router ID assigned. In addition the OSPF priority has a default value of 1. The router assigns the router ID with the highest IP address for the network segment. The switches create two separate network segments for OSPF multicasting. As a result the designated Router (DR) for Router-1 is Router-4 with a router ID (RID) of **172.16.4.1**. Router-5 is on a separate network segment connected to Switch-2 and not assignable to routers on Switch-1.

The highest IP address is calculated from left to right and based on numbering for any IP address. The numbers for each IP address match until octet 3 where subnet 4 is higher.

- 172.16.1.1
- 172.16.2.1
- 172.16.3.1
- 172.16.**4**.1

101. What does "128" refer to in the routing table for that route?

router-1# show ip route

```
   192.168.12.0/24 is variably subnetted, 9 subnets, 3 masks
C    192.168.12.64 /28 is directly connected, Loopback1
C    192.168.12.32 /28 is directly connected, Ethernet0
C    192.168.12.48 /28 is directly connected, Loopback0
O    192.168.12.236 /30 [110/128] via 192.168.12.233, 00:35:36, Serial0
C    192.168.12.232 /30 is directly connected, Serial0
O    192.168.12.245 /30 [110/782] via 192.168.12.233, 00:35:36, Serial0
O    192.168.12.240 /30 [110/128] via 192.168.12.233, 00:35:36, Serial0
O    192.168.12.253 /30 [110/782] via 192.168.12.233, 00:35:37, Serial0
O    192.168.12.249 /30 [110/782] via 192.168.12.233, 00:35:37, Serial0
```

A. OSPF hop count

B. OSPF process identifier

C. OSPF path cost

D. OSPF administrative distance

E. OSPF priority

Correct Answer (C)
Subject Matter: Routing Table Components

Each routing table entry includes a square bracket with two values such as [110/128]. The first entry is the administrative distance (110) and the second entry is the metric (128). The route is OSPF and the metric is path cost.

102. What two statements correctly describe the OSPF process identifier?

    A. assigned per OSPF area

    B. identifies a unique instance of an OSPF database local to a router

    C. assigned per OSPF domain to enable routing exchange

    D. OSPFv2 supports multiple process identifiers on the same router

    E. can be assigned any number from 0 to 1024

Correct Answers (B,D)
Subject Matter: OSPF

The OSPF process ID is a unique number (1 - 65,535) assigned to an OSPF routing instance. It is only locally significant to the router. The routing instance includes a separate OSPF topology database for each process ID.

103. What is the destination IP address of OSPF hello packets forwarded on the same multi-access (Ethernet) segment?

    A. 172.16.0.1

    B. 223.0.0.1

    C. 224.0.0.5

    D. 254.255.255.255

    E. 192.168.0.5

Correct Answer (C)
Subject Matter: OSPFv2 for IPv4

All OSPF routers send hello packets to neighbors on the same segment (subnet) using multicast 224.0.0.5 as the destination IP address.

104. What are two advantages of a default route?

    A. enable connectivity to network addresses not in the routing table

    B. default route administrative distance = 0

    C. default route to an ISP is always available

    D. default route provides additional security

    E. default routes minimize routing advertisements

Correct Answers (A,E)
Subject Matter: IPv4/IPv6 Static Routing

The default route enables connectivity to the internet with a single route in the routing table. That minimizes the routing table size and router CPU utilization. Route processing and forwarding is offloaded to the internet service provider.

105. Refer to the network topology drawing and output from the **show arp** command on Router-1. Host-1 sends a ping to Server-1. What packet rewrite events occur on Router-1 before the packet is forwarded to Router-2? (select three)

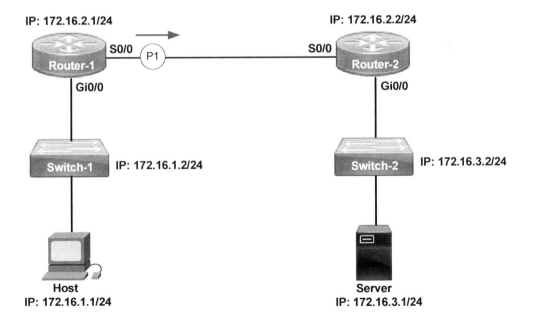

273

router-1# show arp

Protocol	Address	Aging (min)	Hardware Address	Type	Interface
Internet	172.16.1.3	-	0000.000c.cccc	ARPA	GigabitEthernet0/0
Internet	172.16.1.2	12	0000.000b.bbbb	ARPA	GigabitEthernet0/0
Internet	172.16.1.1	12	0000.000a.aaaa	ARPA	GigabitEthernet0/0
Internet	172.16.2.2	12	0000.000d.dddd	ARPA	
Internet	172.16.3.1	12	0000.1234.5678	ARPA	

A. Router-1 rewrites the frame with destination MAC address 0000.000d.dddd

B. Router-1 rewrites the frame with destination MAC address 0000.000a.aaaa

C. Router-1 rewrites the frame with source MAC address 0000.000b.bbbb

D. Router-1 rewrites the frame with destination MAC address 0000.000a.aaaa

E. Router-1 forwards the packet out Serial0/0 interface to Router-2

F. Router-1 rewrites the destination IP address to 172.16.2.2

Correct Answers (A,C,E)
Subject Matter: Routing Concepts

The output from **show arp** command lists the IP address and associated hardware address. That includes all ARP requests performed by Router-1. Match the IP address from the network topology drawing with the ARP table MAC address.

The Aging field with (-) indicates the MAC address of the interface (Gi0/0) on Router-1. It does not age out from the table. The default ARP entry aging timer is 240 minutes. At that point the entry is flushed and new ARP request is required. The interface field signifies where the MAC address was learned. The serial interfaces do not have a MAC address.

The IP address does not change between source and destination. The router will update (rewrite) the source and destination MAC address. The router rewrites the source MAC address to use the MAC address of Router-1 interface (Gi0/0). The destination MAC address assigned is the device MAC address of Router-2. If the link was Metro Ethernet for example, the router WAN interface MAC addresses would then be used.

source MAC address = 0000.000c.cccc
destination MAC address = 0000.000d.dddd

Internet 172.16.1.3 - 0000.000c.cccc ARPA GigabitEthernet0/0
Internet 172.16.2.2 12 0000.000d.dddd ARPA

106. Select two features available with RIPv2 that aren't supported with RIPv1?

A. does not send the subnet mask with routing updates

B. higher maximum hop count

C. less routing updates

D. classless subnet masks

E. route authentication

F. lower administrative distance

Correct Answers (D,E)
Subject Matter: RIPv2 for IPv4

The primary enhancements to RIPv2 includes the following:

- MD5 route authentication
- Classless subnets (VLSM/CIDR)

107. Refer to the output from the following IOS command. Why are there two OSPF DR routers listed on Router-3?

router-3# show ip ospf neighbor

Neighbor_ID	Pri	State	Dead Time	Address	Interface
172.16.254.1	1	Full/DR	00:00:12	172.16.1.2	GigabitEthernet0/0
172.16.254.2	1	Full/DR	00:00:13	172.16.1.1	GigabitEthernet0/1
172.16.1.1	1	Full/BDR	00:00:12	172.16.1.25	GigabitEthernet0/1

A. router configuration error

B. Router-3 is directly connected to each DR router

C. Router-3 is connected to separate layer 2 switches

D. DR routers are assigned to different OSPF areas

Correct Answer (C)
Subject Matter: OSPF

Router-3 is a spoke connected to two different designated routers (DR) shown with 2 x FULL/DR states. Router-3 has two Ethernet interfaces with a unique DR router connected to each segment (switch). The DR election is per network segment (switch). The elected DR router would have FULL/DROTHER state for each connected spoke. The **show ip ospf neighbor** command lists the following status for connected OSPF neighbors:

- Neighbor_ID = neighbor router ID
- Pri = neighbor priority
- State = neighbor DR/BDR/DROTHER status
- Dead Time = dead timer age
- Address = neighbor connected router interface IP address
- Interface = neighbor connected router interface

108. What is the default OSPF hello timer on a multi-access (broadcast) type network?

A. 10

B. 40

C. 30

D. 20

Correct Answer (A)
Subject Matter: OSPF

The default hello timer interval for a multi-access (broadcast) network is 10 seconds. The dead timer is a default of 4 times the hello interval. Ethernet is an example of a multi-access network type.

109. What two statements accurately describe usage of the OSPF process identifier?

A. valid range for any OSPF process ID number is 1 to 65,535

B. Cisco supports multiple OSPF instances per router defined by a separate process ID

C. hello packets advertise the process ID

D. Cisco supports multiple OSPF instances per area defined by a single process ID

E. OSPF process ID is optional

Correct Answers (A,B)
Subject Matter: OSPF

Cisco supports multiple OSPF instances per router defined with a process identifier. The valid range for a process identifier number is 1 - 65,535. It is similar to a VRF where a routing instance is created for a specific purpose such as partner connectivity. There is a maximum of 32 processes permitted per router. The process ID is locally significant and any OSPF interface can only be assigned to a single process identifier.

110. What are two primary advantages of deploying a single OSPF area network design?

A. decreases LSA advertisements sent per routing domain

B. scalability

C. less CPU utilization on area routers

D. permits virtual links

E. faster convergence

Correct Answers (A,E)
Subject Matter: Single Area OSPF

The single OSPF area design reduces the number of LSAs advertised between routers. There are Intra-Area LSAs only comprised of Router (Type 1) and Network (Type 2) links. All areas must be connected directly to the backbone (area 0). The virtual link is not required where there is only a single area. It connects an area to the backbone area through an already connected area.

111. What IOS command will advertise all interfaces to area 0?

A. network 255.255.255.255 0.0.0.0 area 0

B. network all-interfaces area 0

C. network 0.0.0.0 0.0.0.0 area 0

D. network 0.0.0.0 255.255.255.255 area 0

Correct Answer (D)
Subject Matter: OSPFv2 for IPv4

The OSPF network statement advertises network prefixes (subnets) with a wildcard mask. The number of zero's masks off the network portion advertised to neighbors. The wildcard mask is 255.255.255.255 translates to any network address can be advertised. As a result all/any network addresses assigned to an IP address are advertised to area 0.

112. What EIGRP route type is characteristic of a feasible successor?

A. backup route installed in topology table

B. primary route installed as a backup route in both tables

C. primary route installed in the topology table

D. backup route installed in the routing table

Correct Answer (A)
Subject Matter: EIGRP

EIGRP is similar to OSPF where there is a routing table, neighbor table and topology table. Feasible successors are backup routes stored in the topology table.

neighbor table: directly connected EIGRP neighbors where adjacency is established.

topology table: all routes learned from each EIGRP neighbors including feasible successors.

routing table: best (successor) routes selected from the EIGRP topology table.

113. Name three advantages of an EIGRP routing design based on a single
     autonomous system (AS)?

  A. scalability

  B. easier to manage and troubleshoot

  C. automatic route propagation

  D. less CPU utilization

Correct Answers (B,C,D)
Subject Matter: EIGRP

The single EIGRP autonomous system (AS) design simplifies routing
significantly. The result is less router processing for a single EIGRP instance.
The configuration is less complex and route propagation is automatic within a
single AS. Route redistribution is required between multiple AS when deployed.

114. How is ARP traffic managed within a shared cloud data center
     infrastructure? (select two)

  A. proxy ARP from the hypervisor

  B. ARP packets are dropped

  C. proxy ARP from physical switch

  D. proxy ARP from virtual router

  E. not required

Correct Answers (A,D)
Subject Matter: Routing Concepts

ARP support in a shared (multi-tenant) cloud infrastructure is provided with
Proxy ARP services. The hypervisor (VMware etc.) and virtual router appliance
typically provide ARP services to hosts and virtual switches.

115. What are three requirements to configure an IPv6 static route on a router?

    A. enable IPv6 on an interface and configure IPv6 address on that interface

    B. configure autoconfig on any interface

    C. configure IPv6 static route (global)

    D. enable IPv6 unicast-routing (global)

    E. enable IPv6 unicast-routing on interface

Correct Answers (A,C,D)
Subject Matter: IPv6 Static Routing

There are three primary steps required to configure an IPv6 static route.

    1. Enable IPv6 on the router interface and configure an IPv6 address.

    2. Configure the IPv6 static route (global)

    3. Configure **ipv6 unicast-routing** (global)

116. What commands will configure an IPv6 static route with next hop as an interface?

    A. router# ipv6 unicast-routing
        router(config-if)# ip route ipv6 [ipv6 address]

    B. router# ipv6 unicast
        router# router# ipv6 [ipv6 adress] gigabitethernet 0/0

    C. router# ipv6 route [ipv6 adress] gigabitethernet 0/0

    D. router# ipv6 unicast
        router(config-if)# ip route [ipv6 adress]

Correct Answer (C)
Subject Matter: IPv6 Static Routing

The following IOS commands configure an IPv6 static route with next hop as an interface. The router forwards all packets out the local egress interface (Gi0/0).

    router# ipv6 route [ipv6 address] gigabitethernet 0/0

The other option for configuring an IPv6 static route include the next hop IPv6 address fully specified to send across a broadcast network.
280

117. Match the OSPF version on the left with the IPv6 protocol feature supported on the right?

OSPFv2	adjacencies over link-local IP address
OSPFv3	multicast 224.0.0.5 (all OSPF routers) / 224.0.0.6 (DR/BDR)
OSPFv3	single IP address per interface
OSPFv2	IPv4 and IPv6 addressing
OSPFv2	IPv4 addressing only
OSPFv2	assigned to a subnet
OSPFv3	multiple IPv6 addresses per interface
OSPFv3	FF02::5 (all OSPF SPF routers) / FF02::6 (DR/BDR routers)

Correct Answers.
Subject Matter: OSPF

The following describe the difference between OSPFv2 and OSPFv3.

OSPFv2:
- Assigned to a subnet
- Single IP address per interface
- IPv4 addressing only
- Multicast 224.0.0.5 (all OSPF SPF routers) / 224.0.0.6 (DR/BDR)

OSPFv3:
- Multiple IPv6 addresses per interface
- Adjacencies over link-local IP address
- IPv4 and IPv6 addressing
- FF02::5 (all OSPF SPF routers) / FF02::6 (all DR/BDR routers)

118. Select the correct IOS command to enable an OSPFv3 routing process that supports IPv4 and IPv6 within a single OSPF process?

A. router ospfv3 [process id]

B. router ipv6 ospf [process id]

C. ipv6 router ospf [process id]

D. router ospfv3 [process id] /all

Correct Answer (A)
Subject Matter: OSPFv3 for IPv6

The OSPFv3 support with current IOS changed the command syntax enabling support for IPv4 and IPv6 within a single OSPF process. The following is the global command to enable OSPFv3 on a Cisco router with process ID 10.

    router(config)# router ospfv3 10

119. What group of IOS commands will configure an OSPFv3 interface on an Ethernet interface based on the following requirements?

- IPv6 globally routable address
- EUI-64 modified format
- Assign interface to area 0
- Assign process ID 1

A. interface gigabitethernet0/0
   no ip address
   ipv6 enable
   ipv6 address 2001:AB3E::/64 eui-64
   ospfv3 1 ipv6 area 0

B. interface gigabitethernet0/0
   no ip address
   ipv6 enable
   ipv6 2001:AB3E::/64 eui
   ospfv3 1 ipv6 area 0

C. interface gigabitethernet0/0
   no ip address
   ipv6 enable
   ipv6 address 2001:AB3E::/64 eui64
   ospfv3 1 area 0

D. interface gigabitethernet0/0
   no ip address
   ipv6 enable
   ipv6 address 2001:AB3E::/64 eui-64
   ospfv3 1 ipv6 area 0

Correct Answer (D)
Subject Matter: OSPFv3 for IPv6

The following assigns a global routable ipv6 address to an interface. The eui-64 converts it to modified format. In addition the interface is assigned to OSPFv3 process ID 1 and area 0.

```
router(config)# interface gigabitethernet0/0
router(config-if)# no ip address
router(config-if)# ipv6 enable
router(config-if)# ipv6 address 2001:AB3E::/64 eui-64
router(config-if)# ospfv3 1 ipv6 area 0
```

120. Match the IOS show commands on the left with the correct description for OSPF routing protocol?

show ipv6 ospf neighbors	link-state advertisements, advertising routers, process ID, router ID
show ipv6 ospf	timers, router type, router ID, areas, interfaces assigned, process ID
show ipv6 ospf database	status (up/down), area assigned, IPv6 address, OSPF network type, DR/BDR
show ipv6 ospf interface	adjacency state, neighbor interfaces, area assigned, ipv6 address, timers

Correct Answers.
Subject Matter: OSPFv3 for IPv6

The following are correct descriptions for standard OSPF show commands.

show ipv6 ospf neighbors	**adjacency state, neighbor interfaces, area assigned, IPv6 address, timers**
show ipv6 ospf	**timers, router type, router ID, areas, interfaces assigned, process ID**
show ipv6 ospf database	**link-state advertisements, advertising routers, process ID, router ID**
show ipv6 ospf interface	**status (up/down), area assigned, IPv6 address, OSPF network type, DR/BDR**

121. Select three correct statements concerning EIGRP for IPv6?

    A. EIGRP is configured per interface

    B. **network** command statements are not supported

    C. **network** command statements are applied to an interface only

    D. EIGRP instances are not enabled until the router ID is configured

    E. EIGRP interface operational status is up/up as a default

    F. router ID is 128 bits in length

Correct Answers (A,B,D)
Subject Matter: EIGRP for IPv6

The support for IPv6 addressing with EIGRP includes the following new features:

- EIGRP is configured per interface
- No support for network statements
- Protocol instance is not enabled until the router ID is configured

122. Select the correct IOS commands that will enable EIGRP for IPv6 globally and on an Ethernet interface?

    A. router(config)# ipv6 eigrp unicast
       router(config-router)# router-id 172.16.1.1
       router(config)# interface gigabitethernet1/0
       router(config-if)# ipv6 enable eigrp
       router(config-if)# ipv6 eigrp 1

    B. router(config)# ipv6 unicast routing
       router(config-router)# router-id 0.0.0.0
       router(config)# interface gigabitethernet1/0
       router(config-if)# enable eigrp
       router(config-if)# ipv6 router eigrp 1

    C. router(config)# ipv6 unicast-routing
       router(config-router)# router-id 172.16.1.1
       router(config)# interface gigabitethernet1/0
       router(config-if)# no shutdown
       router(config-if)# ipv6 enable
       router(config-if)# ipv6 eigrp 1
       router(config-if)# ipv6 router eigrp 1

D. router1(config)# eigrp unicast-routing
    router1(config-router)# router-id 0.0.0.0
    router1(config)# interface gigabitethernet1/0
    router1(config-if)# shutdown
    router1(config-if)# ipv6 enable
    router1(config-if)# router ipv6
    router1(config-if)# eigrp 1

Correct Answer (C)
Subject Matter: EIGRP for IPv6

The following commands enable IPv6 globally for the router and assigns a router ID. The interface is enabled with EIGRP in autonomous system 1.

    router(config)# ipv6 unicast-routing
    router(config-router)# router-id 172.16.1.1
    router(config)# interface gigabitethernet1/0
    router(config-if)# no shutdown
    router(config-if)# ipv6 enable
    router(config-if)# ipv6 eigrp 1
    router(config-if)# ipv6 router eigrp 1

123. Match the IOS show commands for troubleshooting EIGRP on the left with the correct description on the right?

show ipv6 eigrp 1 interfaces	show the neighbor link-local address, interfaces, timers
show ipv6 eigrp neighbors	list all EIGRP interfaces enabled with IPv6 per process, number of peers per interface
show ipv6 route eigrp	list all IPv6 specific EIGRP routes in the routing table

Correct Answers.
Subject Matter: EIGRP for IPv6

The following are correct descriptions for EIGRP show commands.

show ipv6 eigrp 1 interfaces	**list all EIGRP interfaces enabled with IPv6 per process, number of peers per interface**
show ipv6 eigrp neighbors	**show the neighbor link-local address, interfaces, timers**
show ipv6 route eigrp	**list all IPv6 specific EIGRP routes in the routing table**

124. Select the two correct statements that describe the difference between RIPv1 and RIPv2?

   A. RIPv1 support classless subnet masks

   B. RIPv2 next hop address is included in routing table entries

   C. RIPv2 routing updates sent every 10 seconds to multicast 224.0.0.9

   D. RIPv2 hop count is 255

   E. RIPv2 permits turning off auto-summary

   F. RIPv2 replaces authentication with encryption

Correct Answers (B,E)
Subject Matter: RIPv2 for IPv4

There are various enhancements with RIPv2 that enables optimization of best path selection. RIPv2 includes the next hop IP address with the advertised route. The next hop IP address is included in routing table entries. As a result the best route is selected to the destination subnet. That is based on support for classless subnet masks. The previous RIPv1 path selection was based on the classful subnet mask advertised by the source.

RIPv2 permits turning off auto-summary as well. Classful routing protocols summarize routes at default class boundaries. That includes class A (/8), class B (/16) and class C (/24). Turning off automatic summarization enables advertising of classless subnet masks with more specific routes to neighbors. Any routers enabled with RIPv1 ignore route advertisements from RIPv2 enabled routers.

125. Match the IOS commands on the left with the correct description on the right for troubleshooting layer 3 connectivity?

show interfaces	verify layer 1 and layer 2 interface status is up/up
show ip interface brief	verify the device configuration is correct
ping	interface status, IP address, MAC address, MTU, bandwidth, packet drops
show running-config	verify layer 3 reachability to remote peer

Correct Answers.
Subject Matter: Troubleshooting Layer 3 Connectivity

The following describe IOS commands available for troubleshooting basic layer 3 connectivity.

show interfaces	**interface status, IP address, MAC address, MTU, bandwidth, packet drops**
show ip interface brief	**verify layer 1 and layer 2 interface status is up/up**
ping	**verify layer 3 reachability to a remote peer**
show running-config	**verify the device configuration is correct**

126. Select the correct IOS commands to enable RIP version 2, advertise network address 172.16.0.0 and turn off automatic summarization?

    A. router
       rip v2
       network 172.16.0.0
       no auto-summary

    B. ripv2 router
       enable v2
       ripv2 network 172.16.0.0
       auto-summary

    C. router rip
       enable v2
       network 172.16.0.0/24
       no auto summary

D. router rip
    version 2
    network 172.16.0.0
    no auto-summary

Correct Answer (D)
Subject Matter: RIPv2 for IPv4

The following IOS commands will enable RIPv2, advertise network 172.16.0.0 to RIPv2 neighbors and turn off automatic summarization. The network address (172.16.0.0) must be configured as a classful address based on the Class default subnet. The subnet mask is not included in the statement.

Any network interface interface configured with an IP address in the range of 172.16.0.0 is enabled for RIPv2. The actual IP address assigned to the interface is advertised as a RIPv2 route. For instance, assigning a classless IP address such as 172.16.1.1 /27 to an Ethernet interface advertises it to RIPv2 neighbors.

    router(config)# router rip
    router(config-router)# version 2
    router(config-router)# network 172.16.0.0
    router(config-router)# no auto-summary

127. Refer to the network topology drawing. The host is sending packets to an application on the server for an established session. What is the source and destination IP address of packets at P1?

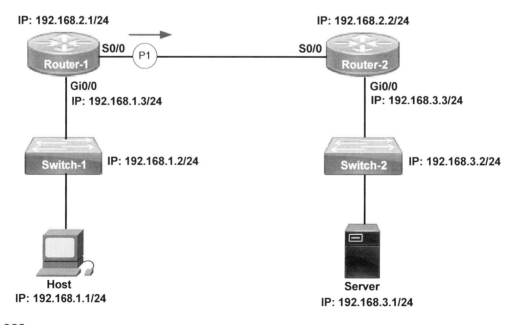

A. source IP = 192.168.2.1/24, destination IP = 192.168.3.3/24

B. source IP = 192.168.1.1/24, destination IP = 192.168.2.2/24

C. source IP = 192.168.1.1/24, destination IP = 192.168.3.1/24

D. source IP = 192.168.2.1/24, destination IP = 172.16.2.2/24

E. source IP = 192.168.1.1/24, destination IP = 255.255.255.255/32

Correct Answer (C)
Subject Matter: Routing Concepts

The source and destination IP address does not change between the host and server. The source IP address is 192.168.1.1/24 (Host) and destination IP address is 192.168.3.1/24 (Server). The MAC addressing does change and is updated by each router hop.

    source IP address = 192.168.1.1/24
    destination IP address = 192.168.3.1/24

128. Refer to the results of the following IOS command. Select two statements that are correct?

router-1# show ip interface brief

Interface	IP address	OK	Method	Status	Protocol
GigabitEthernet0/0	172.16.1.1	YES	NVRAM	up	down
GigabitEthernet0/1	172.16.2.1	YES	Manual	up	up
Serial0/0	172.16.3.1	YES	Manual	up	up
Serial0/1	Unassigned	YES	Unset	administratively down	down
Loopback0	172.16.254.254	YES	NVRAM	up	up

A. GigabitEthernet0/0 interface has a layer 1 error

B. GigabitEthernet0/0 interface changes were not saved to startup config

C. GigabitEthernet0/1 interface changes were saved to startup config

D. Serial0/1 interface was detected however no IP address is configured

E. GigabitEthernet0/0 interface error is sometimes caused by encapsulation mismatch

Correct Answers (D,E)
Subject Matter: Troubleshooting Layer 3 Connectivity

The output of the IOS command **show ip interface brief** lists all Router-1 interfaces. That includes the status of all configured and unconfigured network interfaces. The status of GigabitEthernet0/1, Serial0/0 and Loopback0 interfaces are normal (up/up). There is an entry for Serial0/1 that is not configured with an IP address. It is detected as an interface that is unassigned and correctly reported as down/down status. GigabitEthernet0/0 interface status is up/down. That is a layer 2 error sometimes the result of an encapsulation mismatch with the peering router.

The **NVRAM** status for GigabitEthernet0/0 indicates an interface change was made to the startup configuration file. For instance the IP address and subnet mask was assigned to the interface. In addition the router was reloaded at some point after the configuration. The **Manual** status indicates some configuration change occurred and currently active however the router was not reloaded yet.

129. Refer to the network topology drawing. Router-1 must select a route to forward packets from 172.16.1.0/27 to 172.16.3.0/24 network. Select the route next hop IP address and router interface selected based on the routing table output for Router-1? (select two)

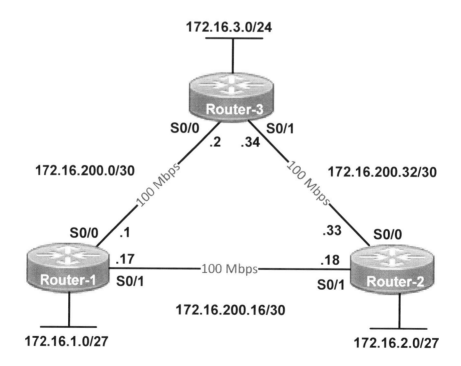

router-1# show ip route

Gateway of last resort is not set

```
    172.16.0.0/24 is variably subnetted, 3 subnets, 2 masks
C     172.16.1.0/27 is directly connected, GigabitEthernet0/0
C     172.16.200.0/30 is directly connected, Serial0/0
C     172.16.200.16/30 is directly connected, Serial0/1
D     172.16.200.32/30 [90/1234567] via 172.16.200.2, Serial0/0
                       [90/1234567] via 172.16.200.18, Serial0/1
D     172.16.3.0/24 [90/1234567] via 172.16.200.2, Serial0/0
D     172.16.3.0/24 [90/3456789] via 172.16.200.18, Serial0/1
```

A. Serial0/0

B. 172.16.200.18

C. 172.16.200.2

D. 172.16.200.16

E. Serial0/1

F. Connected

Correct Answers (A,C)
Subject Matter: Routing Concepts

There are two EIGRP (D) routes advertised to 172.16.3.0/24 subnet. The subnet is on an Ethernet segment of Router-3. The route is advertised by Router-3 (Serial0/0 interfaces) and Router-2 (Serial0/1 interface). Router-2 learned the route via the Router-3 link. The lowest metric is selected where there are multiple routes to the same subnet (172.16.3.0) with the same prefix length (/24) from the same routing protocol (EIGRP). The route from Router-3 shown with next hop 172.16.200.2 has a lower metric and selected as the preferred route.

```
D     172.16.3.0/24 [90/1234567] via 172.16.200.2, Serial0/0
D     172.16.3.0/24 [90/3456789] via 172.16.200.18, Serial0/1
```

130. Refer to the network topology drawing. What wildcard mask will enable advertising of OSPF routes from Router-1 interface Serial0/0 (S0/0) to Router-3 interface Serial0/0 (S0/0)?

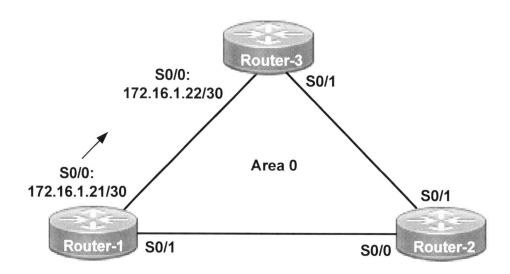

A. network 172.16.1.16 0.0.0.15 area 0

B. network 172.16.1.15 0.0.0.15 area 0

C. network 172.16.1.0 0.0.0.16 area 0

D. network 172.16.1.16 0.15.255. area 0

Correct Answer (A)
Subject Matter: OSPFv2 for IPv4

The OSPF **network** command specifies a single or range of network addresses (subnets) for a router process. Any router interfaces assigned an IP address within that range are included in the OSPF process. There is support for defining multiple OSPF process numbers per router. Each OSPF process identifier is assigned a number and becomes a separate OSPF instance.

Router-1 interface S0/0 is assigned IP address 72.16.1.21/30 to the WAN link. The following **network** command with network address 172.16.1.16 and wildcard mask 0.0.0.15 includes S0/0 interface IP address.

    router-1(config)# router ospf 1
    router-1(config-router)# network 172.16.1.16 0.0.0.15 area 0

The range of IP addresses from **172.16.1.16 - 172.16.1.31** are enabled by the wildcard mask. Interface S0/0 (172.16.1.21/30) for Router-1 is within that IP address range.

The wildcard mask zeros match on the first 3 octets (172.16.1) of the network address. The **15** causes a match on the leftmost 4 bits of the 4th octet. In addition it masks (1s) off the rightmost 4 bits of the 4th octet. it does the opposite of what a subnet mask does.

```
    172.        16.         1.      .16-31
00000000.00000000.00000000.0000 1111
     0.          0.         0.         15
```

131. Refer to the network topology drawing. All routers are enabled with RIPv2 routing protocol. What path will packets take from Router-3 to Router-5?

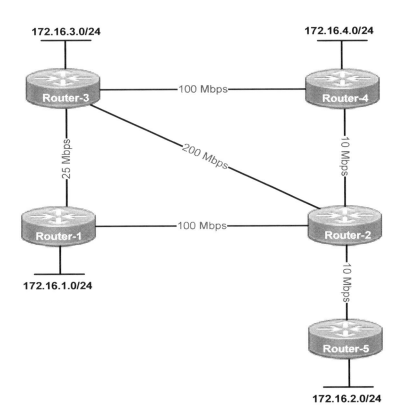

A. R3 to R1 to R2 to R5 and R3 to R4 to R2 to R5

B. R3 to R1 to R2 to R5

C. R3 to R2 to R5

D. R3 to R4 to R2 to R5

E. Path 1: R3 to R1 to R2 to R5
   Path 2: R3 to R4 to R2 to R5

Correct Answer (C)
Subject Matter: RIPv2 for IPv4

RIPv2 routes are selected based on the lowest hop count only. The hop metric is comprised of all routers between source and destination. The bandwidth of a link is not considered. The smallest hop count is from Router-3 to Router-2 to Router-5 (2 hops). RIPv2 does support load balancing across a maximum of 4 paths between source and destination. The paths must have the lowest and equal hop count to load balance packets.

132. Refer to the network topology drawing. All routers are enabled with OSPF and have default settings. What path/s will the router select to forward packets from Router-3 to Router-5?

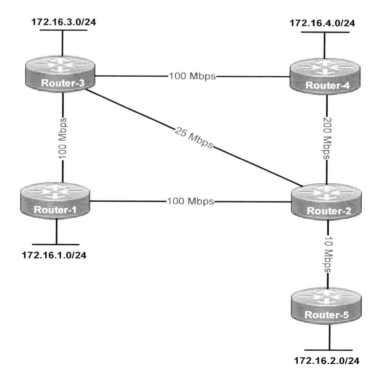

A. Router-3 to Router-2 to Router-5

B. Router-3 to Router-1 to Router-2 to Router-5

C. Router-3 to Router-4 to Router-2 to Router-5

D. Path 1: Router-3 to Router-4 to Router-2 to Router-5
   Path 2: Router-3 to Router-4 to Router-2 to Router-5

Correct Answer (D)
Subject Matter: OSPFv2 for IPv4

OSPF selects a path based on link cost (bandwidth) between source and destination. The cost of each link is calculated and added to arrive at a cumulative metric cost for the path. The minimum cost that can be assigned to any link is 1. The default OSPF reference bandwidth is 100 Mbps. The following formula is used to calculate OSPF link cost.

cost = 100 Mbps / link bandwidth

for example: cost = 100 Mbps / 25 Mbps = 4

default link bandwidth examples:

- 10 Mbps = 10
- 100 Mbps = 1
- 200 Mbps = 1
- 1000 Mbps = 1

Path 1: Router-3 - Router-2 - Router-5 = 4+10 = 14
Path 2: Router-3 - Router-1 - Router-2 - Router-5 = 1+1+10 = 12
Path 3: Router-3 - Router-4 - Router-2 - Router-5 = 1+1+10 = 12

There are two equal lowest cost (highest bandwidth) paths to Router-5. The cost for Path 2 and Path 3 is 12. OSPF will load balance packets across each path as a result. There is no support for unequal-cost load balancing of OSPF routes.

133. How is the OSPF router ID assigned with a default router configuration?

A. router priority

B. highest loopback IP address

C. lowest loopback IP address

D. highest physical interface IP address

Correct Answer (B)
Subject Matter: OSPF

The default OSPF configuration has no router ID assigned. The router assigns the highest IP address of any loopback interface. The physical interface with the highest IP address is assigned where no loopbacks exist.

134. Match the routing protocol on the left with the routing protocol code from a routing table on the right?

EGP	S*
EIGRP	IA
Host (/32)	E
OSPF (Inter-Area)	S
Default Route	D
Static Route	L

Correct Answers.
Subject Matter: Routing Protocol Code

The output of **show ip route** command lists the available routes. The protocol code assigned to the route signifies the source where the route was learned.

EGP	**E**
EIGRP	**D**
Host (/32)	**L**
OSPF (Inter-Area)	**IA**
Default Route	**S***
Static Route	**S**

296

135. What two statements accurately describe route summarization?

A. RIPv1 is a classful routing protocol that cannot summarize routes at default network boundaries

B. EIGRP and OSPF summarize at classless network boundaries only

C. automatic summarization is disabled as a default for classless routing protocols

D. classless routing protocols advertise the subnet in routing updates

E. RIPv2 is a classful routing protocol that summarizes all routes by default

Correct Answers (C,D)
Subject Matter: Routing Concepts

Automatic summarization is disabled as a default for classless routing protocols. Classless routing protocols advertise the subnet in routing updates.

136. Match the EIGRP route type on the left with the correct description?

EIGRP Successor	best advertised route to a destination subnet. It is the route in the routing table
EIGRP AD	backup route with advertised distance less than the feasible distance of the current successor route
EIGRP Feasible Successor	advertised cost from an EIGRP neighbor to the destination subnet
EIGRP FD	advertised distance (cost) + cost between the local router and the next-hop router

Correct Answers.
Subject Matter: EIGRP

The following correctly describe the EIGRP route types available.

EIGRP Successor	**best advertised route to a destination subnet. It is the route in the routing table**
EIGRP AD	**advertised cost from an EIGRP neighbor to the destination subnet**
EIGRP Feasible Successor	**backup route with advertised distance less than the feasible distance of the current successor route**
EIGRP FD	**advertised distance (cost) + cost between the local router and the next-hop router**

137. What three statements correctly describe EIGRP operation for a router with default EIGRP settings?

 A. EIGRP only uses a backup route if the advertised distance (AD) is less than the feasible distance (FD)

 B. EIGRP only uses a backup route if the feasible distance (FD) is less than the advertised distance (AD)

 C. backup route selection rule prevents routing loop

 D. backup route selection rule provides shortest path

 E. feasible distance does not consider bandwidth metric

 F. turn off auto summarization when classless subnet masks are configured

Correct Answers (A,C,F)
Subject Matter: EIGRP

The following correctly describes EIGRP operation with default settings.

- EIGRP only uses a backup route if the advertised distance (AD) is less than the feasible distance (FD).
- Backup route selection rule prevents routing loops.
- Turn off auto summarization when classless subnet masks are configured.

298

138. What is the correct sequence of neighbor states that occurs to establish adjacency between OSPF enabled routers?

1. Loading

2. Down

3. Attempt

4. Exchange

5. Full

6. Exstart

7. Init

8. Two-Way

Correct Answers.
Subject Matter: OSPF

The following describe the correct sequence of states that occurs for OSPF enabled routers to establish adjacency. The IOS command **show ip ospf neighbor** lists the adjacency state with all neighbors. In addition the IOS commands **debug ip ospf hello** and **debug ip ospf adj** are used for troubleshooting adjacency issues.

1. Down: no hello packets received from neighbor

2. Attempt: hello packet has not been received from NBMA neighbor where configured. The local router sends a hello packet to neighbor.

3. Init: hello packet is received from neighbor. Local router verifies neighbor settings such as hello/dead timers and subnet mask are matching.

4. Two-Way: hello packet received from neighbor with router ID of local router listed and DR/BDR election occurs for initial adjacency.

5. Exstart: DR starts exchanging link-state advertisements. Router with higher router ID is assigned as master. The master router manages database synchronization to neighbor/s (slave).

6. Exchange: routers exchange database descriptor packets (DBD).

7. Loading: routers exchange all link-state information (LSA).

8. Full: normal state where adjacency is established between neighbors.

139. What information is advertised in OSPF hello packets from a neighbor? (select three)

A. link speed

B. hello and dead timer settings

C. router priority

D. network type

E. process ID

F. DR/BDR assigned to local segment (subnet)

Correct Answers (B,C,F)
Subject Matter: OSPF

The hello packet advertises various OSPF configuration settings between adjacent neighbors. In addition it detects the operational status of a neighbor. Any routes advertised from a neighbor with the interface down are deleted from the routing table. Neighbor adjacency is not permitted between settings that must match such as timers and common interface subnet. The following is a list of all items advertised with the OSPF hello packet.

- Hello timer and dead timer (sec)
- Router priority
- DR/BDR assigned to local segment
- Area assigned to neighbor interface
- Subnet mask of neighbor interface
- Authentication method

140. Refer to the network topology drawing. Host-1 is assigned to VLAN 10 and cannot access any application on Server-1 assigned to VLAN 12. What two IOS commands are used to verify Inter-VLAN routing is configured and working correctly on Router-1?

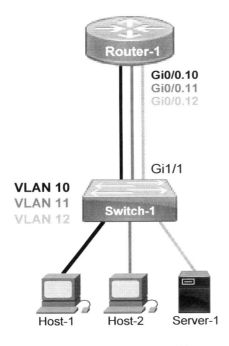

Host-1 = 172.16.10.1/27
Host-2 = 172.16.11.1/27
Server-1 = 172.16.12.1/27

A. router-1# show startup-config

B. router-1# show vlan

C. router-1# show running-config

D. router-1# show ipconfig

E. router-1# show ip route

F. router-1# show interfaces trunk

Correct Answers (C,E)
Subject Matter: Inter-VLAN Routing

Troubleshooting any problem with Inter-VLAN routing requires verifying connectivity between all network devices. The router is configured with subinterfaces that each have a unique IP address. The switch is configured with VLANs and a trunk on the uplink to the router. The trunk forwards VLANs to the router for Inter-VLAN routing

The primary IOS command used for troubleshooting router configuration is **show running-config**. The primary IOS command used to verify routing is **show ip route**.

The IOS command **show running-config** lists the configuration changes made to Router-1. The physical router interface (Gi0/0) is enabled with no IP address and matching speed/duplex settings. There are subinterfaces for VLAN 10, 11 and 12 that are assigned to different subnets. Encapsulation is enabled per subinterface with the correct VLANs assigned. Encapsulation allows the router interface to identify VLAN membership however it isn't a standard trunk interface as with a switch.

```
router-1# show running-config

interface gigabitethernet0/0
no ip address
speed auto
duplex auto
!
interface gigabitethernet0/0.10
encapsulation dot1q 10
ip address 172.16.10.254 255.255.255.224
!
interface gigabitethernet0/0.11
encapsulation dot1q 11
ip address 172.16.11.254 255.255.255.224
!
interface gigabitethernet0/0.12
encapsulation dot1q 12
ip address 172.16.12.254 255.255.255.224
```

The IOS command **show ip route** verifies all three subinterfaces and associated IP address are listed in the routing table. The routes are correctly installed as directly connected (local interface).

router-1# show ip route

Gateway of last resort is not set

    172.16.0.0/24 is subnetted, 3 subnets
C   172.16.10.0 is directly connected, GigabitEthernet0/0.10
C   172.16.11.0 is directly connected, GigabitEthernet0/0.11
C   172.16.12.0 is directly connected, GigabitEthernet0/0.12

The following include additional troubleshooting commands to verify configuration and connectivity between router, switches and hosts.

router-1# **show ip interface brief**

Verify router subinterfaces have layer 1 and layer 2 connectivity (up/up). In addition the IP addresses for subinterface are listed.

switch-1# **show running-config**

Verify VLANs and trunk interface is configured correctly and assigned to the correct switch port.

switch-1# **show vlan**

Verify VLANs are active and assigned to the correct switch port.

c:\> **ipconfig /all**

Verify the host settings are correct for IP address, subnet mask and default gateway.

switch-1# **show interfaces trunk**

Verify the switch trunk interface (uplink) to the router is operational.

device# **ping**

Ping the following devices to verify layer 3 connectivity from the host:
- host default gateway (router)
- destination host (server)

141. What three statements accurately describe the configuration and usage of the following IOS command?

router(config)# ip default-network 172.16.1.254

A. advertises classful routes only

B. configured on layer 2 network device

C. gateway of last resort for a classful route

D. routing must be enabled

E. single **ip default-network** statement permitted per router

F. routing must be disabled

Correct Answers (A,C,D)
Subject Matter: IPv4 Static Routing

The purpose of **ip default-network** command is to configure a gateway of last resort on a router for a classful route. The network administrator can configure multiple **ip default-network** statements. Any classful routes in the routing table to that subnet are flagged as a candidate default routes.

The following features accurately describe the **ip default-network** command:

- Advertises classful routes only
- Configures gateway of last resort for a classful route
- IP routing must be enabled

142. The network administrator issues **ipconfig /all** command from a desktop to determine connectivity status. What three connectivity settings can be verified?

A. MAC address

B. default gateway is assigned from DHCP

C. default static route to the internet is correct

D. assigned default gateway is correct

E. IPv4 address

Correct Answers (A,B,E)
Subject Matter: Troubleshooting Layer 3 Connectivity

The Windows command **ipconfig /all** is used for troubleshooting desktop connectivity issues. The output displays host IPv4/IPv6 addressing and that DHCP has assigned the default gateway. In addition the network administrator can verify the MAC address and operational status of all network adapters. Any issues with network connectivity from the client side can be confirmed.

143. The IP address of a web server has been resolved. Select the protocol that will resolve the destination MAC address to be written into frames directed toward the server?

   A. HTTP

   B. DNS

   C. DHCP

   D. ARP

   E. RARP

Correct Answer (D)
Subject Matter: Routing Concepts

The DNS request will resolve the IP address assigned to any host or network device. The sending host cannot forward packets to a web server for example until the MAC address is known. The ARP broadcast will use the known IP address of the web server to request it's MAC address. The web server then sends a reply to the host with its MAC address.

144. Refer to the network topology drawing. What two statements are correct?

- VLAN 10 = 172.16.10.0/24
- VLAN 11 = 172.16.11.0/24
- VLAN 12 = 172.16.12.0/24

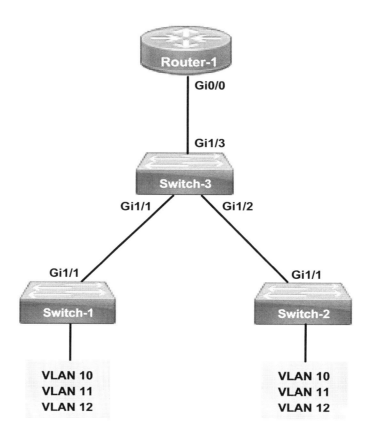

A. Switch-1 and Switch-2 ports must be configured as access mode

B. Switch-3 ports must be configured as access mode

C. Router-1 is required to forward packets between the same VLANs

D. Gi0/0 interface on Router-1 must be configured with subinterfaces

E. Gi1/3 interface on Switch-3 must be configured with subinterfaces

F. all switch ports must be configured as trunk mode

Correct Answers (D,F)
Subject Matter: Inter-VLAN Routing

The trunk link between switches enables forwarding of all VLANs between switches. The layer 2 switches can only forward frames between the same VLANs. Inter-VLAN routing requires a layer 3 network device such as a router to forward packets between different VLANs. It is sometimes referred to as Router on a Stick. The following describes the configuration required to enable Inter-VLAN routing.

- Router-1 physical interface (Gi0/0) must be configured with a subinterface for each VLAN on the switches where Inter-VLAN routing should be enabled.

- All switch port uplinks must be configured for trunk mode.

The frame sent from VLAN 10 of Switch-1 for instance to VLAN 12 of Switch-2 is forwarded to Router-1 first for routing.

145. What two statements correctly describe Switch Virtual Interfaces (SVI)?

A. layer 3 VLAN interface on a switch

B. layer 2 interface

C. enables switch management

D. assigned to an access port

E. assigned to a trunk port

Correct Answers (A,C)
Subject Matter: Inter-VLAN Routing

The SVI is a layer 3 VLAN interface configured on a network switch for routing. purposes. The layer 2 switch is typically configured with a management SVI and assigned to the same subnet as the default gateway (router) for the switch.

146. What two statements correctly describe OSPFv3 operation and packet forwarding?

A. OSPFv3 runs per link instead of per subnet

B. OSPFv3 runs per interface where configured

C. OSPFv3 neighbor subnets must match to form adjacency

D. OSPFv3 neighbor subnets do not have to match when establishing adjacency

E. OSPFv3 does not support multiple instances per link

Correct Answers (A,D)
Subject Matter: OSPFv3 for IPv6

The default for OSPFv3 enabled interfaces is IPv6 addressing. As a result OSPFv3 runs per link instead of per subnet packet forwarding. Multiple IP addresses can be assigned to a single interface and multiple OSPF processes can be assigned per link. There is no requirement for OSPFv3 neighbors to share the same subnet assignment to form an adjacency. In addition OSPFv3 neighbor adjacencies are established over link-local addresses.

147. Refer to the result of the following IOS command on router-1. Select the statement that is correct?

router-1# debug ip ospf adjacency

OSPF adjacency events debugging is on

router-1#

Dead R 40 C 40, Hello R 15 C 10 Mask R 255.255.255.0 C 255.255.255.0

A. router-1 hello timer is 15 seconds

B. router-1 dead timer is 15 seconds

C. neighbor hello timer is 10 seconds

D. router-1 dead timer is 40 seconds

Correct Answer (D)
Subject Matter: OSPF

The IOS command **debug ip ospf adj** is used for troubleshooting OSPF adjacency issues. It lists the packet exchange between neighbors and any errors. Router-1 (where the command was issued) received a hello packet from the neighbor with a mismatched hello timer setting. The received (R) hello timer advertised from the neighbor is 15 seconds. The hello timer of Router-1 is configured (C) as 10 seconds. The dead timers of both routers are set at 40 seconds. The hello timer determines how often hello packets are sent between OSPF neighbor interfaces.

Dead R 40 C 40, Hello **R 15 C 10** Mask R 255.255.255.0 C 255.255.255.0

In addition to timer mismatches, the **debug ip ospf adj** command can detect subnet mismatches and area ID mismatches. The area ID configured on the interfaces that connect OSPF neighbor routers must match.

148. Refer to the network topology drawing. What is required to fix the IP addressing issue on Router-1?

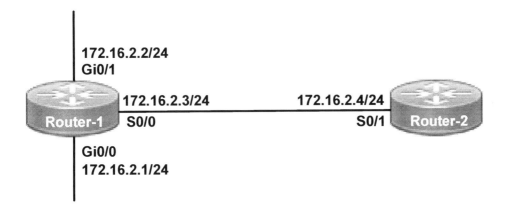

A. assign 172.16.3.3/24 to Router-1 (Gi0/0)

B. assign 172.16.3.3/24 to Router-1 (Gi0/1)

C. assign 172.16.3.1/24 to Router-1 (S0/0)
   assign 172.16.3.2/24 to Router-2 (S0/1)

D. assign 172.16.1.1/24 to Router-1 (Gi0/0)
   assign 172.16.3.1/24 to Router-1 (Gi0/1)

Correct Answer (D)
Subject Matter: Troubleshooting Layer 3 Connectivity

All network interfaces on a router must be assigned to a separate subnet. The interfaces on Router-1 (Gi0/0, Gi0/1 and S0/0) are assigned to the same 172.16.2.0/24 subnet causing routing errors. Assigning each interface to a different subnet would fix the issue. Router-1 interface S0/0 is already assigned 172.16.2.3/24 from 172.16.2.0 subnet. The following assigns Gi0/0 and Gi0/1 interfaces to different subnets.

- 172.16.2.3/24 already assigned to Router-1 (S0/0)
- **assign 172.16.1.1/24 to Router-1 (Gi0/0)**
- **assign 172.16.3.1/24 to Router-1 (Gi0/1)**

Module 4: WAN Technologies

1. When should a network administrator configure the clock rate on a WAN serial interface?

    A. local or remote router interface on any point-to-point serial link

    B. router serial interface that is DTE for the WAN connection

    C. any router serial interface with no CSU/DSU connected

    D. router serial interface that is DCE for the WAN connection

Correct Answer (D)
Subject Matter: WAN Connectivity

Serial interfaces connect devices that are assigned as a DCE or DTE. The DCE provides clocking for the serial interface. The DTE is the device receiving the clock signal. The router is a DTE that typically connects to a DCE such as a CSU/DSU or modem. The CSU/DSU connects to the ISP DCE equipment. The remote peering router is a DTE as well. The clocking and framing is typically set by the ISP on a WAN serial link.

DTE - DCE - **[DCE ISP DCE]** - DCE - DTE

The clock rate is only configured on a router serial interface when the interface is terminated using the DCE end of the cable. That is required when the routers are directly connected in a lab. The DTE side of the cable is terminated at the neighbor router.

2. What is the default synchronous serial interface encapsulation for a Cisco router?

    A. Frame Relay

    B. PPP

    C. none

    D. HDLC

Correct Answer (D)
Subject Matter: WAN Connectivity

The Cisco default synchronous serial interface encapsulation type is HDLC.

3. What IOS interface command is required to change the serial interface operational status to up?

A. restart

B. default is up

C. enable

D. no shutdown

E. reload

Correct Answer (D)
Subject Matter: WAN Connectivity

The serial interface on a router is disabled by default. The following IOS command enables the serial interface.

router(config-if)# no shutdown

4. Refer to the network topology drawing. Router-1 cannot authenticate to Router-2. What is the cause?

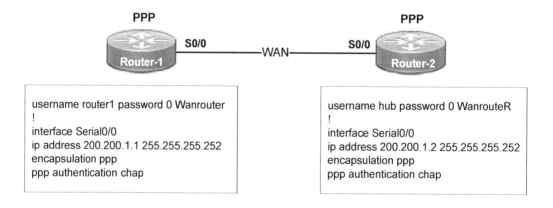

A. device usernames do not match

B. public IP addressing is not supported

C. CHAP authentication requires HDLC encapsulation

D. device passwords do not match

Correct Answer (D)
Subject Matter: PPP and MLPPP

CHAP authentication requires the passwords to match between local and remote peering routers.

5. What three security services are provided by a VPN?

    A. privacy

    B. data integrity

    C. access control lists

    D. authentication

    E. routing

Correct Answers (A,B,D)
Subject Matter: WAN Connectivity

The VPN is characterized by the following attributes:

- Privacy (data encryption)
- Data integrity (hashing)
- Authentication (RSA)

6. Select the TCP handshake exchange between source and destination hosts?

    A. SYN flag set, SYN/ACK flag sent, ACK bit set

    B. ACK bit set, SYN flag set, SYN/ACK flag sent

    C. SYN flag set, ACK flag sent, ACK bit set

    D. SYN flag set, SYN/ACK flag sent, SYN bit set

Correct Answer (A)
Subject Matter: WAN Connectivity

TCP-based applications require a three-way handshake for host-to-host connectivity. The host starts the session by sending a **SYN flag** to the server. The server responds with a **SYN/ACK** flag. The host sends an **ACK** with bit set to acknowledge and establish a TCP connection.

    SYN flag set, SYN/ACK flag sent, ACK bit set

7. What two statements summarize the services provided by LCP and NCP to establish PPP peering between routers?

A. NCP provides Layer 3 protocol encapsulation

B. NCP provides Layer 2 encapsulation

C. PPP includes LCP to establish, manage and terminate WAN connection

D. PPP includes LCP for WAN authentication and error detection

Correct Answers (A,C)
Subject Matter: PPP and MLPPP

LCP establishes, manages and terminates the WAN connection. In addition LCP negotiates PAP/CHAP authentication with the remote peer router. It is the data link (layer 2) of the PPP session. NCP provides protocol encapsulation for multiple layer 3 network protocols where configured.

8. What two statements correctly describe features of CHAP authentication?

A. challenge messages sent at random intervals verify peer router identity

B. one-way authentication per link

C. passwords are sent across the link

D. peering router initiates any identity challenge

Correct Answers (A,D)
Subject Matter: PPP and MLPPP

CHAP is an authentication protocol supported with PPP. It provides secure authentication of the remote peer router with a username and password. The number of retry attempts is controlled by the peer router. In addition messages are sent periodically to verify peering devices is authentic.

9. What two services are provided by WAN connectivity?

A. enable connectivity between branch offices, data center and cloud

B. decrease costs to send data

C. increase network performance

D. information sharing among internal and external organizations

316

Correct Answers (A,D)
Subject Matter: WAN Connectivity

The following describe the standard reasons for deploying WAN connectivity:

- Enable connectivity between branch offices, data center and cloud
- Information sharing among internal and external organizations

10. Refer to the output from the following IOS command. What is the default WAN encapsulation?

    router# show interfaces serial 0/0

    A. ATM

    B. HDLC

    C. PPPoE

    D. PPP

Correct Answer (B)
Subject Matter: WAN Connectivity

The output of **show interfaces** lists the WAN data link protocol that is enabled. The serial interface is using the default HDLC encapsulation.

11. Select three statements that correctly describe WAN device termination?

    A. router analog interface provides PSTN connectivity for voice failover

    B. connecting two routers in a lab requires DCE/DCE cable

    C. CSU/DSU terminates PSTN analog circuit

    D. router is DCE device on a serial WAN interface

    E. router is DTE device on a serial WAN interface

    F. CSU/DSU terminates a digital circuit from internet service provider

Correct Answers (A,E,F)
Subject Matter: WAN Connectivity

The router is a (DTE) device that connects to a local CSU/DSU (DCE) for serial WAN interfaces. The CSU/DSU terminates the digital local loop from the service provider network (ISP). Analog interfaces terminate an analog local loop and converts between digital and analog signaling. The DSL modem terminates a service provider local loop and converts between Ethernet and DSL signaling.

12. Select three correct statements concerning PPP?

    A. WAN link speed faster than T1/E1 is supported

    B. encapsulation type must match between peering routers

    C. supports Multilink PPP

    D. error detection is not supported

    E. layer 3 protocol

Correct Answers (A,B,C)
Subject Matter: PPP

The maximum speed supported on a single PPP link is T1/E1 however MLPPP enables bundling for increased bandwidth. Encapsulation must match between peering routers configured with PPP.

13. What three statements concerning PPP authentication are correct?

    A. CHAP is less secure than PAP

    B. CHAP supports data hashing

    C. PAP sends clear text passwords

    D. CHAP periodically verifies identity (authentication) of peer router

    E. CHAP requires matching device usernames

Correct Answers (B,C,D)
Subject Matter: PPP and MLPPP

CHAP is an enhanced authentication protocol supported with PPP. The purpose of CHAP is to authenticate the remote PPP router. The username and password is hashed with CHAP for optimized security. In addition CHAP periodically verifies the identity (authentication) of the remote peer router. There is no hashing available with PAP authentication. The username and password is sent as clear text only.

14. What three statements accurately describe Multilink PPP (MLPPP) feature support?

   A. encapsulation of serial, Ethernet and DSL frames

   B. encapsulation type per bundle must match for all member links

   C. interface **bandwidth** command is not supported for logical bundle

   D. MLPoE EtherChannel is supported

   E. maximum of 10 Ethernet links per bundle

   F. load balancing not supported

Correct Answers (A,B,C)
Subject Matter: MLPPP

Multilink PPP (MLPPP) enables bundling of multiple links into a single logical link. That includes encapsulation of serial or broadband (Ethernet/DSL) WAN services. Metro Ethernet is now being deployed as a WAN service. The primary advantages include increased bandwidth and link redundancy.

There is a limit of 10 links per serial bundle and 8 link per Ethernet/DSL bundle. The encapsulation type per bundle must match for all member links. In addition the interface **bandwidth** command is not supported for a logical bundle. The **bandwidth** command is sometimes configured to influence routing on a physical interface. It does not however have any effect on the interface speed or forwarding rate. The physical interface speed (1000 Mbps etc.) would determine that. There are QoS techniques that can shape interface speed to a lower rate.

15. What two statements accurately describe the effects of the following IOS commands?

> router(config)# aaa authentication ppp default local
> router(config-if)# ppp authentication pap chap

A. RADIUS server authentication is enabled

B. local username database is used for authenticating peer router

C. enables PAP and CHAP authentication

D. encrypts PAP and CHAP username and passwords

Correct Answers (B,C)
Subject Matter: PPP and MLPPP Local Authentication

The first IOS command **aaa authentication ppp default local** enables use of the local username database for authenticating peer router.

The second IOS command **ppp authentication pap chap** enables PAP and CHAP authentication. The router will attempt PAP authentication first then CHAP based on the order.

16. Select the correct configuration to enable PPP on a serial interface with CHAP authentication and password to *cisco*?

A. router(config)# interface serial1/0/0
    router(config-if)# encapsulation ppp
    router(config-if)# ppp authentication chap cisco

B. router(config)# interface serial1/0/0
    router(config-if)# encapsulation ppp
    router(config-if)# ppp chap authentication
    router(config-if)# ppp chap password cisco

C. router(config)# interface serial1/0/0
    router(config-if)# encapsulation ppp
    router(config-if)# ppp authentication chap
    router(config-if)# ppp chap password cisco

D. router(config)# interface serial1/0/0
    router(config-if)# encapsulation ppp
    router(config-if)# ppp authentication chap
    router(config-if)# ppp password cisco

Correct Answer (C)
Subject Matter: PPP and MLPPP

The following IOS commands will enable PPP on serial interface 1/0/0 with CHAP authentication and password *cisco*.

```
router(config)# interface serial1/0/0
router(config-if)# encapsulation ppp (enables PPP)
router(config-if)# ppp authentication chap (enables CHAP)
router(config-if)# ppp chap password cisco (password = cisco)
```

17. What two statements are true of the following Multilink PPP interface configuration?

```
interface multilink 10
ip address 172.16.1.1 255.255.0.0
no keepalive
ppp multilink
ppp multilink group 10
```

A. enables CHAP authentication type as a default

B. creates Multilink 10 (bundle)

C. enables MLPPP feature

D. enables group number 10 for subinterfaces

E. enables unlimited subinterfaces to join group

Correct Answers (B,C)
Subject Matter: MLPPP

The Multilink bundle starts with creating the Multilink interface and assigning a bundle number. The configuration assigns number 10 to the bundle and enables the mlppp feature. In addition it allows only physical interfaces assigned to Multilink interface 10 to join the bundle. Any WAN interface with the IOS command **ppp multilink group 10** is assigned to bundle 10.

- interface multilink 10 *(assigns bundle number)*
- ip address 172.16.1.1 255.255.0.0
- no keepalive
- ppp multilink *(enables multilink)*
- ppp multilink group 10 *(allow only physical link assigned to bundle 10)*

18. What IOS command verifies the interface status and encapsulation type for Multilink bundle 1?

A. show interfaces multilink 1

B. show interfaces group 1

C. show interfaces mlppp 1

D. show multilink group 1

E. show ppp multilink 1

Correct Answer (A)
Subject Matter: MLPPP

The following IOS command will verify the interface status and encapsulation type for Multilink bundle 1.

router# show interfaces multilink 1

19. What IOS command verifies multilink bundle member settings and errors?

A. show multilink ppp

B. show mlppp /all

C. show ppp multilink

D. show multilink

E. show multilink group

Correct Answer (C)
Subject Matter: MLPPP

The following IOS command displays the status of all bundle member (physical) interfaces. In addition any interface errors are listed as well.

router# show ppp multilink

20. Select two correct statements for PPPoE?

    A. PPPoE encapsulates PPP inside Ethernet frames

    B. PPPoE encapsulates Ethernet inside HDLC frames

    C. PPPoE encapsulates Ethernet inside PPP frames

    D. Ethernet provides authentication, encryption and compression

    E. NCP is not required

    F. PPPoE provides authentication, encryption and compression

Correct Answers (A,F)
Subject Matter: PPPoE

PPPoE was designed to encapsulate PPP inside Ethernet frames. PPP enables authentication, encryption and compression across the internet.

21. Match the descriptions on the left with the protocol that supports the feature on the right?

peer to peer	PPP
security features	PPPoE
multipoint broadcast	PPPoE
easy to deploy	PPPoE
layer 2 transport independent	PPP
Ethernet only router	PPP
WAN serial transport	PPP
router	PPPoE
bridge	PPPoE

Correct Answers.
Subject Matter: PPP/PPPoE

The following correctly match the characteristics for PPPoE and PPP.

peer to peer	PPP
security features	PPP
multipoint broadcast	PPPoE
easy to deploy	PPPoE
layer 2 transport independent	PPPoE
Ethernet only router	PPPoE
WAN serial transport	PPP
router	PPP
bridge	PPPoE

22. How does a PPPoE client receive an IP address assignment?

    A. static only

    B. DHCP

    C. IPCP

    D. LCP

    E. not required

Correct Answer (C)
Subject Matter: PPPoE

IPCP is the Network Control Protocol (NCP) for IPv4 traffic across a PPP link. The client IP address request is processed through IPCP for a PPP link. In addition IPCP allows for requesting the IP address from a DHCP server.

23. What two statements correctly describe the Link Quality Monitoring (LQM) feature for PPP?

A. Link Quality Report (LQR) packet is sent across the WAN at regular intervals

B. Link Quality Report (LQR) packet determines the percentage of packets transmitted that were received

C. PPP will reset a link where packet loss is 10%

D. Link Quality Report (LQR) packet interval is equal to three keepalives

E. Link Quality Report (LQR) is a Network Control Protocol (NCP)

Correct Answers (A,B)
Subject Matter: PPP

The purpose of Link Quality Monitoring (LQM) is to detect packet drop errors on a PPP WAN link. It provides error detection and correction across the PPP link. The link quality report packet (LQR) is sent across the WAN at regular intervals. The LQR calculates the percentage of packets transmitted from packets that were received. It is disabled by default however is configurable with the **ppp quality [percent]** command.

24. Select two encapsulation protocols supported by a WAN serial interface?

A. ATM

B. PPP

C. MPLS

D. HDLC

E. SONET

Correct Answers (B,D)
Subject Matter: WAN Connectivity

- The serial WAN encapsulation protocols include PPP and HDLC. The default encapsulation for Cisco routers is HDLC.

- MPLS is unique as WAN protocol that is IP layer 3 aware. It is a shim between layer 2 and layer 3 (layer 2.5). MPLS adds a label to the data link WAN protocol (T1/E1, Frame Relay, Ethernet, PPP). The packet is forwarded (routed) across the MPLS network.

- SONET does not provide any framing of upper layer protocols. As a result it is a WAN protocol between layer 1 and layer 2 of sorts.

25. What information is provided by the following IOS command for troubleshooting PPP? (select three)

   router# debug ppp negotiation

A. CHAP authentication message exchange

B. IPCP request

C. LCP link establishment status

D. TCP session setup

E. serial interface operational status

F. routing

Correct Answers (A,B,C)
Subject Matter: PPP

The command **debug ppp negotiation** is used to troubleshoot PPP link errors. The output lists LCP link establishment and PAP/CHAP negotiation with the remote router. IPCP packets such as IP address requests are displayed as well.

26. How is a PPPoE client uniquely identified across the broadcast domain?

    A. session ID and MAC address

    B. MAC address and IP address

    C. session ID and password

    D. MAC address and hostname

Correct Answer (A)
Subject Matter: PPPoE

The PPPoE client is uniquely identified with a MAC address and session ID. There is a MAC address exchange between peers before NCP (layer 3) starts. That is required to identify the MAC address of the remote peer router. The session ID is assigned to the PPPoE session after MAC address discovery.

27. What two statements accurately describe Cisco support for PPPoE over Ethernet client feature?

    A. support for PPPoE client mode only

    B. support for PPPoE server mode only

    C. client mode routers connect to the ISP for IP addressing

    D. server mode routers connect to the ISP for IP addressing

    E. client mode router negotiates authentication with server

Correct Answers (C,E)
Subject Matter: PPPoE

The PPPoE over Ethernet Client feature for Cisco routers has a client/server peering model. The client router is at the customer premises and the server device is at the ISP. It is typically deployed for DSL connectivity from a Cisco router with Ethernet only interfaces. The DSL modem is connected to the Cisco router Ethernet interface. The client mode router requests an IP address from the ISP with IPCP negotiation. In addition the client mode router negotiates authentication with the ISP server. PPPoE client mode enables multiple hosts on an Ethernet segment to access DSL services.

28. What two IOS commands provide status information for the PPPoE client router?

A. show pppoe session

B. show pppoe client summary

C. show ip interface brief

D. show ip protocols

E. show pppoe status

Correct Answers (A,C)
Subject Matter: PPPoE

The following describe the two easiest IOS commands used to verify basic PPPoE network connectivity.

show ip interface brief - displays the status of network interfaces with an IP address assigned. That verifies the ISP has assigned an IP address via IPCP to the client router. In addition the dialer IP address virtual interface should have up/up status.

show pppoe session - displays the PPPoE client session status with the ISP. That include assigned MAC address, Ethernet interface and dialer interface status (up/up).

29. What IOS command enables GRE tunneling over DMVPN?

A. tunnel mode gre mtp

B. tunnel mode gre dmvpn

C. tunnel mode gre multipoint

D. tunnel mode gre point-to-point

E. tunnel mode dmvpn

Correct Answer (C)
Subject Matter: GRE Tunneling

The purpose of GRE is to enable layer 3 network protocols across the WAN. It is typically deployed to support routing protocol advertisements across a VPN. That is accomplished by tunneling (encapsulating) the routing protocol. The following IOS command will enable GRE tunnel support across the DMVPN.

    router(config-if)# tunnel mode gre multipoint

30. Select two primary advantages of Generic Routing Encapsulation (GRE)?

    A. encryption and authentication

    B. routing protocol support across internet

    C. dynamic tunnel setup

    D. increase hop count for layer 3 protocols

    E. load balancing

Correct Answers (B,D)
Subject Matter: GRE Tunneling

The two primary advantages of GRE tunneling include the following:

- Routing protocol support across the internet
- Increase hop count for layer 3 protocols

Some advantages of GRE/DMVPN connectivity include the following:

- Lower support costs and easier management
- Tunnel multiple protocols across the internet
- Increase the hop count where required
- Dynamic VPN tunnel setup and configuration
- Enable increased VPN deployment across WAN
- Redundant (backup) WAN connectivity across the internet

31. What two statements describe the GRE tunnel source address?

    A. private routable IP address space

    B. public or private IP address space

    C. public routable IP address space

    D. local interface

    E. virtual interface

Correct Answers (C,D)
Subject Matter: GRE Tunneling

GRE assigns a tunnel source and tunnel destination IP address. They are public (NBMA) routable IP addresses. In addition the tunnel source address refers to a local interface. The tunnel destination address is the remote router interface.

- Public routable IP address
- Local router interface

32. What is the purpose of Next Hop Resolution Protocol (NHRP)?

    A. map public IP address to public GRE tunnel interface

    B. map private IP address to tunnel interface

    C. map public IP address to router hostname

    D. map tunnel interface to public GRE tunnel address

Correct Answer (D)
Subject Matter: GRE Tunneling

Next Hop Resolution Protocol (NHRP) enables the dynamic tunnel setup between hub and spokes. There is an automatic detection of all spoke public IP addresses (NBMA). The public routable (tunnel source) IP address is often dynamically assigned to the spoke (branch) by the ISP. The spoke then registers it's NBMA IP address with the hub router.

NHRP at the hub router maps the spoke tunnel source address to spoke tunnel interface. The tunnel interface (logical) is the private IP address. The hub router at the data center builds a table with mappings for all connected spoke routers. The tunnel interface is often a loopback address. Packet forwarding is enabled with next hop addressing (routes) between hub router and all connected spokes.

33. Select the IOS commands that will configure GRE tunnel 10 with correct IP addressing?

   A. router(config)# interface Tunnel
      router(config-if)# ip address [ip address] [subnet mask]
      router(config-if)# source tunnel 10 [ip address]
      router(config-if)# destination tunnel 10 [ip address]

   B. router(config)# interface Tunnel10
      router(config-if)# ip address [ip address] [subnet mask]
      router(config-if)# tunnel source [ip address] destination [ip address]

   C. router(config)# interface Tunnel
      router(config-if)# ip address [ip address] [subnet mask]
      router(config-if)# tunnel 10 source [ip address]
      router(config-if)# tunnel 10 destination [ip address]

   D. router(config)# interface Tunnel10
      router(config-if)# ip address [ip address] [subnet mask]
      router(config-if)# tunnel source [ip address]
      router(config-if)# tunnel destination [ip address]

Correct Answer (D)
Subject Matter: GRE Tunneling

The following IOS commands will configure GRE tunnel 10 with IP addressing for a spoke router. The tunnel source can be configured as either a physical interface or an IP address.

   router(config)# interface Tunnel10
   router(config-if)# ip address [private ip address] [subnet mask]
   router(config-if)# tunnel source [local egress interface]
   router(config-if)# tunnel destination [remote public ip address]

The hub router would be configured with an mGRE (multipoint GRE) interface. That is required to connect all spoke routers to the hub. In addition there is only a tunnel source IP address configured at the hub.

34. What is the reason for configuring IPsec with GRE tunneling?

    A. IPsec provides the tunneling for GRE

    B. IPsec is required to enable GRE

    C. IPsec provides encryption for GRE traffic

    D. GRE provides tunneling for IPsec

    E. IPsec provides encryption for non-GRE traffic

Correct Answer (C)
Subject Matter: GRE Tunneling

GRE tunneling provides no security at all for packets traversing the internet. IPsec provides encryption and authentication for GRE tunnels.

35. What IOS troubleshooting command will provide Tunnel1 interface status and configuration settings?

    A. show ip interface tunnel 1

    B. show gre tunnel /all

    C. show interface tunnel 1

    D. show interfaces gre

Correct Answer (C)
Subject Matter: GRE Tunneling

The following IOS command provides both interface status (up/up) for the tunnel, configured settings and performance.

    router# show interface tunnel 1

36. What three statements are true of GRE protocol?

    A. stateless

    B. no flow control

    C. connection-oriented

    D. IP protocol 47

    E. 26 byte header

    F. secure

Correct Answers (A,B,D)
Subject Matter: GRE Tunneling

GRE is a stateless protocol with no flow control and assigned IP protocol 47.

37. Match the network topology on the left with the correct description?

hub and spoke	no link redundancy, some broadcast traffic, fast convergence, easy to manage, branch offices
point-to-point	any to any connectivity, maximum link redundancy, expensive, high broadcast traffic, difficult to manage, WAN core
full mesh	single link, cost effective, no link redundancy, low broadcast traffic, easiest to manage

Correct Answers.
Subject Matter: WAN Topologies

The following describe standard network topologies and characteristics.

hub and spoke	**no link redundancy, some broadcast traffic, fast convergence, easy to manage, branch offices**
point-to-point	**single link, cost effective, no link redundancy, low broadcast traffic, easiest to manage**
full mesh	**any to any connectivity, maximum link redundancy, expensive, high broadcast traffic, difficult to manage, WAN core**

38. What three statements are true for WAN homing topologies?

A. single homed provides router redundancy

B. dual homed provides link redundancy

C. single homed provides no link redundancy

D. dual homed provides two connections to different ISPs

E. dual homed provides two connections to the same ISP

F. single homed supports two connections to the same ISP

Correct Answers (B,C,E)
Subject Matter: WAN Topologies

WAN homing describes the network topology between customer and ISP for internet access. In addition along with topology there are levels of redundancy. The following are correct statements concerning WAN homing topologies.

- Dual homed provides link redundancy
- Single homed provides no link redundancy
- Dual homed provides two connections to the same ISP

39. What are four advantages of MPLS?

A. multiprotocol transport support

B. cost effective

C. service provider managed routing

D. any-to-any connectivity

E. QoS support

F. low latency

G. bandwidth on demand

Correct Answers (A,C,D,E)
Subject Matter: WAN Access

MPLS is a layer 2.5 WAN transport solution that encapsulates any data link protocol. Internet routing is provided to customers across the MPLS network. It is popular for connecting branch offices to the enterprise WAN. The following are four standard advantages available with MPLS:

- Multiprotocol transport support
- Service provider managed routing
- Any-to-any connectivity
- QoS support

40. Match the WAN protocol on the left with the most suitable usage?

SSL VPN	branch office, multiprotocol support, WAN access solution, layer 2, layer 3 VPN
MPLS	internet-based, layer 2, DSL, cable, static configuration
IPsec VPN	internet-based VPN, layer 3, cloud connectivity, IWAN, dynamic
DMVPN	web-based encryption, dynamic, easy to deploy, granular application security
Metro Ethernet	static VPN, private, point-to-point topology, difficult to deploy, router peering
PPPoE	easy to deploy, layer 2, bandwidth on demand, distance limits

Correct Answers.
Subject Matter: WAN Access

The following describes the characteristics of each WAN protocol.

SSL VPN	**web-based encryption, dynamic, easy to deploy, granular application security**
MPLS	**branch office, multiprotocol support, WAN access solution, layer 2, layer 3 VPN**
IPsec VPN	**static VPN, private, point-to-point topology, difficult to deploy, router peering**
DMVPN	**internet-based VPN, layer 3, cloud connectivity, IWAN, dynamic**
Metro Ethernet	**easy to deploy, layer 2, bandwidth on demand, distance limits**
PPPoE	**internet-based, layer 2, DSL, cable, static configuration**

41. What IOS commands will add routes to the BGP routing table? (select two)

    A. default route

    B. ip route

    C. network

    D. neighbor

    E. route-map

Correct Answers (B,C)
Subject Matter: Single-Homed eBGP for IPv4

BGP advertises routes based on the configured static routes (**ip route**) and the **network** command. The router installs all static routes in the routing table. The **network** command advertises the network prefixes assigned. In addition the **network 0.0.0.0** command advertises the default route in the routing table.

42. Select two reasons why static routes are required for BGP route propagation when there is no IGP running?

A. BGP is not a dynamic routing protocol

B. routes must exist in routing table for advertising to peer router

C. BGP neighbor adjacency requires static routes

D. static routes have lowest administrative distance

E. route is not directly connected

Correct Answers (B,E)
Subject Matter: Single-Homed eBGP for IPv4

Static routes provide BGP route propagation when there is no IGP (EIGRP etc.) configured. BGP doesn't learn routes dynamically as with IGP routing protocols. All routes must exist in the routing table for BGP advertising to peer routers. Any subnets not directly connected must be added to the router configuration as well. In addition BGP requires an exact match for the route in the routing table.

43. Refer to the network topology drawing. Select the correct IOS commands that will configure Router-1 based on the following requirements?

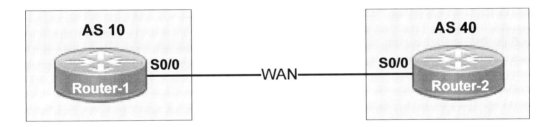

- Enable BGP with local AS 10
- Add eBGP peering neighbor from AS 40
- Assign IP address 172.16.1.2 to remote peer
- Advertise network 10.10.34.1/24 to remote peer

A. router ebgp 10
    neighbor 172.16.1.2 remote-as 40
    network 10.10.34.1 mask 255.255.255.0

B. router bgp 10
    neighbor 172.16.1.2 remote-as 40
    network 10.10.34.1 mask 255.255.255.0

C. router bgp 10
    neighbor 172.16.1.2 remote 40
    network 10.10.34.1 mask 255.255.0.0

D. router bgp AS10
    neighbor 172.16.1.2 remote AS40
    network 10.10.34.1 mask 255.255.255.0

Correct Answer (B)
Subject Matter: Single-Homed eBGP for IPv4

The following IOS commands will configure a BGP routing instance and assign it to AS 10. The **neighbor** command creates an eBGP session with a remote BGP router 172.16.1.2 (AS 40). The **network** command will advertise subnet prefix 10.10.34.1 /24 to the BGP neighbor.

router(config)# router bgp 10
router(config-router)# neighbor 172.16.1.2 remote-as 40
router(config-router)# network 10.10.34.1 mask 255.255.255.0

44. What two statements are true of the following BGP configuration?

router bgp 10
neighbor 172.16.1.2 remote-as 40
network 10.10.34.1 mask 255.255.255.0
network 0.0.0.0

A. BGP will peer between router loopback interfaces as a default

B. this is an iBGP peering configuration

C. default route is configured

D. this is an eBGP peering configuration

E. automatic summarization is enabled

Correct Answers (C,D)
Subject Matter: Single-Homed eBGP for IPv4

The eBGP session is created when BGP routers assigned to different BGP autonomous systems (AS) are peering.

The IOS commands enable eBGP peering between the local router in AS 10 and neighbor BGP router in AS 40. In addition the default route is advertised to BGP neighbors with **network 0.0.0.0** command.

45. What two statements are true concerning the following BGP command?

    router(config-router)# network 0.0.0.0/0

    A. default route must already exist in routing table

    B. default route is not installed in routing table

    C. injects default route into BGP routing table and advertises to BGP peers

    D. redistributes default route to IGP protocols

Correct Answers (A,C)
Subject Matter: Single-Homed eBGP for IPv4

The **network 0.0.0.0** command requires the default route already exist in routing table. BGP will inject the default route into the **BGP** routing table and advertise it to BGP peers.

46. What IOS troubleshooting command lists all BGP peers, adjacency state and TCP connectivity?

    A. router# show ip bgp interfaces

    B. router# show ip bgp

    C. router# show bgp neighbors

    D. router# show ip bgp neighbors

Correct Answer (D)
Subject Matter: Single-Homed eBGP for IPv4

The following IOS command will list all BGP peers for the local router and neighbor adjacency state. The normal adjacency state = **established** for a BGP session where routing updates are exchanged. BGP is a routing protocol with connectivity based on TCP transport. As a result there is a lot of TCP connection status information available as well.

> router# show ip bgp neighbors

47. What are the two correct statements concerning BGP router ID (RID)?

   A. default RID is highest loopback IP address

   B. purpose is recovery from TCP session collisions

   C. default RID is lowest loopback IP address

   D. default RID is the hostname of router

   E. IP address of BGP designated router (DR)

Correct Answers (A,B)
Subject Matter: Single-Homed eBGP for IPv4

The BGP router ID provides recovery from TCP session collisions. The highest loopback IP address is assigned as router ID by default.

48. Match the Quality of Service (QoS) technique on the left with the correct description on the right?

class map	WRED, tail drop, thresholds
classification	shaping, policing
congestion avoidance	class of service, DSCP, NBAR, access list
service-policy	traffic marking, point to class map
bandwidth management	FIFO, WFQ, PQ, CBWFQ (queuing)
policy map	attach policy to interface
congestion management	access groups, traffic matching

Correct Answers.
Subject Matter: QoS Concepts

The following describe features of standard QoS techniques:

class map	access groups, traffic matching
classification	class of service, DSCP, NBAR, access list
congestion avoidance	WRED, tail drop, thresholds
service-policy	attach policy to interface
bandwidth management	shaping, policing
policy map	traffic marking, point to class map
congestion management	FIFO, WFQ, PQ, CBWFQ (queuing)

49. Select the four statements that describe the purpose of QoS?

   A. guarantee SLAs for defined traffic classes

   B. avoid and manage network congestion

   C. increase network capacity

   D. prioritize traffic classes and assign bandwidth

   E. eliminate network peak events

   F. minimize packet loss and network latency

Correct Answers (A,B,D,F)
Subject Matter: QoS Concepts

The following are primary reasons for deploying Quality of Service on a network:

- Guarantee SLAs for defined traffic classes
- Avoid and manage network congestion
- Prioritize traffic classes and assign bandwidth
- Minimize packet loss and network latency

QoS is only applied when network congestion is detected. The purpose is to manage the available network bandwidth for optimizing network performance.

50. What three performance issues does QoS minimize?

A. packet loss

B. low throughput

C. network latency

D. peak traffic events

E. jitter

Correct Answers (A,C,E)
Subject Matter: QoS Concepts

QoS techniques are enabled to decrease latency, packet loss and jitter. It is particularly significant to delay sensitive voice and video traffic.

51. Match the traffic class with the recommended DSCP packet marking?

best effort	EF
scavenger	0
signaling	CS2
voice	CS6
video	AF41
routing	CS1
management	CS3

Correct Answers.
Subject Matter: QoS Concepts

The following are Cisco recommended DSCP markings with decimal value.

best effort	**0 (0)**
scavenger	**CS1 (8)**
signaling	**CS3 (24)**
voice	**EF (46)**
video	**AF41 (34)**
routing	**CS6 (48)**
management	**CS2 (16)**

52. Match the traffic class with Class of Service (CoS) packet marking?

best effort	1
scavenger	3
signaling	2
voice	4
video	0
routing	6
management	5

Correct Answers.
Subject Matter: QoS Concepts

The following are the Cisco recommended Class of Service packet markings.

best effort	**0**
scavenger	**1**
signaling	**3**
voice	**5**
video	**4**
routing	**6**
management	**2**

53. Refer to the network topology drawing. What three statements accurately describe QoS trust boundary?

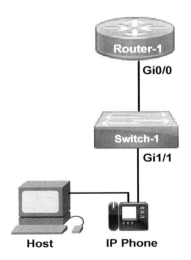

A. packets from a trusted device are remarked

B. packets from a trusted device are not remarked on upstream device

C. trust boundary defines the point where trusted packets start

D. trust boundary is configured with **mls qos trust cos | dscp** command

E. trust boundary describes where queuing starts

F. untrusted packets are dropped

Correct Answers (B,C,D)
Subject Matter: QoS Concepts

Defining trust boundaries across the network topology affects how packets markings are processed. All network devices within a trust boundary won't remark packets as they traverse. The following describe the key points concerning QoS trust boundary configuration.

- Packets from a trusted device are not remarked on upstream device
- The trust boundary defines the point where trusted packets start
- Trust boundary is configured with **mls qos trust cos | dscp** command

54. What two statements are correct concerning the following IOS commands when configured on a Cisco switch port interface?

    switch(config-if)# mls qos trust device cisco-phone
    switch(config-if)# mls qos trust cos

A. switch detects Cisco IP phone and reset CoS packet marking to zero

B. they are global IOS commands

C. switch will trust Cisco IP phone connected and trust CoS packet marking

D. switch detects Cisco IP phone instead of CDP

E. CDP is required

Correct Answers (C,E)
Subject Matter: QoS Concepts

The switch will trust the Cisco IP phone connected and trust the CoS packet marking. CDP must be enabled at the switch for the feature to work.

55. Select the four statements that correctly describe the features supported with policing and/or shaping?

   A. shaping can be applied to ingress and egress interfaces

   B. policing does not queue packets

   C. policing does not support ACL classification

   D. shaping does support queueing

   E. policing can be applied to ingress and egress interfaces

   F. policing drops or remarks traffic that exceeded CIR

Correct Answers (B,D,E,F)
Subject Matter: QoS Concepts

The following statements describe the supported features for shaping and policing. In addition the differences are noted as well.

- Policing does not queue packets
- Shaping does support packet queueing
- Policing is applied to ingress and egress interfaces
- Policing drops or remarks traffic that exceed CIR

There is no support for traffic shaping on ingress interfaces (egress only). In addition policing does allow access lists as a classification method.

56. Match the queuing technique on the left with the description on the right?

Priority Queuing	default hardware queuing (QoS disabled)
FIFO	assigns specific bandwidth to traffic classes
WFQ	assigns bandwidth based on weights to traffic flow
WRED	traffic assigned to queue is serviced and emptied first
CBWFQ	congestion avoidance to avoid queue tail drops

Correct Answers.
Subject Matter: QoS Concepts

The following describe standard queuing techniques available:

Priority Queuing	**traffic assigned to queue is serviced and emptied first**
FIFO	**default hardware queuing (QoS disabled)**
WFQ	**assigns bandwidth based on weights to traffic flow**
WRED	**congestion avoidance to avoid queue tail drops**
CBWFQ	**assigns specific bandwidth to traffic classes**

57. What statement is true of the priority queue when any assigned traffic is not using it?

    A. priority queue bandwidth is not available

    B. bandwidth is available to the assigned traffic class

    C. bandwidth is available when WRED is configured

    D. bandwidth is only available when **percent** command is used

Correct Answer (B)
Subject Matter: QoS Concepts

The bandwidth assigned to the priority queue (PQ) is allocated whether the interface is congested or not. It works as a minimum bandwidth guaranteed to the assigned traffic class at all times. Packets assigned to the priority queue are discarded when the bandwidth is exceeded.

The bandwidth assigned to Class Based Weighted Fair Queues (CBWFQ) are used only when there is congestion. That allocated bandwidth is available to all traffic classes until then. In addition they are serviced (dequeued) only after the priority queue is emptied.

58. Select the two most common network congestion points where QoS is most effective?

A. access switch

B. aggregation uplink

C. WAN to LAN transition

D. LAN to WAN transition

E. network server

Correct Answers (B,D)
Subject Matter: QoS Concepts

The congestion points where QoS is most recommended and crucial include aggregation uplinks and LAN to WAN transition. The aggregation uplinks of network switches is often oversubscribed with traffic. That increases with bulk transfers and peak events where latency can increase for VoIP traffic.

The transition from LAN to WAN is the highest congestion point in the network. The campus Gigabit (1000 Mbps) uplink from a switch or firewall forwards packets to a slower WAN link. In fact the WAN speed is typically 10x - 100x less bandwidth than a switch link. All external traffic from a location is forwarded across the WAN. Any additional latency across the ISP network could cause packet drops as well.

59. What IOS command is used to verify BGP neighbor connection status, memory usage and routing activity?

A. show ip bgp router

B. show ip bgp summary

C. show ip bgp status

D. show bgp neighbor

Correct Answer (B)
Subject Matter: Single-Homed eBGP for IPv4

The IOS command **show ip bgp summary** provides a quick summarized lists of all BGP neighbor connections. That includes BGP AS number and up/down connection status. In addition there is detailed memory usage and session activity listed.

60. Refer to the network topology drawing. Select the two points where most traffic congestion occurs?

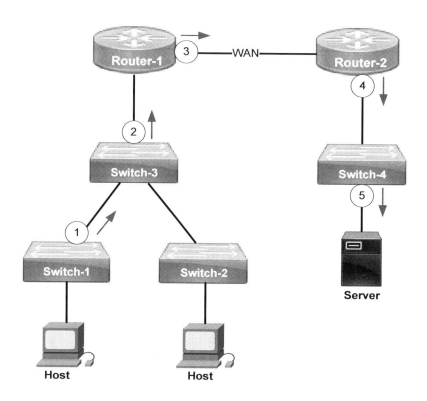

A. 1

B. 2

C. 3

D. 4

E. 5

Correct Answers (B,C)
Subject Matter: QoS Concepts

LAN aggregation (2) and WAN interfaces (3) are the two points where most network congestion typically occurs. The aggregation uplink forwards traffic from multiple switches or interfaces. In addition, the traffic from any LAN to WAN transition forwards packets from a high bandwidth Gigabit LAN interface to a significantly lower WAN bandwidth speed.

61. Refer to the network topology drawing. Match the GRE IP address on the left with the correct description on the right?

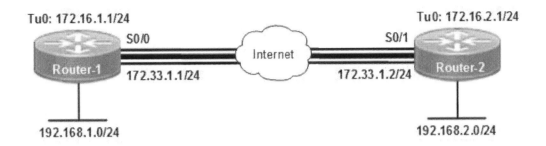

172.33.1.1/24	GRE tunnel source IP address for Router-2
172.16.1.1/24	GRE tunnel source IP address for Router-1
172.16.2.1/24	Tunnel interface IP address for Router-1
172.33.1.2/24	Tunnel interface IP address for Router-2

Correct Answers.
Subject Matter: GRE Tunneling

The GRE tunnel is configured with a Tunnel (virtual) interface and a public routable Tunnel source IP address for each peering router.

GRE Tunnel interface IP addresses are from the private network and not routable. They are assigned to the Tunnel interface on each router with a number. The network topology drawing assigned the following IP addresses to Tunnel0 (Tu0) interface.

   172.16.1.1/24 = Tunnel0 interface IP address (Router-1)
   172.16.2.1/24 = Tunnel0 interface IP address (Router-2)

GRE Tunnel source IP addresses are public routable and assigned by the ISP. They are assigned to the public facing physical interface on each router. The Tunnel source IP address assigned to the remote router is referred to as the Tunnel destination IP address. The network topology drawing assigned the following IP addresses.

   172.33.1.1/24 = GRE tunnel source IP address (Router-1)
   172.33.1.2/24 = GRE tunnel source IP address (Router-2)

62. What is the normal state for LCP when peering with a remote PPP neighbor across WAN?

A. established

B. full

C. active

D. open

E. forwarding

F. send

Correct Answer (D)
Subject Matter: PPP

The normal operational status for LCP (layer 2) is *Open* when the PPP link is working correctly. In addition NCP, IPCP and Multilink interface also show as *Open*.

63. What IOS command is used to verify all active member links and packet drops for a MLPPP interface?

A. show multilink interfaces

B. show multilink /all

C. show ppp multilink

D. show interface mlppp

E. show mlppp

Correct Answer (C)
Subject Matter: Multilink PPP (MLPPP)

The IOS command **show ppp multilink** is used to verify all active member links of a multilink bundle. It confirms the multilink interface is up and forwarding packets. In addition the bundle name is listed and number of packet drops.

64. What IOS command is used to verify LCP and NCP operational state for Multilink interface Serial0/1?

A. debug ip mlppp

B. show interfaces serial 0/1

C. show multilink interfaces serial 0/1

D. show multilink serial 0/1

Correct Answer (B)
Subject Matter: Multilink PPP (MLPPP)

The IOS command **show interfaces serial0/1** can verify LCP, NCP and IPCP operational status. The Open status is normal and indicates the multilink interface is established and multilink bandwidth available. The same IOS command is used for a standard PPP link as well.

router# show interfaces serial 0/1

The IOS command **show interfaces multilink** provides all of the same status information except NCP (layer 3).

65. What three options best describe where traffic shaping is most effective?

A. provides multiple packet handling options

B. prevents ISP from dropping packets that exceed maximum data rate

C. allows oversubscription on a physical interface with burst

D. minimizes effect of any single user or application traffic on network performance

E. most effective when configured on layer 2 switches

F. shapes traffic to lower rate than what is available with customer physical interface

G. delay sensitive traffic

Correct Answers (B,D,F)
Subject Matter: QoS Concepts

The primary purpose of traffic shaping is to limit the maximum data rate on an egress network interface. The queuing of packets is used to prevent packet forwarding from exceeding CIR. There is support for applying traffic shaping to a single user or application. That minimizes the effect of any internet traffic and bandwidth hogging for instance. The queuing of packets can affect delay sensitive traffic with higher latency. The following is a list of the correct features and operation of shaping.

- Minimize the effect of any single user traffic on network performance.
- Prevent ISP from dropping packets that exceed maximum data rate (CIR)
- Shape traffic to lower rate than what is available with customer physical interface.

66. What statement best describes where traffic policing is most effective?

A. layer 2 switches

B. ingress interface only

C. granular packet handling based on data rate

D. granular packet handling based on network latency

E. delay sensitive traffic

Correct Answer (C)
Subject Matter: QoS Concepts

The primary purpose of policing is to provide multiple options for packet handling based on allowed data rate and burst rate. The conditions include conforming, exceeding and violating. The following describe standard conditions and possible actions:

conforming = packet forwarded with option to remark
exceeding = packet has exceeded limits and is dropped or remarked
violating = data rate is faster than CIR and allowed, dropped or remarked

Note that remark can refer to either marking up or down of a packet. The network administrator could decide for instance to remark packet to a higher (preferred) DSCP marking.

There is support for policing on ingress and egress interface queues. It is most effective at WAN interfaces and aggregation points. There is no guaranteed minimum bandwidth configurable with traffic shaping or policing. Queuing techniques are available for that purpose. There is no queuing of packets with policed traffic so packet drops are common during periods of congestion.

67. Select the correct order for how QoS is applied to packets?

1. policing

2. classification

3. congestion avoidance

4. shaping

5. queuing

6. marking

Correct Answers.
Subject Matter: QoS Concepts

QoS is applied to packets (and frames) based on a specific order when configured. It starts with selecting traffic to apply QoS using classification. The most popular classification is accomplished with ACLs. The selected traffic is then marked and assigned to a queue. Any traffic shaping is applied before testing conditions for policing. Congestion avoidance drops queued packets based on configured settings. The flow management for applying QoS is described with the following:

1. Classification

2. Marking

3. Queuing

4. Shaping

5. Policing

6. Congestion Avoidance

68. What two statements accurately describe switch port trust state operation?

A. trust state examines ingress packets and forwards them unaltered

B. trust state examines ingress packets and remarks them to CoS = 0

C. trusted state is switch default setting

D. untrusted state is switch default and packets are remarked to CoS = 0

E. AutoQoS configures untrusted state as a default

Correct Answers (A,D)
Subject Matter: QoS Concepts

The trust state of a switch determines how the packet marking is interpreted for ingress traffic. The default trust setting for a Cisco switch is untrusted. The switch will remark the CoS or DSCP value to zero (0) for all ingress packets on an untrusted interface.

The switch will examine ingress packets and forwards them unaltered when trust state is enabled. For instance voice packets marked as Cos 5 from an IP phone are forwarded with that value. Packets from a host are remarked from a default zero (0) to a configured value on a trusted interface.

69. What IOS command will reset all BGP sessions with all neighbors?

A. clear ip bgp soft

B. clear ip bgp

C. clear ip bgp *

D. clear ip bgp /all

Correct Answer (C)
Subject Matter: Single-Homed eBGP for IPv4

The following IOS command will reset all BGP sessions with all neighbors. It is used to do a hard reset of all BGP sessions and rebuild the BGP routing table.

router# clear ip bgp *

70. What queuing solution is recommended when voice, video and data traffic is present?

A. WRED

B. Class Based Weighted Fair Queuing (CBWFQ)

C. Priority Queuing (PQ)

D. Shaping

E. Weighted Fair Queuing (WFQ)

F. Policing

Correct Answer (C)
Subject Matter: QoS Concepts

The delay sensitive nature of voice and video traffic requires a dedicated queue. The priority queue assigns guaranteed bandwidth to voice and/or video packets. The priority queue is serviced first and emptied before any other configured queues can forward packets. It is referred to as Low Latency Queuing (LLQ) and deployed along with CBWFQ. Any traffic classes assigned to CBWFQ is assigned a minimum bandwidth or remaining bandwidth. The traffic assigned to CBWFQ queues are serviced after emptying the priority queue.

71. What network protocol provides security as packets are traversing the internet?

A. MD5

B. RSA

C. PPP

D. IPsec

E. GRE

Correct Answer (D)
Subject Matter: WAN Access

IPsec is an open standard deployed as part of a VPN for data encryption. It provides end-to-end data security for packets traversing the internet.

72. Select the network interface where Class of Service (CoS) marking is supported?

A. layer 3 interface

B. switch trunk

C. any network interface

D. switch access port

E. serial interface

Correct Answer (B)
Subject Matter: Quality of Service (QoS)

The only network interface that supports Class of Service (CoS) marking is an Ethernet switch trunk. The 802.1q tag is added to an Ethernet frame when trunking is enabled. The 802.1q field is used for VLAN membership tagging. That allows forwarding of multiple VLANs between switches. There is a 3 bit field used for CoS marking and prioritization (queuing) of traffic.

Routers can only examine the CoS marking of a frame and trust or remark the layer 3 packet. The router would specifically strip off the original frame and rewrite MAC addressing. In addition the router would either trust the CoS value or rewrite a DSCP value equal to the CoS marking. Serial interfaces do not use frames and have no MAC address. Layer 2 switches are configured with a trust state that determines frame handling.

Cisco IP phones mark all voice traffic to the switch with default CoS 5. In addition a trunk is created from the IP phone to the switch when the voice VLAN feature is enabled. The trunk tags voice packets from the phone and data from the host to an access port on the switch.

Module 5: Infrastructure Services

1. How is an IP address conflict managed by a DHCP server?

    A. hosts are assigned new IP addresses immediately

    B. IP addresses are removed from the DHCP pool

    C. IP address conflict detected by Ping or GARP is automatically unassigned

    D. host receives an error message to restart

    E. hosts are disconnected from the network

Correct Answer (B)
Subject Matter: DHCP Connectivity

The DHCP server will remove any IP address from the DHCP pool until the conflicts are resolved.

DHCP uses Ping or Gratuitous ARP to detect IP address conflicts. The DHCP server will Ping the proposed IP address to confirm it isnt assigned. The ICMP echo reply is sent from any network device or host if it is already in use. The DHCP server will log the conflict error with a Syslog server. That is enabled with the **ip dhcp conflict logging** feature as a default.

In addition Gratuitous ARP (GARP) is sent by a router to detect IP addresses in use. The network device would reply with an ARP to confirm IP address is not available. The following IOS command lists all IP address conflicts detected on a Cisco router configured as a DHCP server.

router# show ip dhcp conflict

IP Address	Detection Method	Detection Time
172.16.1.32	Ping	July 16 2016 9:30 AM
172.16.1.64	Gratuitous ARP	July 16 2016 10:30 AM

2. Host-1 is connected to a DHCP server through a switch and router. The DHCP server was upgraded over the weekend and now Host-1 cannot access the network. What is the first recommended action to resolve the problem based on the network topology drawing?

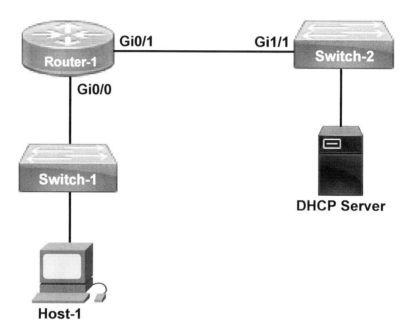

A. clear ARP cache on Switch-1

B. issue command **ipconfig /release /renew** on Host-1

C. clear ARP cache on Host-1

D. clear MAC address table on Switch-1

Correct Answer (B)
Subject Matter: DHCP Connectivity

The IP address pool is defined on the DHCP server along with the lease time. The IP address pool is a range of addresses that are reserved for dynamic assignment typically for hosts. In addition the host often receives the default gateway and DNS server settings as well. Any configuration changes whether required or errors could affect host connectivity.

The Windows desktop command **ipconfig /release /renew** will release the current IP address and request a new IP address. The DHCP server would assign a random IP address from the pool along with additional settings.

3. What two IP addresses should never be included in the DHCP pool?

    A. leased IP address

    B. interface IP address

    C. network address

    D. manually assigned address

    E. dynamic IP address

    F. network broadcast address

Correct Answers (C,F)
Subject Matter: DHCP Connectivity

The network address and broadcast address should not be included with the DHCP pool for dynamic assignment. The host assignment would include anything else unless it is statically assigned already.

4. What are the two primary services provided by Dynamic Host Configuration Protocol (DHCP)?

    A. provide additional network security

    B. assign and renew IP addresses from a designated pool

    C. detect errors with IP addressing

    D. configure default route with IPv6 addressing

    E. configure TCP/IP address settings on hosts

Correct Answers (B,E)
Subject Matter: DHCP Connectivity

The DHCP server is responsible for dynamic configuration of host IP settings. In addition it manages the renewal of new IP addresses from an address pool.

5. How does a DHCP server dynamically assign an IP address to a host?

    A. IP address is assigned to each host for a fixed lease time. The host will then request the DHCP server renew the same IP address.

    B. IP address is assigned to each host until it restarts then host must request a new lease.

    C. IP address is automatically assigned to each host until the host sends a request for a new IP address.

    D. IP address is assigned to each host for a fixed lease time and renewed automatically with an available IP address from the pool.

Correct Answer (A)
Subject Matter: DHCP Connectivity

The host IP address renewal is based on the lease time setting. The host will typically keep using the same IP address assigned. The lease renewal request is sent to the DHCP server when the lease time expires. The DHCP server will extend the lease again for the lease time setting.

6. What are two primary services provided by Network Address Translation?

    A. decrease the number of subnets required on a private network

    B. provides packet filtering

    C. translate private IP addressing to a public routable IP address

    D. translate public routable IP address to private IP addressing

Correct Answers (C,D)
Subject Matter: Inside Source NAT

Network Address Translation (NAT) translates private IP addressing (RFC1918) to a public routable IP address for outbound internet traffic. The inbound traffic from the internet is translated (mapped) to a private IP address.

7. What feature is not an advantage of Network Address Translation (NAT)?

    A. optimizes internet access with a single public routable IP address

    B. promotes internet cloud access

    C. optimizes network security at the internet edge

    D. enables multiple different ISP connections from a single public routable IP address

Correct Answer (D)
Subject Matter: Inside Source NAT

The disadvantage to NAT is the IP address renumbering when switching internet service providers (ISP). The public routable (internet) IP address is used to configure translation for any static or dynamic NAT configuration.

8. Refer to the results of the following IOS command for NAT translation. Define the purpose or usage of the outside local address?

    router# show ip nat translations

    A. IP address of an outside host as it appears to the inside private network

    B. IP address assigned to a host on the inside private network

    C. IP address that translates multiple inside local IP addresses to a public routable address

    D. IP address that translates the public IP address to a private address

Correct Answer (A)
Subject Matter: Inside Source NAT

The IOS command **show ip nat translations** lists inside global, inside local, outside local and outside global addresses.

The **outside local address** is the IP address of an outside host as it appears to the inside (private) network.

9. What IOS command is used to create a static NAT between an inside local IP address and inside global IP address?

    A. ip nat outside

    B. ip nat dmz

    C. ip nat inside source

    D. ip nat pool

Correct Answer (C)
Subject Matter: Inside Source NAT

The static NAT statement creates a 1:1 mapping between a local IP address and a global IP address. The following configures a static NAT between inside local IP address 192.168.1.1 (private) and inside global IP address 200.16.1.1 (internet routable).

    router(config)# ip nat inside source static 192.168.1.1 200.16.1.1

Inside Local IP Address
private IP address assigned to a host on the inside network (RFC 1918).

Inside Global IP Address
public internet routable IP address assigned by the ISP.

Outside Global IP Address
public internet routable IP address assigned to outside (remote) host device

Outside Local IP Address
public internet routable IP address of outside host as appears to inside network.

10. What statement best describes a static NAT configuration?

    A. manually configured many-to-one address mapping

    B. manually configured one-to-one address mapping

    C. automatically assigned from a NAT address pool

    D. one-to-many address mapping

    E. any-to-any address mapping

Correct Answer (B)
Subject Matter: Inside Source NAT

The static NAT statement consists of a one-to-one persistent mapping between IP addresses. It is manually configured mapping of an inside local address to an outside global address.

    router(config)# ip nat inside source static [inside address] [mapped address]

11. Examine the router configuration and select the correct statement?

    router(config)# ip nat inside source list 1

    A. refers to an access control list configured on the router to filter traffic

    B. refers to a route map configured on the router to filter traffic

    C. refers to a router inside interface on the private network

    D. refers to a static NAT configuration on the inside interface of the router

Correct Answer (A)
Subject Matter: Inside Source NAT

The IOS command **ip nat inside source list 1** enables dynamic NAT with access-list number 1 for filtering. The packets arriving on the inside interface are filtered by access-list 1. Any packets matching access list 1 have their source IP address translated to a public IP address from the NAT pool.

    router(config)# ip nat inside source list 1

12. What two statements accurately describe the operation of static NAT translations?

    A. enable host sessions to be started from an inside host only

    B. optimize use of the available public assigned IP addresses

    C. persistence in the translation table while the router is operational

    D. allow host sessions to be started from an internet host

Correct Answers (C,D)
Subject Matter: Inside Source NAT

The static NAT translation is a 1:1 configured mapping between local and global addresses. As a result they are a permanent entry in the NAT translation table. They enable a remote host connection from an outside (external) network.

13. What are two advantages of Network Address Translation (NAT)?

    A. increases the private IP address space that can be assigned

    B. enables security of packets while in transit across the internet

    C. conceals private IP address assignments from the internet

    D. eases management of internet connectivity

    E. eliminates the need for DNS requests

Correct Answers (C,D)
Subject Matter: Inside Source NAT

The primary advantage of NAT is to map multiple private IP addresses to a single or multiple public routable IP addresses. The ISP does not have a public routable IP address available for every private IP address. NAT allows for configuring a pool of public IP addresses. The private IP address is dynamically mapped for that internet session only. As a result there is no requirement to readdress local hosts for internet access.

The NAT translation has the advantage of protecting the private IP address assignments. The private addresses are not advertised providing additional security for internet connectivity. The remote hosts send packets to the public destination IP address.

14. What design feature is required to create a single virtual router from two separate routers?

    A. routers must share a virtual IP address and MAC address

    B. routers must share a virtual MAC address only

    C. assign a loopback IP address to each router

    D. create a port channel between routers with a virtual IP address

Correct Answer (A)
Subject Matter: HSRP

The virtual router is based on a shared virtual IP address and MAC address. The virtual addressing is assigned to the active router. The standby router is assigned the virtual addressing when the active router isn't available. The redundancy feature allows for fast failover to the standby router.

15. Select the virtual MAC address for HSRP version 1 that is valid?

   A. 0007.c700.ac00

   B. 0000.0c07.a0c0

   C. 0000.0c07.ffff

   D. 0000.0c07.ac01

Correct Answer (D)
Subject Matter: HSRP

The HSRP virtual MAC address for version 1 is **0000.0c07.ac01**. This is for the group 1. The rightmost 2 bits (01) indicate the group number. The default HSRP group 0 would be assigned virtual MAC address **0000.0c07.ac00** for version 1.

16. What three statements accurately describe HSRP operation?

   A. HSRP virtual IP address must be assigned to a different subnet than the HSRP enabled physical interfaces

   B. HSRP virtual MAC address is derived from the physical interface of the HSRP active router

   C. HSRP default timers are 3 second hello interval and 10 second hold interval (timers)

   D. HSRP supports physical interfaces and VLAN interfaces

   E. HSRP groups enable load sharing among multiple HSRP enabled interfaces

   F. HSRP does not support MD5 authentication

Correct Answers (C,D,E)
Subject Matter: HSRP

The active HSRP active router is assigned the virtual IP address and MAC address for packet forwarding. Hello packets are sent between active and standby router at 3 second intervals by default. In addition the hold timer is 10 seconds. There is support for assigning a maximum 255 groups per physical interfaces or VLAN interfaces. Multiple groups across multiple routers enable configuration of load balancing.

17. What four statements correctly describe configuration and connectivity of HSRP on a Cisco router?

  A. standby IP address assigned to the HSRP group is configured on all group members

  B. HSRPv2 hello messages are advertised to multicast address 224.0.0.102

  C. HSRP group is associated with at least 2 routers

  D. HSRP is an open standard with multiple vendor support

  E. The active router has a higher priority than the standby router

Correct Answers (A,B,C,E)
Subject Matter: HSRP

The following statements correctly describe standard HSRP operation:

  • At least one HSRP group is associated with at least two routers.

  • The active router is configured with a higher priority than standby router.

  • HSRP version 2 sends hello messages to multicast address 224.0.0.102

  • The virtual IP address assigned to the HSRP group is configured on both router members with the **standby ip** command.

368

18. What IOS command provides HSRP operational status of a router?

    A. router# show standby

    B. router(config)# show standby

    C. router(config)# show standby hsrp

    D. router# show ip hsrp

Correct Answer (A)
Subject Matter: HSRP

The following IOS command lists the HSRP status for all groups. The status includes active router, standby IP address, virtual addressing and timers.

router# show standby

19. Refer to the network topology drawing. Order the following events in their proper sequence when a DNS request is made to connect from Host-1 to www.cisco.com?

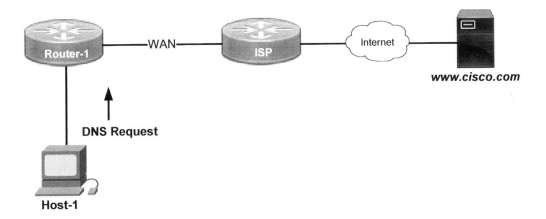

1. The local resolver creates a DNS query and sends it to DNS name server listed with TCP/IP settings.

2. The DNS name server sends IP address of www.cisco.com to the web browser.

3. The DNS name server listed with TCP/IP settings sends a new DNS request to name server for www.cisco.com

4. The web browser (DNS client) uses resolver to request resolution of www.cisco.com hostname to an IP address.

5. The root server responds with addresses of name servers that are authoritative for cisco.com

6. DNS name server for web browser checks cache for hostname. The DNS name server forwards query to root server for domain (.com etc) if the hostname is not in the DNS cache.

Correct Answers.
Subject Matter: DNS

The following describes the sequence of events that occurs when a web browser makes a DNS request. The DNS server resolves a hostname to the unknown IP address of www.cisco.com for the web browser.

Step 1: The web browser (DNS client) uses resolver to request resolution of www.cisco.com hostname to an IP address.

Step 2: The local resolver creates a DNS query and sends it to DNS name server listed with TCP/IP settings.

Step 3: The DNS name server for web browser checks cache for hostname. The DNS name server forwards query to root server for domain (.com etc) if the hostname is not in the DNS cache.

Step 4: The root server responds with addresses of name servers that are authoritative for cisco.com

Step 5: The DNS name server listed with TCP/IP settings sends a new DNS request to name server for www.cisco.com

Step 6: The DNS name server sends IP address of www.cisco.com to the web browser.

20. What three desktop host commands verify that DNS is working correctly?

    A. ping www.google.com

    B. iperf

    C. nslookup 127.0.0.0 [dns server ip address]

    D. nslookup www.google.com

    E. nslookup [ip address]

    F. ping [default gateway ip address]

Correct Answers (A,C,D)
Subject Matter: DNS

DNS servers resolve a known IP address to an unknown hostname. In addition they can resolve a known hostname to an unknown IP address. Connecting to web servers for instance is based on domain name.

The following techniques will verify the DNS server is reachable and resolving hostnames properly. The **ping** will return a request timed out error message. The **nslookup** command provides DNS information such as DNS server, IP address and domain name. The second **nslookup** command does a host loopback to test the DNS server.

- ping www.google.com
- nslookup www.google.com
- nslookup 127.0.0.0 [dns server ip address]

21. What are three possible reasons why a host cannot connect to a server?

    A. TCP/IP settings configured on the host are incorrect

    B. DNS name server is not configured on the default gateway

    C. UDP Port 53 is filtered by an ACL

    D. TCP Port 69 is filtered by an ACL

    E. WAN connection from ISP is unavailable

Correct Answers (A,C,E)
Subject Matter: DNS

The following are some common problems that could affect DNS services.

- **Host TCP/IP settings incorrect** - DHCP configures the DNS server IP address for each host. The host cannot send requests to the DNS server unless the correct IP address is configured.

- **UDP Port 53 filtered** - DNS is a network protocol that requires UDP port 53 for proper operation. DNS is sometimes assigned to TCP port 53 as well. Verify that UDP or TCP port 53 isn't filtered by an ACL.

- **WAN connection from ISP is unavailable** - The DNS server won't be available if it is located across a WAN link that is unavailable.

22. What desktop command lists the IP address, DNS server and DHCP server address configuration for the host?

   A. netstat

   B. show interface

   C. ipconfig /all

   D. show config /all

   E. nslookup

Correct Answer (C)
Subject Matter: DHCP

The host command to list all IP addressing is **ipconfig /all.** It provides the current TCP/IP settings including IP address, DHCP server and DNS server address. In addition MAC address and default gateway address can be verified.

23. What is the reason for configuring a DNS name server on a Cisco device?

   A. enable Telnet access between routers using IP address

   B. enable SSH access between routers

   C. enable Telnet access between switches using device hostname

   D. enable Telnet and/or SSH access between layer 3 devices

Correct Answer (C)
Subject Matter: DNS

The DNS name server enables Telnet hopping between network devices that is based on a hostname. The IOS command **ip name-server** allows for specifying a DNS server IP address. The DNS queries sent to the DNS server resolve the IP address from a hostname.

24. What is the correct order of network protocols required for establishing a desktop host to server connection?

    A. Layer 1, Layer 2, DHCP, DNS, ARP, Server Authentication

    B. Layer 1, Layer 2, DNS, ARP, DHCP, Server Authentication

    C. Layer 1, Layer 2, DHCP, DNS, ARP, Server Authentication

    D. Layer 1, Layer 2, DNS, ARP, DHCP, Server Authentication

Correct Answer (C)
Subject Matter: DHCP/DNS

The following describes the correct order for enabling network connectivity between a desktop host and server:

1. **Layer 1:** network connectivity between a host and server requires all layers to work starting with layer 1

2. **Layer 2:** connectivity is established from desktop host to switch

3. **DHCP Request:** host sends a request to the nearest DHCP server for IP addressing. That enables layer 3 connectivity from the host to the router.

4. **DNS Query:** server IP address is resolved with a DNS query sent to the configured DNS name server.

5. **ARP Request:** host sends an ARP request for the server MAC address based on the server IP address. The server replies with its MAC address.

6. **Server Authentication:** host authenticates to the server and starts an application.

25. Refer to the network drawing. Host-1 sends a DHCP broadcast request to obtain IP address settings. What are two typical causes for DHCP failure?

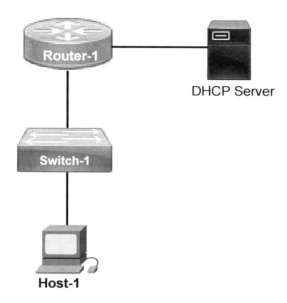

A. DHCP server configuration error

B. DHCP relay agent configuration error

C. IP address of DHCP server is not configured correctly on Host-1

D. DHCP server is on a different subnet than client (Host-1)

E. broadcasts are filtered at router

Correct Answers (A,B)
Subject Matter: DHCP

Layer 3 connectivity is verified with a ping of the DHCP server IP address. The cause of DHCP address assignment is often configuration errors on the DHCP server. In addition configuring DHCP relay agent with the wrong DHCP server IP address will cause errors.

26. What is the default IP address lease renewal period for a Cisco DHCP server?

    A. 1 day

    B. 30 days

    C. 10 days

    D. unlimited

Correct Answer (A)
Subject Matter: DHCP

The default lease time for an IP address assigned from a Cisco based DHCP server is 1 day. The routers and switches would renew the IP address after 24 hours when triggered by a host request.

27. What network device sends DHCP option 82?

    A. DNS server

    B. DHCP relay agent

    C. DHCP server

    D. desktop

    E. server

    F. firewall

Correct Answer (B)
Subject Matter: DHCP

DHCP relay agent forwards DHCP request from hosts with option 82 where it is enabled. The purpose of option 82 is to provide additional host connectivity information. That is required when the default gateway of the host is unknown. Option 82 allows for proper assignment of IP address for the host request.

28. What Cisco IOS command disables DHCP services?

   A. disable dhcp service

   B. no run dhcp

   C. no service dhcp

   D. no dhcp service

Correct Answer (C)
Subject Matter: DHCP

DHCP server and relay agent are enabled by default on Cisco routers and switches. To disable DHCP services use the following IOS command:

   router(config)# no service dhcp

29. DHCP server feature is supported on Cisco routers and switches?

   A. True

   B. False

Correct Answer (True)
Subject Matter: DHCP

DHCP is a network service typically configured on multiple third party network servers for redundancy. Cisco does support DHCP server feature as well with IOS that can be deployed on switches and routers.

30. Select the correct IOS commands to configure a DHCP server IP address pool on a router, DNS server and default gateway IP addressing to hosts?

   A. router(config)# ip dhcp pool [name]
       router(dhcp-config)# network [ip address]
       router(dhcp-config)# dns server [ip address]
       router(dhcp-config)# default router [ip address]

   B. router(config)# ip dhcp pool [name]
       router(dhcp-config)# network [ip address]
       router(dhcp-config)# dns-server [ip address]
       router(dhcp-config)# default-router [ip address]

C. router(config)# ip dhcp pool [name]
router(dhcp-config)# network [ip address]
router(dhcp-config)# dns-server [ip address]
router(dhcp-config)# default-gateway [ip address]

D. router(config)# dhcp pool [name]
router(dhcp-config)# network [ip address]
router(dhcp-config)# dns-server [ip address]
router(dhcp-config)# default-router [ip address]

Correct Answer (B)
Subject Matter: DHCP

The following are the correct IOS commands for configuring a DHCP server on a Cisco router. The IOS commands configure a DHCP pool of IP addresses for the hosts. The DHCP server will dynamically assign IP addresses to the hosts. In addition the DNS server and default gateway addresses are sent to the hosts.

router(config)# ip dhcp pool [name]
router(dhcp-config)# network [ip address range]
router(dhcp-config)# dns-server [ip address]
router(dhcp-config)# default-router [ip address]

31. What is the purpose of the following IOS command?

router(config)# ip dhcp excluded-address [low address] to [high address]

A. excludes IP address range from being assigned to non-DHCP clients

B. excludes IP address range from being assigned to any network devices

C. excludes IP address range from being assigned to DHCP clients

D. excludes IP address range from being assigned to any hosts

E. excludes IP address range from network devices that are assigned static addressing

Correct Answer (C)
Subject Matter: DHCP

The purpose of the following IOS command is to exclude an IP address range from the DHCP pool. There are some IP addresses that are reserved and should not be assigned to a DHCP enabled host.

router(config)# ip dhcp excluded-address [low address] to [high address]

32. What is the purpose of the following IOS commands?

> router> enable
> router# configure terminal
> router(config)# interface vlan10
> router(config-if)# ip helper-address 172.16.3.1

A. configures the IP address of DHCP server

B. configures default gateway for DNS requests

C. configures the IP address of DHCP relay agent

D. forwards DNS broadcast requests to VLAN interface

Correct Answer (A)
Subject Matter: DHCP

The IOS commands configure the DHCP relay agent for hosts on VLAN 10. There is support for assigning physical interfaces as well.

The **ip helper-address** command is configured with the IP address of the DHCP server. All DHCP requests arriving from hosts are forwarded to the DHCP server (172.16.3.1) on a remote subnet. The DHCP relay agent is the router configured with the **ip helper-address** command.

33. What sequence of events occurs when a host requests an IP address from a DHCP server?

A. server discovery, IP lease offer, IP lease request, IP lease acknowledgement

B. server discovery, IP lease request, IP lease offer, IP lease acknowledgement

C. IP lease request, server discovery, IP lease offer, IP lease acknowledgement

D. IP lease request, server discovery, IP lease acknowledgement, IP lease offer

Correct Answer (A)
Subject Matter: DHCP

The DHCP request for a IP address starts with **server discovery**. The DHCP server replies with an IP address **lease offer**. The host replies with an **IP lease request** for the proposed IP address. The DHCP server confirms the IP address with a **lease acknowledgement** to the host. The DHCP server will send the lease time and any additional address settings as well. The following are standard DHCP message types.

Step 1: Server Discovery = DHCPDISCOVERY

Step 2: IP Lease Offer = DHCPOFFER

Step 3: IP Lease Request = DHCPREQUEST

Step 4: IP Lease Acknowledgement = DHCPACK

34. What are four problems that could affect proper operation of HSRP?

A. virtual IP address is assigned to the wrong subnet

B. HSRP timers mismatch

C. HSRP version mismatch

D. VTP modes mismatch

E. HSRP assigned to a VLAN interface

F. **preempt** command configured on standby router

G. **ip helper-address** command assigned to physical interface

Correct Answers (A,B,C,D)
Subject Matter: HSRP

The virtual IP address must be assigned from the same subnet as the router interfaces. All timers must match between HSRP router peers. The HSRP version must match between routers as well. There are features enabled with HSRPv2 not supported with HSRPv1. The VTP modes for both routers must match. The active router configured as VTP server requires the same VTP mode for standby.

35. What IOS command will show HSRP operational state, priority and standby IP address?

A. router# show interfaces virtual

B. router# show ip standby

C. router# show ip hsrp

D. router# show standby

E. router# show standby interfaces

Correct Answer (D)
Subject Matter: HSRP

The following is typical output from **show standby** IOS command. It includes the HSRP state, priority and standby (virtual) IP address assigned.

router# show standby

Ethernet0/1 - Group 1
Local state is **Active, priority 110**, may preempt
Hello time 3 holdtime 10
Next hello sent in 00:00:01.154
Virtual IP address is **172.16.1.1** configured
Active router is 172.16.1.2 expires in 00:00:03
Active router is local
Standby router is 172.16.1.3 expires in 00:00:07
Virtual mac address is 0000.0c07.ac01
Name is cisco

36. Select the correct configuration for deploying router-1 as the active router assigned to group 1 with HSRP version 2?

A. router-1(config)# interface gigabitethernet0/1
   router-1(config-if)# ip address 172.16.1.1 255.255.255.0
   router-1-(config-if)# hsrp 2
   router-1(config-if)# standby 1 preempt
   router-1(config-if)# standby 1 priority 110
   router-1(config-if)# standby 1 ip 172.16.1.3

B. router-1(config)# interface gigabitethernet0/1
   router-1(config-if)# ip address 172.16.1.1 255.255.255.0
   router-1(config-if)# hsrp v2
   router-1(config-if)# standby preempt
   router-1(config-if)# standby 1 priority 100
   router-1(config-if)# standby 1 ip 172.16.1.3

C. router-1(config)# interface gigabitethernet0/1
   router-1(config-if)# ip address 172.16.1.1 255.255.255.0
   router-1(config-if)# standby version 2
   router-1(config-if)# standby 1 preempt
   router-1(config-if)# standby 1 priority 110
   router-1(config-if)# standby 1 ip 172.16.1.3

D. router-1(config)# interface gigabitethernet0/1
   router-1(config-if)# ip address 172.16.1.1 255.255.255.0
   router-1(config-if)# standby 1 version 2
   router-1(config-if)# standby preempt
   router-1(config-if)# standby 1 priority 110
   router-1(config-if)# standby 1 172.16.1.3

Correct Answer (C)
Subject Matter: HSRP

The following IOS commands will configure HSRP on an interface. In addition router-1 will be assigned as active for group 1 with HSRPv2 enabled. The **priority 110** command assigns router-1 as the active router. That is higher that the default priority 100. The group (**1**) designator applies settings to the group and interface assigned.

router-1(config)# interface gigabitethernet0/1
router-1(config-if)# ip address 172.16.1.1 255.255.255.0
router-1(config-if)# standby version 2 *(enables HSRPv2)*
router-1(config-if)# standby 1 preempt *(compare router priorities for group 1)*
router-1(config-if)# standby 1 priority 110 *(active router)*
router-1(config-if)# standby 1 ip 172.16.1.3 *(virtual IP address)*

37. Select the correct values for a default HSRP configuration? (select two)

  A. hello timer = 3 seconds, hold timer = 10 seconds

  B. HSRPv2

  C. standby priority = 100

  D. group = 0

  E. standby priority = 90

Correct Answers (A,C)
Subject Matter: HSRP

The default HSRP values include the following settings:

- Hello timer = 3 seconds
- Hold timer = 10 seconds
- Standby priority = 100
- HSRP version = HSRPv1
- Enabled groups = none
- Default group = 0

38. What default amount is the priority value decremented for a tracked interface when the state goes to down?

  A. 10

  B. 1

  C. 100

  D. 110

  E. 90

  F. 0

Correct Answer (A)
Subject Matter: HSRP

HSRP provides a tracking feature that detects when the active HSRP router isn't available. That triggers a failover to the standby router. The priority of the active router is decremented by **10** as a default. The standby router has a higher priority and becomes the active router.

39. What is the default HSRP priority and how is the active router selected when priorities are equal?

    A. priority 100, highest IP address

    B. priority 0, any loopback address

    C. priority 90, lowest IP address

    D. priority 110, highest IP address

Correct Answer (A)
Subject Matter: HSRP

The default HSRP priority is 100. The router with the highest IP address is elected the active router when all priorities are equal.

40. What is the effect of the following HSRP command?

    router(config-if)# standby 1 preempt

    A. decreases the priority for the HSRP standby router

    B. configured on all HSRP enabled routers so the router with highest priority becomes active

    C. configured on HSRP primary router to make it active

    D. configured on HSRP standby router only so it isn't active router

Correct Answer (B)
Subject Matter: HSRP

The **preempt** command enables comparison of priority between routers to elect an active HSRP router. It is configured on all HSRP enabled routers so the router with highest priority becomes active.

41. Select two statements that describe the difference between HSRPv1 and HSRPv2?

    A. multicast IP address is the same

    B. HSRPv2 has additional groups

    C. HSRPv1 group number range is 0-4096

    D. HSRPv2 supports IPv6

    E. HSRPv1 provides msec timer support

    F. HSRPv2 is the current default

Correct Answers (B,D)
Subject Matter: HSRP

There are additional features supported with HSRPv2. The number of groups available with HSRPv2 is 4096 (0-4095). In addition IPv6 is supported with HSRPv2 as well.

42. Select the correct virtual MAC address per HSRP version? (select three)

    A. HSRPv1 = 0000.0c07.acxx

    B. HSRPv1 = 0000.0c07.afxx

    C. HSRPv2 = 0000.0c9f.fxxx

    D. HSRPv2 = 0000.0c9e.fxx

    E. HSRP for IPv6 = 0005.73a0.0000 through 0005.73a0.0fff

    F. HSRP for IPv6 = 0005.73a0.0000 through 000a.73a0.0ffe

Correct Answers (A,C,E)
Subject Matter: HSRP

The following are virtual MAC addresses based on the HSRP version.

- HSRPv1 = 0000.0c07.acxx
- HSRPv2 = 0000.0C9f.fxxx
- HSRP for IPv6 = 0005.73a0.0000 through 0005.73a0.0fff

43. Select three valid HSRP interface states from the following list?

A. standby

B. idle

C. block

D. init

E. active

F. established

Correct Answers (A,D,E)
Subject Matter: HSRP

The valid HSRP states from the list include Standby, Init and Active. In addition there is Listen and Speak states.

Initial (Init): This is the start state indicating that HSRP isn't running.

Learn: The virtual IP address is unassigned and no hello message was received from the active router yet.

Listen: The virtual IP address and MAC address is known by the router. The active and standby router is unassigned. It listens for hello messages from HSRP enabled routers.

Speak: The router sends hello messages to elect active and standby router.

Standby: The router is in standby mode and monitors hello packets sent from the active router. It becomes active when active router fails

Active: The router forwards packets to the HSRP group. In addition the active router sends regular hello packets.

44. Match the time source on the left with the correct description on the right?

ntp peer	initializes software clock after restart
system calendar	initially set by hardware clock
software clock	backup time server
ntp server	external time server

Correct Answers.
Subject Matter: Network Time Protocol (NTP)

The following describe time sources available with Cisco network devices.

ntp peer	**backup time server**
system calendar	**initializes software clock after restart**
software clock	**initially set by hardware clock**
ntp server	**external time server**

45. What four statements are correct for Network Time Protocol (NTP)?

A. time source for logging and time stamp transactions

B. NTP is based on UDP connectionless transport protocol

C. **ntp server** command configures private time server

D. reference is UTC coordinated universal time

E. **ntp peer** command specifies an external time server

F. DNS is required for resolving time server IP address

Correct Answers (A,B,D,F)
Subject Matter: Network Time Protocol (NTP)

The following are all correct statements concerning NTP network protocol.

- Provides time source for logging and time stamp transactions
- NTP is based on UDP connectionless protocol
- Reference is UTC coordinated universal time
- DNS is required for resolving time server IP address

46. What three statements accurately describe NTP operations?

A. higher numbered stratum time servers are preferred

B. only a single router can connect to the external clock server

C. server mode routers provide time source to client mode network devices

D. time servers are hierarchical

E. server mode routers poll external time server

Correct Answers (C,D,E)
Subject Matter: Network Time Protocol (NTP)

The following statement correctly describe NTP operation:

- Server mode routers provide time source to client mode devices

- Time servers are hierarchical

- Server mode routers poll an external time server

47. What IOS command is used to show NTP server synchronization and stratum level?

A. router# show ntp server

B. router# show ntp status

C. router# show ntp detail

D. router# show ntp status /all

Correct Answer (B)
Subject Matter: Network Time Protocol (NTP)

The following IOS command is used to show NTP server synchronization status and stratum level for a router.

router# show ntp status

48. What statement is true of the following IOS command?

    router(config)# ntp server 172.16.1.1

    A. configures unidirectional time synchronization between devices

    B. configures local router as NTP server

    C. configures external time server as authoritative time source

    D. configures bidirectional time synchronization between devices

Correct Answer (C)
Subject Matter: Network Time Protocol (NTP)

The following IOS command configures an external time server as authoritative time source for a router.

    router(config)# ntp server 172.16.1.1

49. What IOS troubleshooting command is used to show the status with NTP neighbors and NTP mode of the local client device (client/server)?

    A. show ntp client

    B. show ntp detail

    C. show ntp server

    D. show ntp associations

Correct Answer (D)
Subject Matter: Network Time Protocol (NTP)

The following IOS command is used to show the NTP association status with neighbors and NTP mode of the local client network device (client/server).

    router# show ntp associations

50. Select the correct configuration to enable Port Address Translation (PAT)?

    A. router(config)# ip nat inside source list 1 pool [pool name] overload

    B. router(config)# ip nat inside source list 1 pool [pool name] nat overload

    C. router(config)# ip nat inside source list 1 pool [pool name] pat

    D. router(config)# ip nat inside source list 1 pool [pool name] no overload

Correct Answer (A)
Subject Matter: Inside Source NAT

The following IOS command enables Port Address Translation (PAT) referred to as NAT overload. The **source list 1** points to ACL 1 that permits a range of internal (private) IP addresses to be translated. The [pool name] refers to a NAT pool that has a single or multiple public routable IP addresses assigned. The **overload** option enables port address translation of multiple internal IP private addresses to a single public IP address.

    router(config)# ip nat inside source list 1 pool [pool name] overload

NAT without overload provides either a static 1:1 or dynamic NAT mapping translation. The static translation manually assigns a private IP address to a public IP address. For instance, three public routable IP addresses will allow three static NAT translations.

Dynamic NAT mapping translates each private IP address to an available public IP address in the NAT pool. The dynamic NAT pool of public IP addresses is shared by all internal IP addresses on a first come first served basis. The maximum number of simultaneous internet connections available is limited to the number of public IP addresses in the NAT pool.

51. How is the IP address of a TFTP server communicated to hosts and Cisco IP phones?

    A. DNS Server Option 150

    B. DHCP Server Option 43

    C. TFTP Server Option 60

    D. DHCP Server Option 150

Correct Answer (D)
Subject Matter: DHCP

The IP address of a TFTP server is communicated to a host via DHCP option 150. It is a Cisco proprietary feature that enables a host or IP phone to request the TFTP server IP address on bootup. There is support as well for a list of TFTP servers. Cisco IP phones require either manual configuration or enabling DHCP option 150 to obtain the TFTP server IP address. The Cisco IP phone device configuration file is downloaded from a TFTP server. DHCP option 66 is the IEEE open standard for multi-vendor support.

52. Refer to the network drawing. What standby (virtual) IP address for HSRP is valid based on the IP addressing assigned to Router-1 and Router-2?

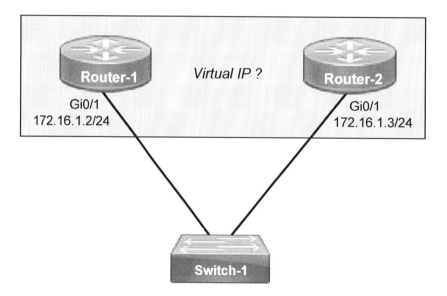

A. 172.16.1.1

B. 172.16.1.3

C. 172.16.1.2

D. 172.16.0.1

Correct Answer (A)
Subject Matter: HSRP

The HSRP virtual IP address is shared between routers. It must be assigned from the same subnet as the physical interfaces of Router-1 and Router-2. Any assignment other than .2 and .3 from the 4th octet are valid with the /24 subnet mask.

- Router-1 = 172.16.1.2/24
- Router-2 = 172.16.1.3/24
- Virtual IP Address = 172.16.1.1

The active router is assigned the HSRP virtual IP address until failover occurs at the standby router. The HSRP configuration is **standby 1 ip 172.16.1.1** where the virtual IP address is assigned to group (**1**). There is support for assigning multiple groups per physical interface or VLAN interface.

53. Refer to the network topology drawing. What network device will be assigned as HSRP standby?

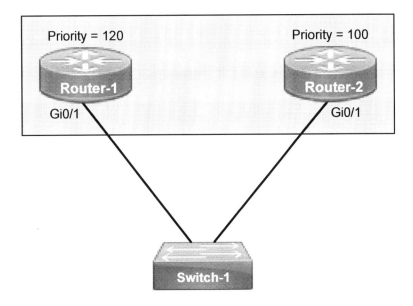

A. Router-1

B. Router-2

C. Switch-1

D. none

Correct Answer (B)
Subject Matter: HSRP

The HSRP enabled router with the lowest priority is elected as standby router. The priority of 120 elects Router-1 as HSRP active. Router-2 with a priority of 100 is HSRP standby (failover).

54. Refer to the network topology drawing. Match the NAT address type with the correct IP address for packets to the server?

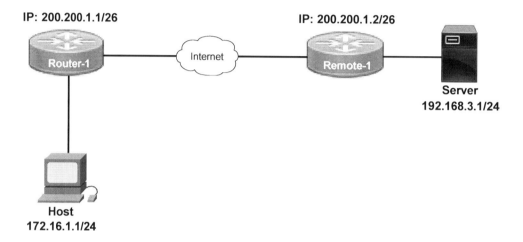

- inside local IP address = 200.200.1.2

- inside global IP address = 172.16.1.1

- outside local IP address = 200.200.1.2

- outside global IP address = 200.200.1.1

Correct Answers.
Subject Matter: Inside Source NAT

The following correctly describe Network Address Translation (NAT) types:

Inside Local IP Address = 172.16.1.1
Private IP address assigned to a host on the inside network.

Inside Global IP Address = 200.200.1.1
Public routable IP address as advertised to remote hosts across the internet. Private inside host addresses are translated to this public address.

Outside Local IP Address = 200.200.1.2
IP address of an outside host as it is advertised to the inside network before NAT has occurred. Typically it is the public WAN interface of the remote router.

Outside Global IP Address = 200.200.1.2
Public routable IP address of network device advertised across the internet. It is typically the WAN interface of the remote router.

Host-1	Remote-1
Inside Local	Outside Local
source IP = 172.16.1.1	destination IP = 200.200.1.2

Router-1 (NAT)	Remote-1
Inside Global	Outside Global
source IP = 200.200.1.1	destination IP = 200.200.1.2

55. What IOS command displays IP address, MAC address and lease expiration of all DHCP enabled hosts?

  A. router# show ip dhcp pool

  B. router# show ip dhcp database

  C. router# show ip dhcp binding

  D. router# show dhcp arp

  E. router# show dhcp bind

Correct Answer (C)
Subject Matter: DHCP

Cisco routers and switches can provide DHCP services to enabled hosts. The following IOS command lists the bindings for all DHCP enabled hosts.

  router# show ip dhcp binding

IP Address	Hardware Address	Lease Expire	Type
172.16.1.1	0000.000a.aaaa	Aug 16 2016 17:00 PM	Auto
172.16.1.2	0000.000b.bbbb	Aug 16 2016 17:00 PM	Auto
172.16.1.3	0000.000c.cccc	Aug 16 2016 17:00 PM	Auto
172.16.1.4	0000.000d.dddd	Aug 16 2016 17:00 PM	Auto

56. Refer to the network topology drawing. The network administrator recently deployed an edge router (Router-1) with NAT for internet connectivity. The ping from Router-1 to Ext-Router for testing layer 3 connectivity is not working. What two IOS commands can verify that NAT is not the issue?

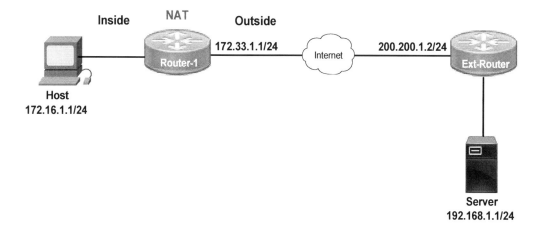

A. router-1# show ip interface brief

B. router-1# show running-config

C. router-1# show ip nat translations

D. router-1# show ip arp

E. router-1# show interfaces serial 0/0

F. router-1# ping 172.16.1.1

Correct Answers (B,C)
Subject Matter: Inside Source NAT

The following IOS commands are used to verify NAT operation. The results of **show running-config** list the current configuration for NAT. That would include any static or dynamic pool address translations, interfaces enabled and access control lists (ACL).

router-1# show running-config

The following IOS command lists the translation from inside local (private) (172.16.1.1) to public (172.33.1.1) IP addressing. The network administrator can verify the IP address is translated to the public routable address. There are often access control lists (ACL) configured to allow only a range of private IP addresses.

router-1# show ip nat translations

Pro	Inside global	Inside local	Outside local	Outside global
---	172.33.1.1	172.16.1.1	---	---

57. What IP address translation technique allows for the most internet connections based on a single public IP address?

  A. static NAT

  B. dynamic NAT (pool)

  C. port address translation (PAT)

  D. source NAT

  E. NAT with no overload

Correct Answer (C)
Subject Matter: Inside Source NAT

Port Address Translation (PAT) is an IP address translation technique that translates the most internal (private) IP addresses to a single or multiple public IP addresses. It is an enhancement to NAT that assigns a unique source port number to each translated IP address. The host IP address for instance could be identified with 200.200.1.1:10 as the translated source IP address. The **10** is the unique source port making the translated IP address unique. The 16 bit source port field allows for translating 65,535 private (internal) IP addresses to a a public IP address. There is support for a pool of addresses or single interface.

    192.168.1.1:10 -> 200.200.1.1:10
    192.168.1.2:11 -> 200.200.1.1:11
    192.168.1.3:12 -> 200.200.1.1:12

Module 6: Infrastructure Security

1. What IOS command will configure local username **admin** and password **cisco** on a switch with privilege level 15?

   A. username admin password cisco privilege 15

   B. username admin 15 cisco

   C. username admin privilege 15 password cisco

   D. username admin cisco privilege 15

Correct Answer (C)
Subject Matter: Basic Device Hardening

The following IOS command will configure a username called **admin** with privilege level 15. In addition the password for the manually configured account is **cisco**. The same command is used on Cisco Catalyst switches and routers.

   device(config)# username *admin* privilege 15 password *cisco*

2. What IOS command will configure the local username **admin** and a hidden password?

   A. username admin privilege 15 password 6

   B. username admin privilege 15 password 7

   C. username admin privilege 15 password 9

   D. username admin privilege 15 password 0

Correct Answer (B)
Subject Matter: Basic Device Hardening

The following IOS command will configure a username called **admin** with privilege level 15 and a hidden password. The 7 designates the password as hidden (encrypted) with the configuration script. The encrypted password is copy/pasted to the command line. It is common to copy the encrypted password from another device where the same password is already configured. The service password-encryption command must be enabled on the device for type 7 encryption.

   device(config)# username admin privilege 15 password 7 [encrypted password]

3. What global IOS command is used to configure username *admin* and a hidden secret password?

    A. username admin privilege 15 secret 0

    B. username admin privilege 15 secret 7

    C. username admin privilege 15 secret 5

    D. username admin privilege 15 secret 15

Correct Answer (C)
Subject Matter: Basic Device Hardening

The following IOS command will configure a username called *admin* with privilege level 15 and a hidden secret password. The 5 designates the password as secret and hidden (encrypted) with the configuration script. The secret password uses an MD5 hash to encrypt the that is more secure than type 7 encryption keyword.

The secret encrypted password is copy/pasted to the command line. It is common to copy the encrypted password from another device. Note that secret passwords do not require service password encryption. Some network devices have multiple password types however so they would use that service.

    device(config)# username admin privilege 15 secret 5 [encrypted password]

4. What two statements are correct concerning the following IOS command?

    device(config)# service password-encryption

    A. service password-encryption command is not supported on routers

    B. encrypts the password in all configuration files

    C. service password does not encrypt secret passwords

    D. service password encrypts secret passwords

    E. service password encryption is a privileged exec level command

Correct Answers (B,C)
Subject Matter: Basic Device Hardening

The purpose of **service password-encryption** command is to encrypt passwords in the running and startup configuration scripts. It applies to all passwords except secret passwords.

5. Select the proper order of commands to configure enable password *cisco*?

   A. device> configure terminal
      device# enable
      device(config)# enable password cisco

   B. device> configure terminal
      device# enable
      device# enable cisco

   C. device> configure terminal
      device(config)# password cisco

   D. device> enable
      device# password cisco

Correct Answer (A)
Subject Matter: Basic Device Hardening

The following IOS commands will configure an enable password on a Cisco switch or router. The enable password will be required before access to privileged EXEC mode is allowed (switch#). That mode then allows access to global configuration mode.

   device> configure terminal
   device# enable
   device(config)# enable password cisco

6. Select the IOS commands that assign password *cisco* to the Cisco device console port?

    A. device(config)# console 0
           device(config-line)# login password cisco

    B. device(config)# line console 0
           device(config-if)# password cisco
           device(config-if)# login

    C. device(config)# line console 0
           device(config-line)# password cisco
           device(config-line)# login

    D. device(config)# console
           device(config-line)# password cisco
           device(config-line)# login cisco

Correct Answer (C)
Subject Matter: Basic Device Hardening

The following commands will assign password *cisco* to the switch or router console port. Any login attempt to the console port will require that password.

    device(config)# line console 0
    device(config-line)# password *cisco*
    device(config-line)# login

7. What order of IOS commands will enable Telnet login, set the password to *cisco* and a timeout value of 5 minutes for all five default VTY lines?

    A. device(config)# line vty 0 4
           device(config-line)# line enable
           device(config-line)# login cisco
           device(config-line)# timeout 600

    B. device(config)# line vty 4
           device(config-line)# enable password cisco
           device(config-line)# login
           device(config-line)# timeout 5

    C. device(config)# line vty 4
           device(config-line)# password cisco
           device(config-line)# login
           device(config-line)# exec-timer 5

D. device(config)# line vty 0 4
   device(config-line)# password cisco
   device(config-line)# login
   device(config-line)# exec-timeout 5

Correct Answer (D)
Subject Matter: Basic Device Hardening

The following IOS commands will enable Telnet login, set the password to *cisco* and a timeout value of 5 minutes for all five default VTY lines.

device(config)# line vty 0 4
device(config-line)# password *cisco*
device(config-line)# login
device(config-line)# exec-timeout 5

8. What is the purpose of the following IOS command?

   device(config-line)# login local

A. password is not required for VTY or console access

B. VTY authentication is from local username and password database

C. network device permits console port access only

D. password is not required for VTY access

Correct Answer (B)
Subject Matter: Basic Device Hardening

The IOS command login local enables the use of the local database for VTY line access. The username and password is manually configured in the local device database for user authentication. The same IOS command is used to configure console access as well. Any AAA server configuration with TACACS or RADIUS takes precedence over any login local when configured.

9. What IOS command enables SSH protocol connection to VTY 0 4 lines and denies Telnet access for security purposes?

A. transport input ssh

B. transport input none

C. transport vty ssh

D. transport none telnet

Correct Answer (A)
Subject Matter: Basic Device Hardening

The following IOS command allows only SSH protocol traffic inbound to the default VTY lines (0 4). It will deny all other protocols inbound access to the VTY lines including Telnet. The Cisco default is to allow all protocols inbound and outbound access.

    device(config-line)# transport input ssh

10. What statement is true for passwords on a Cisco network device?

A. no default password is configured

B. type 5 passwords are uncrackable

C. type 7 passwords are uncrackable

D. type 0 passwords are uncrackable

Correct Answer (B)
Subject Matter: Basic Device Hardening

Cisco Type 5 device passwords are based on MD5 hash algorithm that is uncrackable. The Type 5 option encrypts the secret password automatically without requiring service password-encryption. Issue the **show version** command to verify whether the IOS image supports secret passwords.

11. What three IOS commands are not required to enable SSH on a Cisco network device?

A. transport input ssh all

B. enable secret password

C. login local

D. crypto key generate rsa

Correct Answers (A,B,C)
Subject Matter: Basic Device Hardening

The IOS command **crypto key generate rsa** is required to enable SSH.

- transport input ssh all *(not required - default is to allow all protocols)*
- enable secret password *(not required)*
- login local *(optional)*

12. What IOS command configures an MOTD banner on a Cisco device?

A. device (config)# banner motd ^ enter text ^

B. device (config)# motd banner # enter text

C. device (config-if)# motd banner # enter text ^

D. device # banner motd # enter text

Correct Answer (A)
Subject Matter: Basic Device Hardening

The following IOS command configures an MOTD banner for a Cisco device.

device(config)# banner motd ^ enter text ^

13. Select the command used to encrypt all plain-text passwords on a router?

A. router# password-encryption

B. router(config)# service password encryption

C. router(config)# service password-encryption

D. router# service password-encryption

Correct Answer (C)
Subject Matter: Basic Device Hardening

The following IOS command is used to encrypt all plain-text passwords on a Cisco device. The passwords are encrypted in the running configuration and startup configuration script.

router(config)# service password-encryption

14. What is the effect of using the service password-encryption command on a Cisco network device?

    A. encrypts all passwords configured including new passwords

    B. encrypts the secret password and remove the enable secret password from the configuration

    C. only the enable password will be encrypted

    D. only the enable secret password will be encrypted

    E. only passwords configured after the command has been entered will be encrypted

Correct Answer (A)
Subject Matter: Basic Device Hardening

The purpose of **service password-encryption** is to make device passwords unreadable for security. That includes authentication key, enable, console, VTY and BGP neighbor passwords. It does not however encrypt secret passwords.

15. What is the purpose of the following VTY line configuration?

    line vty 0 4
    password 7 [encrypted password]
    login
    transport input ssh

A. configures an unencrypted password on VTY lines 0 and 4 only and allows inbound SSH traffic

B. configures a hidden encrypted password on the default VTY lines and allows inbound SSH traffic only

C. configures a secret password on the default VTY lines and allows inbound SSH traffic or Telnet

D. configures the password 7 on the default VTY lines only and allows inbound SSH traffic

Correct Answer (B)
Subject Matter: Basic Device Hardening

The IOS command **password 7** enables a hidden password that is encrypted and not listed with show running-config command. It is a password for the default VTY lines. The encrypted password is copied from another Cisco device. In addition the command **transport input ssh** enables inbound SSH traffic only for VTY access.

```
line vty 0 4
password 7 [encrypted password]
login
transport input ssh
```

The following describe usage of the **transport** command to filter protocols. The **output** keyword is available as well that applies to outbound traffic.

```
transport input all = allow all protocols (telnet, ssh etc.)
transport input telnet ssh = allow telnet and ssh only
```

16. What IOS command is used to monitor and verify configured ACLs?

A. show ip access-list

B. show running-config

C. show access-group /all

D. show access-lists

Correct Answer (D)
Subject Matter: IPv4 Access Control Lists (ACL)

The following IOS command lists all IPv4 ACLs configured on a router.

router# show access-lists

The following IOS command lists all IPv6 ACLs configured on a router.

router# show ipv6 access-list

17. What are the components of a standard access control list (ACL)?

   A. source address, subnet mask, destination address

   B. source address and subnet mask

   C. destination address, wildcard mask, protocol

   D. source address and wildcard mask

Correct Answer (D)
Subject Matter: Access Control Lists (ACL)

The standard access list allows for only specifying a source address and wildcard mask. The wildcard mask is used for filtering purposes.

18. Refer to the network topology drawing. The following access control list (ACL) was configured on Router-2. What is the effect of the following ACL?

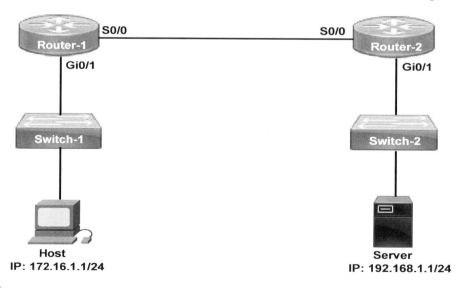

router-2(config)# access-list 100 deny tcp any host 192.168.1.1 eq 21

A. deny all FTP traffic destined for server 192.168.1.1

B. deny all Telnet traffic destined for server 192.168.1.1

C. deny all DNS traffic destined for server 192.168.1.1

D. deny all SSH traffic destined for server 192.168.1.1

Correct Answer (A)
Subject Matter: IPv4 Access Control Lists (ACL)

The following extended access list is configured to deny all FTP traffic destined for server 192.168.1.1 host IP address.

router-2(config)# access-list 100 deny tcp any host 192.168.1.1 eq 21

- Extended access list numbering is > 99
- FTP = TCP port 21
- ACL denies all other traffic explicitly

19. Refer to the network topology drawing. Router-1 is configured with the following access control list (ACL) configuration. The purpose is to deny access from all hosts on subnet 192.168.0.0/24 to the server. Select the correct network device, interface and direction to apply the ACL?

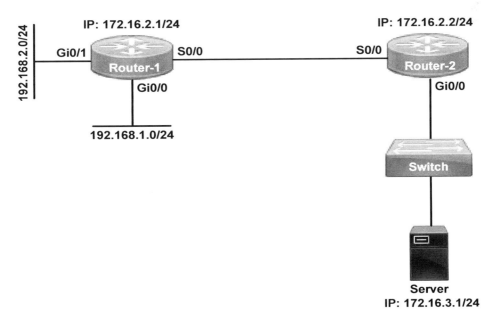

router-1(config)# ip access-list extended hosts-deny
router-1(config-ext-nacl)# deny ip 192.168.0.0 0.0.255.255 any

A. Router-1, Gi0/0, inbound

B. Router-1, S0/0, outbound

C. Router-1, Gi0/1, inbound

D. Router-1, S0/0, inbound

E. Router-2, Gi0/0, outbound

F. Router-2, S0/0, inbound

Correct Answer (B)
Subject Matter: IPv4 Access Control Lists (ACL)

The named ACL denies traffic from all host IP addresses assignable to 192.168.0.0/24 subnets. That is accomplished with the wildcard mask **0.0.255.255.** The host portion for a Class C address is the 4th octet. The ACL is applied outbound on interface S0/0 of Router-1. That filters traffic nearest to the source with the extended access control list. Applying the ACL inbound on interface Gi0/0 or Gi0/1 of Router-1 would only deny access from that local subnet (192.168.1.0 and 192.168.2.0) and not both.

20. Select the standard IP access control list (ACL) statement?

A. access-list 100 deny tcp any host 192.168.34.1 eq 22

B. access-list 199 deny tcp any host 172.16.1.1

C. access-list 110 permit ip any any

D. access-list 99 deny host 172.33.1.1

Correct Answer (D)
Subject Matter: IPv4 Access Control Lists (ACL)

The standard access list (ACL) has a numbered range from 1-99. It specifies permit/deny traffic from a source address with a wildcard mask.

The extended access list (ACL) has a numbered range from 100-199. It specifies permit/deny with source and destination IP address, IP/TCP/UDP protocols and destination ports.

21. Refer to the following router configuration. ACL 100 is not configured correctly and denying all traffic from all subnets. What interface level IOS command immediately removes the effect of ACL 100?

    access-list 100 deny tcp 172.16.0.0 0.0.255.255 any eq 80
    access-list 100 deny ip any any

    router# show ip interface gigabitethernet 1/1

    GigabitEthernet1/1 is up, line protocol is up
    Internet address is 192.168.1.1/24
    Broadcast address is 255.255.255.255
    Address determined by DHCP
    MTU is 1500 bytes
    Helper address is not set
    Directed broadcast forwarding is enabled
    Outgoing access list is **100**
    Inbound access list is not set
    Proxy ARP is enabled

    A. no ip access-group 100 in

    B. no ip access-group 100 out

    C. no ip access-class 100 in

    D. no ip access-list 100 in

    E. no ip access-class 100 out

Correct Answer (B)
Subject Matter: IPv4 Access Control Lists (ACL)

The ACL must be applied to an interface for it to inspect and filter any traffic. In addition the **in | out** keywords specify the direction to filter packets at the interface. The output from **show ip interface** command lists the ACL and direction configured for the interface. As a result there is ACL 100 applied outbound on GigabitEthernet0/0 interface. The ACL is applied with interface level IOS command **ip access-group 100 out**. To remove filtering requires deleting the **ip access-group** from the interface. The **ip access-group in | out** command refers to an ACL by name or number. The **access-class in | out** command filters VTY line access only.

    router(config-if)# no ip access-group 100 out

Any ACL with a single deny statement would deny all traffic outbound on a particular interface. The ACL adds an implicit deny statement at the end of each ACL effectively denying any traffic that does not match.

22. ACL statements 1, 2, 3 and 4 are configured in the sequence shown and applied to interface Gi0/0 inbound.

    1. permit ip any any
    2. deny 172.16.1.128 0.0.0.15
    3. permit 172.16.1.129 0.0.0.0
    4. permit 172.16.1.142 0.0.0.0

The ACL should permit only the first and last IP address of subnet 172.16.1.128/28 from accessing the network. The current configuration permits all network traffic however. What is the correct order of statements that would fix the configuration error?

A. 4,2,1,3

B. 3,4,2,1

C. 1,3,4,2

D. 2,1,4,3

Correct Answer (B)
Subject Matter: IPv4 Access Control Lists (ACL)

The ACLs are comprised of a single or multiple permit/deny statements. In addition they are ordered to control how traffic is filtered. There must be at least one permit statement or all traffic is denied. Each ACL adds an explicit deny as a last statement. The ACL starts at the first (top) statement and cycles through each ACL until there is a match. The packet is discarded where no match exists.

The first two ACLs only allow 172.16.1.129 and 172.16.1.142 hosts. The wildcard mask matches every bit from the host portion for the Class B address. The deny statement is then ordered next to deny any specific traffic. Without a deny statement, all traffic is allowed. The permit is to allow any existing traffic that should not be filtered by the ACL. The permit allows any additional traffic that isn't a match for the previous statements.

    1. permit 172.16.1.129 0.0.0.0
    2. permit 172.16.1.142 0.0.0.0
    3. deny 172.16.1.128 0.0.0.15
    4. permit ip any any

23. Select the statement that accurately describes how access lists can be applied to network interfaces?

   A. one access list can be applied inbound or outbound per interface per layer 3 protocol

   B. one access list can be applied inbound or outbound per interface per layer 2 protocol

   C. multiple access lists can be applied inbound or outbound per interface per layer 3 protocol

   D. one access list can be applied inbound only per interface per layer 3 protocol

Correct Answer (A)
Subject Matter: Access Control Lists (ACL)

The access lists are characterized by a single or multiple permit/deny statements. The purpose is to filter traffic inbound or outbound on a selected interface. In addition ACLs filter layer 3 traffic protocols. The result is a single ACL can be applied in one direction only per layer 3 protocol. There is support for a maximum of two ACLs per interface per protocol. That would include for instance a single IP ACL applied inbound and single IP ACL applied outbound.

24. The network administrator must allow temporary network access for a remote user with a username and password. Select the ACL type that supports the security requirement?

   A. dynamic

   B. standard

   C. reflexive

   D. extended

   E. global

Correct Answer (A)
Subject Matter: Access Control Lists (ACL)

The dynamic ACL provides temporary access to the network for a remote user. The ACL configured defines the type of access permitted and the source IP address. In addition there is a timeout value that limits the amount of time for network access. The remote user sign-on is available with a configured username and password.

411

25. What two statements describe the characteristics of port security?

    A. requires security feature license upgrade

    B. supports MAC address and/or IP address filtering

    C. permits Ethernet frames from both configured or dynamically learned MAC addresses

    D. sticky learning updates any dynamically learned addresses to the running configuration script

Correct Answers (C,D)
Subject Matter: Port Security

The following statements describe primary characteristics of port security.

- The sticky learning feature adds dynamically learned addresses to the running configuration script.

- Switch ports configured with port security only accept frames from addresses that have been dynamically learned or manually configured.

26. What security solution prevents connecting any unauthorized network device hardware to the corporate network?

    A. port security

    B. access control list (ACL)

    C. BPDU guard

    D. VLAN access control list (VACL)

    E. dynamic ACL

Correct Answer (A)
Subject Matter: Port Security

The purpose of port security is to optimize security through network switch access control. For instance plugging a laptop from home into the Ethernet jack at work could affect network operations. The switch port enabled with Port Security would deny access based on the unknown MAC address.

27. What is the effect of configuring the following commands on a switch?

> switch(config-if)# switchport port-security
> switch(config-if)# switchport port-security mac-address sticky

A. dynamically learned MAC addresses are added to the startup configuration file

B. dynamically learned MAC addresses are added to the VLAN database

C. dynamically learned MAC addresses are added to the running configuration file

D. statically configured MAC addresses are added to the startup configuration file

E. static and dynamically learned MAC addresses are added to the switch ARP table only

Correct Answer (C)
Subject Matter: Port Security

The IOS commands enable port security on a switch port interface. In addition the **sticky** keyword saves the dynamically learned MAC address to the running configuration script. The sticky MAC addresses do not age out of the MAC address table. The switch does have to relearn the MAC addresses after every reboot unless the running configuration is saved to startup configuration file. Removing the **sticky** keyword causes dynamically learned the MAC addresses to persist in the MAC address table only for the connected session.

28. What switch feature automatically disables the port enabled with PortFast when a BPDU is advertised?

A. Root guard

B. BPDU guard

C. BackboneFast

D. BPDU Filter

E. UplinkFast

F. Loop guard

Correct Answer (B)
Subject Matter: Port Security

The purpose of BPDU guard is to errdisable a switch port when a BPDU is advertised to it. It applies specifically to switch ports with PortFast enabled.

29. What two IOS commands are used to verify port security configuration on a switch port interface?

   A. show running-config

   B. show port-security interface

   C. show switchport interface

   D. show port security interface

   E. show port security detail

Correct Answers (A,B)
Subject Matter: Port Security

Each of the following IOS commands can verify that port security is configured on a switch port interface. In addition **show port-security** interface command provides status information.

    switch# show port-security interface gigabitethernet 1/1
    switch# show running-config

30. Refer to the port security configuration on switch interface Gi1/1. Ethernet frames with source MAC address *0000.000a.aaaa* arrives at switch interface Gi1/1. What two events occur when the frames arrives on Gi1/1?

    switch(config-if)# switchport port-security
    switch(config-if)# switchport port-security mac-address sticky
    switch(config-if)# switchport port-security maximum 1

   A. switch will discard frame

   B. switch won't update MAC address table with static address

   C. switch will update ARP table with MAC address

   D. switch will permit frames to access the network

   E. MAC address is dynamically learned

414

Correct Answers (D,E)
Subject Matter: Port Security

Port security is configured to allow the host connected to port Gi1/1 access to the network. The source MAC address **0000.000a.aaaa** is assigned to the host. Ethernet frames with destination MAC address **0000.000a.aaaa** are forwarded out (egress) Gi1/1 as well.

switch(config-if)# switchport port-security *(enables port security)*

switch(config-if)# switchport port-security mac-address sticky
(add MAC address 0000.000a.aaaa to running configuration)

switch(config-if)# switchport port-security maximum 1 *(single device only)*

31. What command/s prevent connecting two network devices to a switch port?

    A. switch(config-if)# switchport port-security maximum 1

    B. switch(config-if)# switchport mode access
       switch(config-if)# switchport port-security mac-address 1

    C. switch(config-if)# switchport mode trunk
       switch(config-if)# switchport port-security maximum 1

    D. switch(config-if)# switchport mode trunk
       switch(config-if)# switchport port-security mac-address 1

Correct Answer (A)
Subject Matter: Port Security

The following IOS command permits connectivity of a single network device only to a switch port.

switch(config-if)# switchport port-security maximum 1

32. What are three features provided by 802.1X port-based authentication?

    A. prevent unauthorized hosts from connecting to network

    B. prevent unauthorized wireless access points from connecting to network

    C. provides RADIUS based authentication

    D. provides TACACS+ based authentication

    E. MAC authentication bypass

Correct Answers (A,C,E)
Subject Matter: 802.1X Port-Based Authentication

802.1X provides user authentication of clients typically from switch ports where there is public access. The RADIUS server authenticates a username and password. In addition there is MAC authentication bypass available. The host MAC address is used as the username and password for identity. 802.1X authentication is an open standard supporting multi-vendor network devices.

Cisco port security is hardware (MAC) based authentication. It controls the MAC address/s allowed and number of devices. The following correctly describe the features of 802.1X port-based authentication:

- Prevent unauthorized hosts from connecting to network
- RADIUS based user authentication
- Supports MAC address authentication

33. What IOS interface command enables switch-side 802.1X authentication?

A. authentication port-control on

B. authentication port-control auto

C. authentication port-control enable

D. authentication port-control any

Correct Answer (B)
Subject Matter: 802.1X Port-Based Authentication

The following IOS command enables 802.1X with switch-side authentication.

switch(config-if)# authentication port-control auto

34. Refer to the network topology drawing. What happens when Host-1 attempts to connect to the network and no EAP request/identity frame was received from Switch-1?

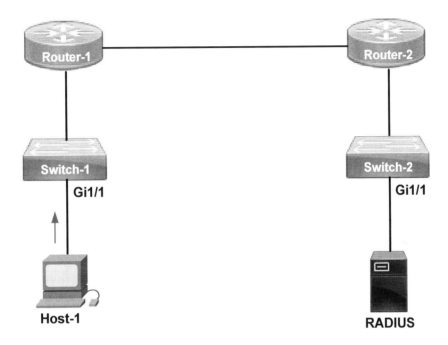

A. client can initiate authentication by sending EAPOL-start frame

B. client can initiate authentication by sending authentication request frame

C. client can request auto authentication from Switch-1

D. Switch-1 sends EAP request/identity frames as a default

E. Switch-1 sends error message to client and port is admin shutdown

Correct Answer (A)
Subject Matter: 802.1X Port-Based Authentication

The host connected to an 802.1X enabled switch port waits for an EAP request/identity frame from the switch. The client can initiate authentication by sending EAPOL-start frame if the EAP request/identity frame isn't sent.

35. What three issues would cause 802.1X authentication to fail?

    A. host (client) does not have 802.1X compliant software

    B. host (client) MAC address not permitted

    C. 802.1X is not enabled on the router

    D. no connectivity to RADIUS server

    E. no connectivity to TACACS+ server

    F. 802.1X timers incorrect

Correct Answers (A,B,D)
Subject Matter: 802.1X Port-Based Authentication

The following are three common causes for 802.1X authentication to fail.

- Host (client) does not have 802.1X compliant software
- Host (client) MAC address is not permitted
- No connectivity to RADIUS server

36. What two 802.1X switch port states can occur as a result of a security violation?

    A. restrict

    B. listening

    C. errdisable

    D. blocking

    E. disable

    F. idle

Correct Answers (A,C)
Subject Matter: 802.1X Port-Based Authentication

The following 802.1X switch port states occur when there is a security violation.

- Restrict
- Errdisable

37. Select the IOS commands required to enable 802.1X authentication on switch port GigabitEthernet1/2?

   A. switch(config)# interface gigabitethernet1/2
      switch(config-if)# switchport mode dot1x
      switch(config-if)# authentication port-control auto

   B. switch(config)# interface gigabitethernet1/2
      switch(config-if)# switchport mode dot1x
      switch(config-if)# dot1x radius authenticator
      switch(config-if)# authentication port-control

   C. switch(config)# interface gigabitethernet1/2
      switch(config-if)# switchport mode access
      switch(config-if)# dot1x authenticator
      switch(config-if)# authentication port-control any

   D. switch(config)# interface gigabitethernet1/2
      switch(config-if)# switchport mode access
      switch(config-if)# authentication port-control auto

Correct Answer (D)
Subject Matter: 802.1X Port-Based Authentication

The following IOS commands are required for enabling 802.1X on switch port GigabitEthernet1/2. The IOS command **authentication port-control auto** enables 802.1X authentication. In addition it configures the switch to initiate authentication when the link-state changes from down to up.

   switch(config)# interface gigabitethernet1/2
   switch(config-if)# switchport mode access
   switch(config-if)# authentication port-control auto

38. What three switch port interface configurations are supported with 802.1X authentication?

   A. access port

   B. layer 2 static trunk

   C. routed port

   D. dynamic port

   E. span port

   F. dynamic trunk

Correct Answers (A,B,C)
Subject Matter: 802.1X Port-Based Authentication

There are only specific switch interface configurations supported with 802.1X security. The supported (but not exclusive) list includes access ports, layer 2 static trunk and routed ports.

39. What IOS show command will verify the authorized state of an 802.1X client along with host mode and timer configuration?

   A. switch# show dot1x interface [interface-id]

   B. switch# show 802.1x interface [interface-id] details

   C. switch# show dot1x interface [interface-id] details

   D. switch# show 802.1 [interface-id] details

Correct Answer (C)
Subject Matter: 802.1X Port-Based Authentication

The following IOS show command will list the authorized state of an 802.1X client along with host mode and timer configuration.

   switch# show dot1x interface [interface-id] details

40. Refer to the network topology drawing. Switch-1 port Gi1/1 is 802.1X enabled. What statement correctly describes the requirement for connecting Cisco IP phones?

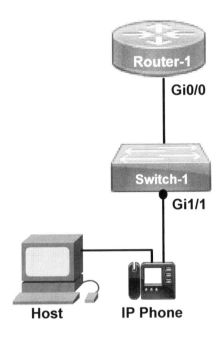

A. not supported with layer 2 switch

B. trunk support only

C. data VLAN and voice VLAN must be assigned to a separate VLAN ID

D. data VLAN and voice VLAN must be assigned to the same VLAN ID

E. multimode support only

Correct Answer (C)
Subject Matter: 802.1X Port-Based Authentication

The data VLAN and voice VLAN must be assigned to a separate VLAN ID. That is required for connecting a Cisco IP phone to an 802.1X enabled switch port.

41. What two services are provided by DHCP snooping?

   A. provide DHCP server authentication

   B. permit DHCP packet types (Discovery, Offer, Request, ACK) to trusted port only

   C. minimize DHCP packet types (Discovery, Offer, Request, ACK) to a single VLAN

   D. prevents rogue DHCP servers from offering IP addresses to hosts

   E. detect layer 2 broadcast storms

Correct Answers (B,D)
Subject Matter: DHCP snooping

DHCP snooping is a security feature that acts like a firewall between untrusted hosts and trusted DHCP servers. The services provided by DHCP snooping include the following:

   • Permit DHCP packet types (Discovery, Offer, Request, ACK) to trusted port only.

   • Prevent rogue DHCP servers from offering IP addresses to hosts.

42. Select the two options where DHCP snooping can be enabled?

   A. per physical interface

   B. per VLAN

   C. per IP address

   D. globally

   E. all of the above

Correct Answers (B,D)
Subject Matter: DHCP snooping

DHCP snooping feature is enabled both globally per network device and per VLAN. The network administrator would enable snooping on VLAN/s assigned to switch access ports and **trunk uplink connected to the router**. Typically the hosts VLANs are configured for snooping.

43. Select two statements that correctly describe DHCP snooping operation?

A. at least one DHCP server must be connected to the switch through a trusted interface

B. all DHCP servers must be connected to the switch through trusted interfaces

C. all DHCP servers must be connected to the same subnet as all clients

D. untrusted DHCP messages are forwarded only to trusted interfaces

E. DHCP snooping is a layer 3 network service

Correct Answers (B,D)
Subject Matter: DHCP snooping

For DHCP snooping to work properly, all DHCP servers must be connected to the switch through trusted interfaces. In addition all untrusted DHCP messages are forwarded only to trusted interfaces.

44. What two statements correctly describe a switch trusted interface for DHCP snooping?

A. only layer 2 trusted interfaces forward all DHCP broadcast messages

B. only layer 3 trusted interfaces forward all DHCP broadcast messages

C. 802.1X authentication is required for proper operation of DHCP snooping

D. layer 2 trusted interface is typically a switch uplink for connectivity to DHCP servers

E. all switch ports assigned to a VLAN enabled with DHCP snooping must be trusted interfaces

F. only layer 2 trusted interfaces forward all DHCP broadcast messages

Correct Answers (A,D)
Subject Matter: DHCP snooping

The following statements are true of a switch trusted interface:

*   Only layer 2 trusted interfaces forward all DHCP broadcast messages.
*   Layer 2 trusted interface is typically a switch uplink for connectivity to DHCP servers.

45. What IOS commands will enable DHCP snooping and configure DHCP trust state on a layer 2 switch interface?

   A. switch(config)# dhcp snooping
       switch(config)# ip dhcp snooping vlan [vlan ID] [vlan range]
       switch(config)# interface [interface]
       switch(config-if)# dhcp snooping trust

   B. switch(config)# dhcp snooping enable
       switch(config)# ip dhcp snooping vlan [vlan ID] [vlan range]
       switch(config)# interface [interface]
       switch(config-if)# ip dhcp snooping enable

   C. switch(config)# ip dhcp snooping
       switch(config)# ip dhcp snooping vlan [vlan ID] [vlan range]
       switch(config)# interface [interface]
       switch(config-if)# ip dhcp snooping trust

   D. switch(config)# service dhcp snooping
       switch(config)# ip dhcp snooping vlan [vlan ID] [vlan range]
       switch(config)# interface [interface]
       switch(config-if)# snooping dhcp enable

Correct Answer (C)
Subject Matter: DHCP snooping

The following commands enables DHCP snooping globally and snooping on VLAN 10. In addition trust state is assigned to switch port GigabitEthernet1/1. That is the uplink that connects to the router with DHCP server enabled. The trust state command is only supported on layer 2 switch interfaces.

   switch(config)# ip dhcp snooping *(enables globally)*
   switch(config)# ip dhcp snooping vlan 10 *(enable snooping on vlan 10)*
   switch(config)# interface gigabitethernet1/1 *(uplink to router)*
   switch(config-if)# ip dhcp snooping trust *(configures interface as trusted)*

Configure switch ports with DHCP clients (hosts) as untrusted with **no ip dhcp snooping trust** interface level command.

46. What three statements are correct concerning the native VLAN?

   A. cannot be assigned VLAN 1

   B. forwards untagged packets across an access port

   C. must match between connected switches

   D. forwards untagged packets across a switch trunk

   E. should not be assigned the default VLAN 1 for switch trunk interface

   F. forwards tagged VLAN packets across an EtherChannel

Correct Answers (C,D,E)
Subject Matter: Nondefault Native VLAN

The native VLAN is used to forward untagged packets across a switch trunk. In addition Layer 2 control plane traffic such as DTP and STP protocols are always sent across native VLAN. The default native VLAN is assigned to VLAN 1. That is the same as the default management VLAN for switches. The native VLAN should not be assigned to VLAN 1 to prevent security or STP issues. As a result assigning a nondefault native VLAN is a security best practice.

The following are correct statements for the nondefault native VLAN:

   • The native VLAN must match between connected switches.
   • It is used to forward untagged packets across a switch trunk.
   • The native VLAN for switch trunk interfaces should not be assigned the default VLAN 1.

47. What three statements are true concerning Cisco switch VLAN 1?

   A. default VLAN for Cisco switches

   B. native VLAN for switch trunk interfaces is assigned to VLAN 1

   C. forwards management traffic and cannot be deleted

   D. VLAN 1 only applies to routers

   E. assigning user traffic to VLAN 1 creates a security vulnerability

   F. Telnet requires VLAN 1 for management access

Correct Answers (A,C,E)
Subject Matter: Default VLAN

VLAN 1 is the default for an unconfigured Cisco switch. The primary purpose of VLAN 1 is to forward management traffic between switches. The following are correct statements concerning VLAN 1:

- Cisco switch default is VLAN 1
- Default VLAN 1 forwards management traffic and cannot be deleted
- Assigning user traffic to VLAN 1 creates a security vulnerability

48. Select the correct IOS command to configure nondefault native VLAN 999?

    A. switch(config-if)# switchport encapsulation native vlan 999

    B. switch(config-if)# switchport mode trunk native vlan 999

    C. switch(config-if)# switchport trunk vlan 999 native

    D. switch(config-if)# switchport trunk native vlan 999

Correct Answer (D)
Subject Matter: Nondefault Native VLAN

The following command configures a nondefault native VLAN 999 instead of the default VLAN 1. It is configured on all switch port interfaces assigned as trunk ports.

    switch(config-if)# switchport trunk native vlan 999

49. What three differences exist between IPv4 and IPv6 support for ACLs?

    A. IPv4 does not support wildcard masks

    B. IPv6 supports only named ACLs

    C. IPv6 permits ICMP neighbor discovery (ARP) as implicit default

    D. IPv6 supports standard and extended ACLs

    E. IPv6 denies all traffic as an implicit default for last line of ACL

    F. IPv4 and IPv6 NAT deny inbound traffic as implicit default

Correct Answers (B,C,E)
Subject Matter: IPv4 and IPv6 Access Control Lists (ACL)

The following are three primary differences between IPv4 and IPv6 support for access control lists (ACL).

- IPv6 supports only named ACLs
- IPv6 permits ICMP neighbor discovery (ARP) as implicit default
- IPv6 denies all traffic as an implicit default for the last line of the ACL

50. What last statement is required for proper IPv6 operation when deploying multiple ACL deny statements?

   A. permit icmp any any nd-na

   B. permit ipv6 any any

   C. permit IPv6 any

   D. deny ipv6 any any

   E. deny ipv6 any any log

Correct Answer (B)
Subject Matter: IPv6 Access Control Lists (ACL)

Proper IPv6 operation requires ACL **permit ipv6 any any** (all traffic) as a last statement when there are multiple ACL deny statements.

51. What is the default network protocol as part of an IPv6 ACL?

   A. TCP

   B. IP

   C. UDP

   D. ICMP

   E. IPv6

Correct Answer (E)
Subject Matter: IPv6 Access Control Lists (ACL)

The IPv6 ACL statement starts with a permit or deny along with a protocol. The default protocol is IPv6 where none is specified. Additional protocols supported include ICMP, TCP and UDP.

52. Refer to the network topology drawing. What does the following IPv6 ACL accomplish when configured on Router-1?

    ipv6 access-list web-traffic
    deny tcp host 2001:0:AD03::1 host 2001:34F:20DC:24DE::1F eq www
    permit ipv6 any any

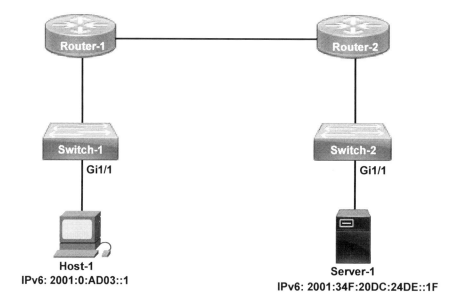

A. deny HTTP traffic for all hosts on a subnet

B. deny HTTP traffic from host 2001:0:AD03::1 to host 2001:34F:20DC:24DE::1F

C. deny HTTP traffic to host 2001:34F:20DC:24DE::1F

D. deny access to all TCP applications for the hosts listed

E. deny all HTTP traffic for the local IPv6 subnet

F. deny HTTP traffic to host 2001:0:AD03::1 from host 2001:34F:20DC:24DE::1F

Correct Answer (B)
Subject Matter: IPv6 Access Control Lists (ACL)

The Cisco ACL for IPv4 and IPv6 use similar syntax from left to right. For instance the ACL reads as - *deny tcp traffic from host address (source) to host address (destination)*. All web-based applications are TCP-based and as such requires **deny tcp**. The **eq www** specifies the TCP-based application to deny.

reads as - *deny http from host 2001:0:AD03::1 to 2001:34F:20DC:24DE::1F*

The **deny tcp** with no application specified will deny traffic from all TCP applications (Telnet, FTP, SSH etc). It would however allow all UDP-based application traffic. The **deny ipv6 host** command when configured won't allow UDP or TCP traffic. IP is a lower layer protocol and required for higher layer protocols.

53. What two statements are true of Cisco Path Trace service?

    A. endpoint support for hosts and/or layer 3 interfaces

    B. enables trace from router loopback interface

    C. enables automated network troubleshooting

    D. Cisco network device support only

    E. endpoint support for layer 2 and layer 3 interfaces only

Correct Answers (A,C)
Subject Matter: APIC-EM Path Trace

Path Trace (PT) is a feature available with Cisco APIC-EM that can identify the exact path between two endpoints. The trace is determined based on the endpoint IP addresses and a 5-tuple description for a flow. This helps automate inspection and enable cost effective faster troubleshooting. The following are correct statements concerning Path Trace:

- Endpoint support for hosts and/or layer 3 interfaces
- Enables automated network troubleshooting

54. How are non-Cisco devices represented with a Path Trace report?

 A. unknown device represented with !

 B. unknown device represented with NCD

 C. unknown device represented with ?

 D. unknown device represented with *

 E. no support is available for third party devices

Correct Answer (C)
Subject Matter: APIC-EM Path Trace

Non-Cisco devices are listed with a question mark (?) in a Path Trace report.

55. What are two requirements before starting an ACL Path Trace?

 A. network discovery

 B. SSH access for controller only

 C. SSH or Telnet access for controller to network devices

 D. IP Anycast enabled

 E. IP device tracking (IPDT) enabled

 F. NetFlow enabled

Correct Answers (A,C)
Subject Matter: APIC-EM Path Trace (ACL)

The network discovery is required before starting an ACL Path Trace. In addition SSH or Telnet is required to enable APIC-EM controller access to the devices. The network discovery feature collects information on all network devices and builds an inventory database.

56. Select two correct statements that describe ACL Path Trace operation?

    A. ACL Trace analyzes egress interfaces only for all devices between endpoints

    B. Path is calculated between the designated endpoints (source and destination IP address)

    C. ACL Trace report describes where packets were permitted and dropped

    D. ACL Trace analyzes how a flow is affected by all ACLs deployed on the path

    E. analysis is based on how each ACL is affected by neighbor ACLs

Correct Answers (B,D)
Subject Matter: APIC-EM Path Trace (ACL)

ACL Path Trace analyzes how a flow is affected by any ACLs deployed on the path. After the path between source and destination is calculated, the ACL Trace analyzes both ingress and egress interfaces of all devices on the path. The analysis is cumulative per ACL and not end-to-end path.

The following are correct statements concerning ACL Path Trace operation:

- Path is calculated between the designated endpoints (source and destination IP address).

- ACL Trace analyzes how a flow is affected by ACLs deployed on the path.

57. What are three disadvantages of AAA authentication?

    A. AAA server is a single point of failure

    B. password management is complex

    C. no redundancy support

    D. not scalable

    E. local account is required as a backup on network devices

    F. same AAA password is used for multiple network devices

Correct Answers (A,E,F)
Subject Matter: AAA Device Security

The following is a list of disadvantages with AAA authentication method.

- AAA server is a single point of failure
- Local account is required as a backup on network devices
- Same AAA password is used for multiple network devices

58. Match the AAA server type on the left with the feature support on the right?

TACACS+	multi-vendor open standard
RADIUS	Cisco proprietary
TACACS+	UDP
RADIUS	TCP
TACACS+	integrates authentication and authorization
RADIUS	separates authentication, authorization and accounting
TACACS+	encrypts passwords only
RADIUS	encrypts all communication

Correct Answers.
Subject Matter: AAA Device Security

The following describes the feature support based on the AAA server type.

TACACS+	**Cisco proprietary**
RADIUS	**multi-vendor open standard**
TACACS+	**TCP**
RADIUS	**UDP**
TACACS+	**separates authentication, authorization and accounting**
RADIUS	**integrates authentication and authorization**
TACACS+	**encrypts all communication**
RADIUS	**encrypts passwords only**

59. Select the three advantages of TACACS+ over RADIUS authentication services?

A. TACACS+ supports UDP

B. TACACS+ supports 15 privilege levels

C. TACACS+ supports controls for user authorization levels

D. TACACS+ allow for device administration

E. TACACS+ requires less server CPU and memory

Correct Answers (B,C,D)
Subject Matter: AAA Device Security

The following are three advantages of TACACS+ over RADIUS server.

- TACACS+ supports 15 privilege levels
- TACACS+ enables controls for user authorization levels
- TACACS+ allow for device administration

RADIUS is limited to privilege mode and provides network access and authentication only.

60. What AAA component enables security control to permit/deny user access to a network server where the FTP application is running?

A. accounting

B. authentication

C. auditing

D. authorization

Correct Answer (D)
Subject Matter: AAA Device Security

The AAA security model includes authentication, authorization and accounting. The authentication component verifies user identity for approving access to the server. The authorization component allows user access to applications and data on the server. The accounting component provides an audit trail of transactions for security analysis and forensics.

61. What IOS command can verify that login access for a AAA account is disabled?

A. show running-config

B. show aaa sessions

C. show aaa local user lockout

D. show aaa user

Correct Answer (C)
Subject Matter: AAA Device Security

The user will typically complain that access to a particular network device isn't available. The following IOS command will verify the login access for a AAA user account is disabled.

device# show aaa local user lockout

62. What server-based authentication protocol allows defining of authorization policies per group?

A. Telnet

B. SSH

C. RADIUS

D. TACACS+

E. ACS

F. 802.1X

Correct Answer (D)
Subject Matter: AAA Device Security

TACACS+ is a server-based authentication protocol that allows defining of authorization policies per group. As a result TACACS+ is well suited to managing the access security for thousands of network devices. The advantage is defining multiple levels of authorization for groups. The groups could include technical support, network engineers, contractors etc.

63. What AAA authentication method verifies access requests from the username and password database local to the router?

A. Local TACACS+

B. TACACS+ Server

C. RADIUS Server

D. Local RADIUS

E. Local AAA

Correct Answer (E)
Subject Matter: AAA Device Security

The local AAA authentication method will use the local username and password database configured on the router.

The IOS command **aaa authentication login default local** enables AAA authentication to use the device local username database. There is an option as well to configure local authentication as failover for AAA as well.

64. Select the network device considered the supplicant as part of the 802.1X authentication process?

A. authentication server

B. host requesting authentication

C. default gateway router

D. switch

Correct Answer (B)
Subject Matter: 802.1X Port-Based Authentication

The client requesting authentication is the supplicant as part of the 802.1X authentication process. The client identity credentials are submitted to the authenticator (access switch). The authenticator forwards the client credentials to the RADIUS authentication server.

65. Refer to the network topology drawing. Select the network point where DHCP snooping trust interface is enabled?

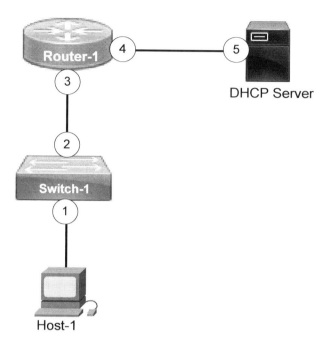

DHCP Server

Switch-1

Host-1

A. 1

B. 2

C. 3

D. 4

E. 5

Correct Answer (B)
Subject Matter: DHCP snooping

DHCP snooping trust interfaces are enabled on a layer 2 Ethernet interface or layer 2 port channel. The trusted interface must have connectivity to DHCP servers where DHCP messages are sent. The layer 2 (access) switch uplink is typically enabled as a DHCP trusted interface for that purpose.

The switch uplink at point 2 is where the trusted interface is enabled. That provides connectivity to the router for packet forwarding to DHCP servers on remote subnets.

66. Refer to the network topology drawing. What network points does ACL Path Trace support? (select two)

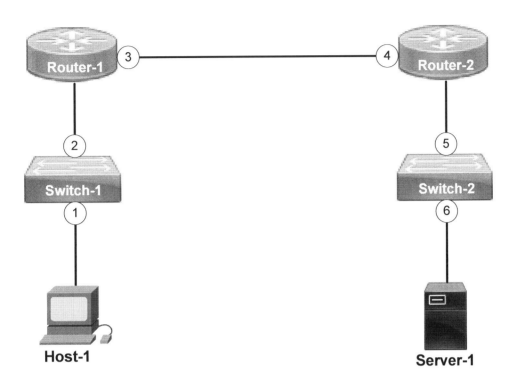

A. 1

B. 2

C. 3

D. 4

E. 5

F. 6

Correct Answers (C,D)
Subject Matter: APIC-EM Path Trace (ACL)

Cisco ACL Path Trace is supported on layer 3 interfaces only.

67. What IOS command can bring a switch port in error-disabled state out of this state when port security is configured?

   A. switch(config)# errdisable recovery

   B. switch(config-if)# errdisable recovery psecure-violation

   C. switch(config)# err-disable recovery reset

   D. switch(config)# err-disable recovery psecure

Correct Answer (B)
Subject Matter: Port Security

The following IOS global configuration command will re-enable a switch port interface in errdisable state caused by a port security violation.

   switch(config)# errdisable recovery cause psecure-violation

The default setting is to re-enable the port with **shutdown** and **no shutdown** interface configuration commands. In addition where the interface is a VLAN, the IOS command **clear errdisable interface** [interface] [vlan] will enable the VLAN interface.

68. What happens when there is a port security violation on a switch port enabled with restrict mode?

   A. switch port is shutdown

   B. error message is sent only

   C. switch only allows a single MAC address

   D. packets from unknown source MAC addresses are dropped

   E. switch deletes MAC address to fix error

Correct Answer (D)
Subject Matter: Port Security

The four configurable violation modes include protect, restrict, shutdown and shutdown VLAN. The switch interface can add up to the maximum number of allowed MAC addresses to the address table. The security violation is triggered when there an attempt from a host with a MAC address not in the MAC address table. The duplicate MAC address error causes a violation as well. The restrict mode causes the switch to drop all packets from what is an unknown source.

438

In addition an SNMP trap alert is sent, syslog message is logged and the violation counter is increased. The protect mode only sends a security violation notification.

69. What are two primary advantages of Named ACLs?

    A. assign the same name to standard and extended access lists

    B. optimized network security

    C. dynamically add or delete statements to an ACL without having to delete and rewrite all lines

    D. easier to manage and troubleshoot

Correct Answers (C,D)
Subject Matter: Access Control Lists (ACL)

Named ACLs allow for dynamically adding or deleting ACL statements without having to delete and rewrite all lines. There is of course less CPU utilization required as well. They are easier to manage and enable troubleshooting of network issues.

70. Select three correct statements that are recommended best practices for creating and applying ACLs?

    A. apply standard ACL near source

    B. apply extended ACL near source

    C. apply extended ACL near destination

    D. apply standard ACL near destination

    E. order ACL with multiple statements from most specific to least specific

    F. order ACL with multiple statements from least specific to most specific

Correct Answers (B,D,E)
Subject Matter: Access Control Lists (ACL)

There are some recommended best practices when creating and applying access control lists (ACL). The network administrator should apply a standard access list closest to the destination. The standard access list is comprised of a source IP address and wildcard mask.

439

It is very general and can inadvertently filter traffic incorrectly. Applying the standard access list near the destination where filtering is required prevents possible over filtering. The extended access list should be applied closest to the source. The extended access list is granular (specific) and filters traffic based on stringent requirements. It includes source address, destination address, protocols and port numbers. Applying an extended access list closest to the source prevents traffic that should be filtered from traversing the network. That conserves bandwidth and additional processing required at each router hop from source to destination.

Some access control lists (ACL) are comprised of multiple statements. The ordering of statements is key to the ACL working as expected. The router starts from the top (first) and cycles through all statements until a matching statement is found. The packet is dropped where no match exists. The network administrator should order ACL statements from most specific to least specific. Assigning least specific statements first will sometimes cause a match to occur with an ACL that wasn't intended for that packet. As a result the match on the intended ACL statement never occurs.

The more specific ACL statement is characterized by source and destination addresses with shorter wildcard masks (more zeros). In addition protocols and port numbers are often specified. The first ACL statement is more specific than the second ACL statement. There is an implicit **deny any any** statement added to the end of each ACL.

> permit tcp 192.168.1.0 0.0.0.255 host 10.10.64.1 eq 23
> deny tcp any any eq 23

71. What IOS command permits Telnet traffic only from host 10.1.1.1/24 to host 10.1.2.1/24?

A. access-list 100 permit ip 10.1.1.1 0.0.0.0 host 10.1.2.1 eq 23

B. access-list 100 permit tcp host 10.1.1.1 host 10.1.2.1 eq 23

C. access-list 100 permit tcp 10.1.1.1 255.255.255.0 host 10.1.2.1 eq 23

D. access-list 100 permit tcp 10.1.1.1 255.255.255.255 host 10.1.2.1 eq 23

Correct Answer (B)
Subject Matter: IPv4 Access Control Lists (ACL)

The following IOS command permits Telnet traffic from host 10.1.1.1/24 to host 10.1.2.1/24

>   access-list 100 permit tcp host 10.1.1.1 host 10.1.2.1 eq 23

The access control list (ACL) statement reads from left to right as - *permit all tcp traffic from source host only to destination host that is Telnet (23)*. The TCP refers to applications that are TCP-based. The UDP keyword is used for applications that are UDP-based such as SNMP for instance. The 0.0.0.0 wildcard mask requires a match on all 4 octets of source address (10.1.1.1)

72. Refer to the network topology drawing. Select the correct IOS commands to configure the following security requirements?

- deny telnet traffic from 10.0.0.0/8 subnets to Router-2
- deny http traffic from 10.0.0.0/16 subnets to Router-2
- permit any traffic not matching

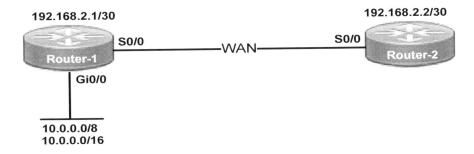

A. access-list 100 deny tcp 10.0.0.0 0.255.255.255 any eq 23
    access-list 100 deny tcp 10.0.0.0 0.0.255.255 any eq 80
    access-list 100 permit ip any any

B. access-list 100 deny tcp 10.0.0.0 0.255.255.255 host 192.168.2.2 eq 23
    access-list 100 deny tcp 10.0.0.0 0.255.255.255 host 192.168.2.2 eq 80
    access-list 100 permit ip any

C. access-list 100 deny tcp 10.0.0.0 0.255.255.255 host 192.168.2.2 eq 21
    access-list 100 deny tcp 10.0.0.0 0.0.0.255 host 192.168.2.2 eq 443
    access-list 100 permit ip any

D. access-list 100 deny tcp 10.0.0.0 0.255.255.255 host 192.168.2.2 eq 23
    access-list 100 deny tcp 10.0.0.0 0.255.255.255 host 192.168.2.2 eq 80
    access-list 100 permit tcp any

Correct Answer (A)
Subject Matter: IPv4 Access Control Lists (ACL)

The following IOS commands will configure the correct ACLs based on the security requirements:

> access-list 100 deny tcp 10.0.0.0 0.255.255.255 any eq 23
> access-list 100 deny tcp 10.0.0.0 0.0.255.255 any eq 80
> access-list 100 permit ip any any

The other options have either a wrong wildcard mask, application port number or no **permit ip any any** statement. All extended access control lists must have a permit all source and destination traffic with **permit ip any any** as a last ACL statement.

The ACL is applied inbound to interface Gi0/0 of Router-1 with the IOS command **ip access-group 100 in**. That would include all access control list statements numbered 100.

73. Refer to the network topology drawing. Select the correct IOS commands to configure the following security requirements?

   1. create a named ACL called ***http-ssh-filter***
   2. add a remark that describes purpose of the ACL
   3. permit http traffic from all 192.168.0.0 subnets to web server
   4. deny all SSH traffic from 192.168.0.0 subnets
   5. permit any traffic not matching

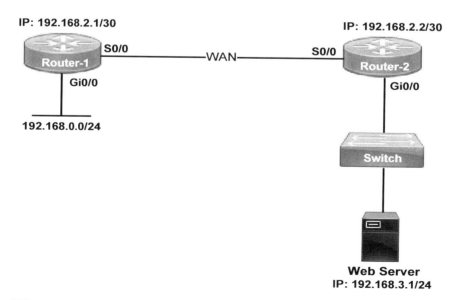

A. access-list extended http-ssh-filter
   remark permit http to web server and deny all ssh traffic
   permit ip 192.168.0.0 0.0.255.255 host 192.168.3.1 eq 80
   deny ip any host 192.168.3.1 eq ssh
   permit any any

B. ip access-list extended http-ssh-filter
   description permit http to web server and deny all ssh traffic
   permit tcp 192.168.0.0 0.255.255.255 host 192.168.3.1 eq 22
   deny ip any any eq 22
   permit ip any any

C. ip access-list extended http-ssh-filter
   remark permit http to web server and deny all ssh traffic
   permit tcp 192.168.0.0 0.255.255.255 host 192.168.3.1 eq 80
   deny ip any host 192.168.3.1 eq ssh
   permit ip any

D. ip access-list extended http-ssh-filter
   remark permit http to web server and deny all ssh traffic
   permit tcp 192.168.0.0 0.0.255.255 host 192.168.3.1 eq 80
   deny tcp any any eq 22
   permit ip any any

Correct Answer (D)
Subject Matter: IPv4 Access Control Lists (ACL)

The following IOS commands will configure the correct ACLs based on the security requirements:

   ip access-list extended http-ssh-filter
   remark permit http to web server and deny all ssh traffic
   permit tcp 192.168.0.0 0.0.255.255 host 192.168.3.1 eq 80
   deny tcp any any eq 22
   permit ip any any

The other options have either a wrong wildcard mask, application port number or no **permit ip any any** statement. All extended access control lists must have a permit all source and destination traffic with **permit ip any any** as a last ACL statement.

The ACL would be applied inbound to interface Gi0/0 of Router-1 with the IOS command **ip access-group http-ssh-filter in**. Sometimes it is preferred to apply an ACL outbound when the access control list is not specific enough and could filter additional traffic (i.e deny tcp any host [ip address]). The ACL could then be applied outbound to Serial0/0.

74. The network administrator must configure an ACL to only permit traffic to a server from host IP addresses 172.16.1.32/24 to 172.16.1.39/24. Select the ACL statement that would accomplish this?

A. access-list 10 permit ip 172.16.1.32 0.0.0.7

B. access-list 10 permit tcp 172.16.1.32 0.255.255.255

C. access-list 10 permit ip 172.16.1.32 0.0.7.255

D. access-list 10 permit ip 172.16.1.0 0.0.1.255

E. access-list 10 permit ip 172.16.40.0 0.0.0.255

Correct Answer (A)
Subject Matter: IPv4 Access Control Lists (ACL)

The ACL must permit traffic from 172.16.1.32 - 172.16.1.39 address range. The wildcard mask is applied to filter the network portion. The wildcard mask 0.0.0.7 applied allows only the specific IP host addresses from the fourth octet. The rightmost 3 bits are masked off permitting a maximum of eight IP addresses from 172.16.1.32/24 to 172.16.1.39/24 range.

```
   172.       16.        1.        32
10101100.00010000.00000001.00100 000
00000000.00000000.00000000.00000 111
   0.         0.         0.         7
```

Module 7: Infrastructure Management

1. What three statements correctly describe Cisco **traceroute** command?

   A. ICMP messages use IP protocol 10

   B. ICMP decrements by one at all network devices

   C. Cisco traceroute is based on UDP transport protocol

   D. Traceroute encapsulates ICMP messages in IP header

   E. TTL value is incremented by one at each layer 3 (router) hop

Correct Answers (C,D,E)
Subject Matter: IOS Troubleshooting Tools

The Cisco version of **traceroute** is based on sending 3 UDP datagrams to each hop between source and destination hosts. ICMP packets contain messages that are encapsulated within the IP layer 3 header. The TTL field of the UDP datagram is incremented by one with each hop that isn't the destination. ICMP sends a *Time Exceeded* message to the source and 3 UDP packets are sent to the next hop. When the UDP datagram arrives at the destination host with the correct IP address, ICMP sends a host unreachable message to the source. The message is the result of the invalid UDP port number.

2. What is the default number of simultaneous Telnet sessions supported by a Cisco router?

   A. 1

   B. 2

   C. 3

   D. 5

   E. 4

   F. 15

Correct Answer (D)
Subject Matter: Configure Device Management

The default number of simultaneous Telnet sessions supported by a Cisco router is five. They are comprised of the default VTY lines 0 4 (0,1,2,3,4).

3. Where is the IOS image file stored on a Cisco network device?

    A. DRAM

    B. NVRAM

    C. Flash

    D. SSD

    E. ROM

Correct Answer (C)
Subject Matter: Device Maintenance

The IOS image file is stored in Flash memory on a Cisco device. The Flash memory is permanent non-volatile file storage. On bootup the IOS image is loaded from Flash to DRAM volatile memory. The startup configuration is stored in permanent non-volatile NVRAM. The running configuration file is the startup configuration file that is loaded to DRAM.

4. What are the default Cisco console port serial settings?

    A. 9600 bps, 8 data bits, 2 stop bit, no parity, no flow control

    B. 9600 bps, 7 data bits, 1 stop bit, no parity, xon/xoff flow control

    C. 9600 bps, 8 data bits, 1 stop bit, no parity, no flow control

    D. 2400 bps, 8 data bits, 3 stop bit, parity, no flow control

Correct Answer (C)
Subject Matter: Initial Device Configuration

The Cisco network devices provide a console port for direct connection from a laptop. It is typically used for initial configuration and troubleshooting purposes. The following are default settings for the Cisco console port interface.

- 9600 bps, 8 data bits, 1 stop bit, no parity, no flow control

5. What IOS commands assign the hostname of *switch-1* and configures PST time zone on a Cisco switch?

A. switch> hostname router-1
   switch# timezone PST

B. switch(config)# hostname switch-1
   switch(config)# clock timezone PST -8

C. switch(config)# host name switch-1
   switch(config)# clock time-zone PST

D. switch(config)# host switch-1
   switch(config)# time PST -8

Correct Answer (B)
Subject Matter: Configure Device Management

The following global IOS commands assigns the hostname *switch-1* and configures **PST** timezone for the Cisco switch.

    switch(config)# hostname switch-1
    switch-1(config)# clock timezone PST -8

6. What commands configure a management IP address for a layer 2 switch?

A. switch(config)# interface vlan [number]
   switch(config)# ip address [ip address] [wildcard mask]
   switch(config)# no shutdown

B. switch(config)# vlan [number]
   switch(config)# ip address [ip address] [subnet mask]

C. switch(config)# interface vlan [number]
   switch(config)# ip address [ip address] [subnet mask]

D. switch(config)# interface vlan [number]
   switch(config-if)# ip address [ip address] [subnet mask]
   switch(config-if)# no shutdown

Correct Answer (D)
Subject Matter: Initial Device Configuration

The following IOS commands configure a management IP address (SVI) for a layer 2 switch. The Cisco recommended best practice is to assign an unused VLAN for remote switch management. The default VLAN 1 is used to forward control traffic (CDP, VTP, PAgP) between switches.

    switch(config)# interface vlan [number]
    switch(config-if)# ip address [ip address] [subnet mask]
    switch(config-if)# no shutdown

7. What IOS command will configure the default gateway for a layer 2 switch?

    A. switch(config)# ip default gateway 172.16.0.1

    B. switch(config)# ip default-network 172.16.0.1

    C. switch(config)# ip default-gateway 172.16.0.1

    D. switch(config)# default-gateway 172.16.0.1

Correct Answer (C)
Subject Matter: Initial Device Configuration

The following IOS command will configure a default gateway for a layer 2 switch. The layer 2 switch with no ip routing enabled will forward packets outside of its local subnet to the default gateway (router). The default gateway is the IP address of the router LAN interface on the same subnet as the switch.

    switch(config)# ip default-gateway 172.16.0.1

8. What IOS command will save the running configuration changes to the startup configuration file?

    A. device# copy start run

    B. device# copy running-config startup-config

    C. device# copy run all

    D. device# copy nvram

    E. device# copy running config startup config

Correct Answer (B)
Subject Matter: Configure Device Management

The following IOS command will save the running configuration changes to the startup configuration file (script).

   device# copy running-config startup-config

The alternate IOS command used is the following:
   device# copy system:running-config nvram:startup-config

9. What IOS command allows network administrators to run show commands from global configuration mode?

   A. device(config)# enable

   B. device(config)# exec

   C. device(config)# run

   D. device(config)# do

Correct Answer (D)
Subject Matter: Initial Device Configuration

The following IOS command allows the network administrator to run IOS show commands from global configuration mode.

   device(config)# do [show command]

10. What IOS commands serves the purpose of erasing the startup configuration file and restarting a Cisco network device? (select two)

   A. device# erase startup-config
      device# reload

   B. device# del nvram
      device# reload

   C. device# write erase
      device# reload

   D. device# erase nvram
      device# restart

   E. device# erase nvram
      device# reload

Correct Answers (A,C)
Subject Matter: Configure Device Management

There are two options available for erasing the startup configuration and restarting a switch or router.

Option 1:
device# erase startup-config
device# reload

Option 2:
device# write erase
device# reload

11. Where does a Cisco network device store the startup configuration file?

A. Disk0:

B. Flash0:

C. DRAM

D. NVRAM

Correct Answer (D)
Subject Matter: Configure Device Management

Cisco network devices store the startup configuration file in NVRAM.

12. Refer to the network topology drawing. What Cisco IOS command issued from Router-1 will list the routing hops from Host-1 to Server-1?

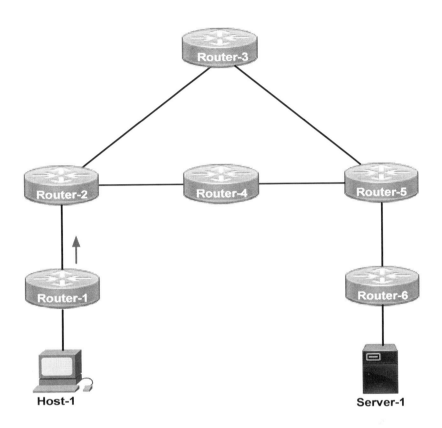

A. tracert

B. ping

C. traceroute

D. ip route

Correct Answer (C)
Subject Matter: IOS Troubleshooting Tools

The **traceroute** command on a Cisco device allows you to view hop by hop packet routing of traffic. The output of **traceroute** lists each layer 3 hop IP address hop taken from source to destination.

    device# traceroute [destination ip address]

The **tracert** command is only available from the Windows command line. The trace is from the desktop source IP address instead of switch or router interface.

13. Refer to the network topology drawing. Router-1 has the startup configuration file erased and restarted. What occurs as a result of this?

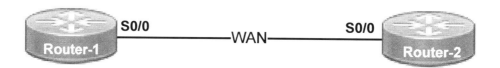

A. all interfaces are shutdown and routers start with user mode prompt

B. all interfaces are active and routers start with the enable prompt

C. only configured interfaces are active and routers start with system configuration dialog prompt

D. all interfaces are shutdown and routers start with system configuration dialog prompt

Correct Answer (D)
Subject Matter: Configure Device Management

Deleting the startup configuration and restarting the network devices will put the network interfaces in shutdown state. Entering **no shutdown** command on Router-1 Gi0/0 and Router-2 Gi0/0 interfaces will enable CDP between the devices.

14. What IOS command is available to verify the changes made to a Cisco device when a new interface is configured?

A. device# show memory

B. device# show flash

C. device# show current-config

D. device# show processes

E. device# show startup-config

F. device# show running-config

Correct Answer (F)
Subject Matter: Configure Device Management

The **show running-config** command is used to verify any changes that were made before saving the running configuration.

    device# show running-config

15. What IOS command provides a list of all active users connected to the VTY lines of a router?

   A. router > show vty

   B. router > show vty user

   C. router > show users all

   D. router > show vty all

Correct Answer (C)
Subject Matter: Configure Device Management

The following IOS command provides a list of all active users connected to the VTY lines of a router.

    router > show users all

16. How does the router select what IOS image to load?

   A. examines the startup configuration file in NVRAM

   B. selects the first IOS image file in Flash memory

   C. examines the running configuration file

   D. examines the configuration register

Correct Answer (D)
Subject Matter: Device Maintenance

The network device starts Power On Self Test (POST) to run diagnostic software from ROM. The router examines the configuration register value that specifies where to load the IOS. The default value of the configuration register is 0x2102.

Configuration Register Settings:

0x2100: Boot from ROM only.

0x2101: Use the first IOS listed in Flash and ignore any boot system command.

0x2102: Load the IOS image based on the location specified with the boot system command configured in startup configuration file. Load IOS from Flash if no boot system command is configured. Load the startup configuration file from NVRAM. Ignore the break key and boot to ROM mode if boot fails. (default setting).

0x2142: Ignore break key, boot to ROM mode if boot fails and ignore the startup configuration file.

17. What IOS command displays CPU utilization on a Cisco network device?

   A. show system

   B. show protocols

   C. show process cpu

   D. show cpu proc

Correct Answer (C)
Subject Matter: IOS Troubleshooting Tools

The following IOS command displays CPU utilization for a Cisco device.

   device# show process cpu

18. What is the advantage of assigning a loopback interface to manage routers?

   A. loopback interface is available as long as any physical interface is up

   B. loopback interface is available as long as the network device is operational

   C. loopback interface does not require an IP address

   D. loopback interface is available when all network interfaces are down

Correct Answer (A)
Subject Matter: Configure Device Management

The loopback interface is virtual and always available when there is at least one physical interface up. Routers have at least two physical interfaces. The loopback interface is unaffected by issues with any single interface. The router cannot be managed when a physical interface assigned for management purposes is unavailable. The following example is typical of a loopback interface configuration. The standard subnet mask for a loopback is a /32 host mask.

```
router(config)# interface loopback0
router(config-if)# ip address 192.168.254.254 255.255.255.255
router(config-if)# end (return to privileged exec mode)
```

19. What must be verified before starting any new IOS upgrade and how is it verified? (select two)

   A. NVRAM available

   B. bootstrap software version

   C. show license

   D. Flash and DRAM available

   E. show running-config

   F. show version

Correct Answers (D,F)
Subject Matter: Device Maintenance

Before doing any IOS upgrade to a Cisco device it is important to verify available device memory. The IOS image file will requires a minimum amount of Flash memory based on file size. In addition there is a minimum amount of DRAM required to boot the IOS image as well. The minimum required Flash/DRAM memory is listed with each IOS filename. The **show version** command will list the amount of available Flash and DRAM memory on the Cisco network device. The following is an example of output from **show version** for router Flash memory usage (bytes).

   [73400320 bytes used, **195035136 available**, 268435456 total]

The total Flash memory installed is 256 MB. The Flash memory used by files including the current IOS is approximately 70 MB including any additional files. That leaves approximately **186 MB available** for any new IOS with the original IOS image left on Flash. Compare the IOS image file size from cisco.com with the available Flash memory.

20. The network administrator configures a new router and issues the following IOS command on the router. The router is rebooted and enters system configuration dialog mode. What is the cause of the problem?

router# copy startup-config running-config

A. router is configured with the **boot system startup** command

B. **boot system flash** command is missing from the configuration

C. configuration register is set to 0x2102

D. configuration register is set to 0x2100

E. network administrator failed to save the running configuration

Correct Answer (E)
Subject Matter: Initial Device Configuration

The IOS command **copy startup-config running-config** will overwrite the running configuration with the startup configuration script. It would cause a reset to initial startup configuration for any new unconfigured device after reboot.

The startup configuration is only as current as when the most recent configuration changes that were saved. Any device configuration changes apply to the running configuration only. The changes are lost unless there is **copy running-config startup-config**.

21. Refer to the results of the IOS command **show log**. What is the cause of the Syslog output message?

%LINK-5-CHANGED: Interface GigabitEthernet0/1, changed state to administratively down

%LINEPROTO-5-UPDOWN: Line protocol on Interface GigabitEthernet0/1, changed state to down

%DUAL-5-NBRCHANGE: IP-OSPF 1:Neighbor 172.16.1.1 (GigabitEthernet0/1) is down: interface down

A. GigabitEthernet0/1 was administratively shutdown causing an OSPF neighbor adjacency error

B. encapsulation mismatch on GigabitEthernet0/1 caused OSPF interface flapping

C. GigabitEthernet0/1 was reset causing OSPF reconvergence event

D. router was rebooted causing GigabitEthernet0/1 to shutdown and reset OSPF adjacency

Correct Answer (A)
Subject Matter: Configure Device Management

The **administratively down** status from the Syslog message indicates that GigabitEthernet0/1 was manually shutdown. The **shutdown** command was administered on that interface causing the OSPF adjacency to go down. The OSPF neighbor was declared unreachable and the adjacency was removed.

22. What IOS command will erase all configuration information from a router?

A. router# erase nvram:

B. router# erase flash

C. router# format flash:

D. router# format nvram:

Correct Answer (A)
Subject Matter: Device Maintenance

All configuration files including certificates are stored in the Cisco device NVRAM. It is smaller amount of non-volatile (permanent) storage where the startup configuration is stored. The IOS command **erase nvram:** will delete all files from NVRAM including startup configuration. That will cause the initial configuration dialog mode to start when the device is reloaded. The IOS command **erase startup-config** will only delete the startup configuration file instead of all files on NVRAM.

23. What Cisco feature set license upgrade is required to enable IPS and VPN on a Cisco router?

A. datak9

B. uck9

C. ipbasek9

D. securityk9

E. ipseck9

Correct Answer (D)
Subject Matter: Configure Device Management

Cisco feature set licensing is based on feature packages. Each package bundle include additional protocols and enhancements from the default (base) package. For instance encryption protocols such as IPsec and SSH would require the **securityk9** feature license upgrade.

24. How do you list the current IOS code and feature set license on a router?

A. router# show version

B. router(config)# show feature udi

C. router(config)# show version /all

D. router# show license

Correct Answer (A)
Subject Matter: Configure Device Management

The output of **show version** command lists the current IOS code version along with feature set license. The **show version** command is also available from user mode prompt as well (router >).

The **show version** command also provides the following operational information to a network administrator:

- Configuration register settings
- Amount of Flash and DRAM memory available
- Most recent router power cycle (reboot) method used

25. What IOS command will copy the IOS image file to Flash memory?

   A. router# copy IOS flash:

   B. router# copy flash: tftp

   C. router# copy tftp: nvram:

   D. router# copy tftp: flash:

Correct Answer (D)
Subject Matter: Device Maintenance

The following IOS command will copy the IOS image file to Flash memory.

   router# copy tftp: flash:

26. What IOS command will list the Flash directory on a Cisco device?

   A. device# list /all

   B. device# do list /all

   C. device# dir /all

   D. device# netdir flash

Correct Answer (C)
Subject Matter: Device Maintenance

The following IOS command will list the Flash directory on a Cisco device.

   device# dir /all

27. What IOS command assigns the IOS filename to use for router bootup?

   A. router# boot system flash [filename]

   B. router(config-boot)# boot system ios flash [filename]

   C. router(config)# boot ios flash [filename]

   D. router(config)# boot system flash [filename]

Correct Answer (D)
Subject Matter: Device Maintenance

The default configuration register setting is **0x2102**. That causes the Cisco device to load the IOS image file specified with the **boot system** command. The following IOS command assigns the IOS image filename to use for bootup. It is a global configuration mode command.

    router(config)# boot system flash [IOS filename]

28. What IOS command will delete a file from Flash memory?

    A. router(config)# delete flash:[filename]

    B. router# erase flash:[filename]

    C. router# delete flash:[filename]

    D. router# erase ios:[filename]

Correct Answer (C)
Subject Matter: Device Maintenance

The following IOS command will delete a file from Flash memory. Include any specific subdirectories for the file location where applicable as well.

    router# delete flash:[filename]

29. Select three standard components of SNMP architecture?

    A. Syslog

    B. SNMP agent

    C. MIB

    D. SNMP manager

    E. NetFlow

    F. SNMP Trap

Correct Answers (B,C,D)
Subject Matter: Device Monitoring Protocols

SNMP is a network management protocol that enables monitoring of network device. The following are three components that enable SNMP communication.

- MIB
- SNMP Manager
- SNMP Agent

30. Select the two alert messages generated by SNMP?

    A. Get

    B. Set

    C. Trap

    D. Inform

    E. Send

    F. MIB

Correct Answers (C,D)
Subject Matter: Device Monitoring Protocols

The alert messages generated by SNMP agents include both Trap and Inform. The purpose of Trap messages is to send alerts to the network management station (NMS). For instance, the network device sends a Trap to the NMS alerting that a network interface status is down. The Inform message is an acknowledgement of a Trap to confirm it arrived.

31. What three features are now available with SNMPv3 that are not supported with SNMPv2?

    A. compression

    B. encryption

    C. error detection

    D. message integrity

    E. authentication protocols

Correct Answers (B,D,E)
Subject Matter: Device Monitoring Protocols

The following three features are enhancements available with SNMPv3.

- Message Integrity
- Authentication
- Encryption

32. What two authentication protocols are used by SNMPv3?

A. HMAC-MD5

B. HMAC-AES

C. HMAC-SHA3

D. HMAC-SHA

Correct Answers (A,D)
Subject Matter: Device Monitoring Protocols

The following are authentication protocols used by SNMPv3.

- HMAC-MD5
- HMAC-SHA

33. What three statements correctly describe feature support available with SNMPv2 and/or SNMPv3?

A. SNMPv3 added Bulk messages

B. SNMPv2 added GetBulk messages

C. SNMPv2 added GetTrap messages

D. SNMPv3 provides enhanced security

E. SNMPv3 supports Inform messages

F. SNMPv2 supports Inform messages

Correct Answers (B,D,F)
Subject Matter: Device Monitoring Protocols

The following are correct statements concerning the features of SNMPv2 and SNMPv3.

- SNMPv3 provides security enhancements
- SNMPv2 added the Inform protocol message to SNMP
- SNMPv2 added the GetBulk protocol message to SNMP

34. What authentication method is used by SNMPv2?

    A. CBC-DES

    B. community strings

    C. HMAC-SHA

    D. HMAC-MD5

Correct Answer (B)
Subject Matter: Device Monitoring Protocols

The authentication type used by SNMPv2 is community strings.

35. Select three locations where system messages are typically saved on a Cisco network device?

    A. local logging buffer

    B. NVRAM

    C. Syslog server

    D. console terminal

    E. Flash

Correct Answers (A,C,D)
Subject Matter: Device Monitoring Protocols

System messages are typically saved to the following locations:

- Local logging buffer
- Console terminal
- Syslog server

36. What three statements correctly describe Syslog feature support?

A. Syslog services provide granular messaging to support enterprise SNMP architecture

B. Syslog server provides a scalable solution for system message storage

C. Syslog provides additional security compared with local router disk space

D. debug messages are automatically time stamped when logging is enabled

E. Syslog is an effective solution for managing logs and alerts

Correct Answers (A,B,E)
Subject Matter: Device Monitoring Protocols

The following are correct statements concerning Syslog utilization.

- Syslog services provides granular messaging to support enterprise SNMP architecture.

- Syslog services provide a scalable network solution for storing system messages.

- Syslog is an effective solution for managing logs and alerts.

37. What IOS command enables timestamp of debug messages (msec) sent to a Syslog server?

A. service timestamps debug datetime localtime

B. service timestamps log datetime msec

C. service timestamps debug datetime msec

D. service timestamps log datetime localtime

Correct Answer (C)
Subject Matter: Device Monitoring Protocols

The following IOS command enables the device to timestamp Syslog debug messages in milliseconds (msec).

device(config)# service timestamps debug datetime msec

38. What SNMP traps generated from the Cisco device are logged when the following IOS command is configured? (select four)

   device(config)# logging trap 4

   A. emergencies

   B. informational

   C. alerts

   D. errors

   E. notices

   F. warnings

Correct Answers (A,C,D,F)
Subject Matter: Device Monitoring Protocols

The IOS command enables a Cisco device to log SNMP trap from 0 (zero) up to and including level 4. The traps are logged to the Syslog server. The Syslog servers receive informational (trap 6) and lower numbered messages as a default. The logging facility default setting is local7 for switches and routers.

   device(config)# logging trap 4

The following alert level traps are generated with level 4 logging:

- Emergencies (level 0)
- Alerts (level 1)
- Errors (level 3)
- Warnings (level 4)

39. What two statements correctly describe SNMPv2 and/or SNMPv3 feature support?

   A. SNMPv3 supports community strings for security

   B. SNMPv2 now support username with MD5 security

   C. SNMPv3 enables message integrity, authentication and encryption

   D. SNMPv3 supports Trap and Inform messages

Correct Answers (C,D)
Subject Matter: Device Monitoring Protocols

The following statements correctly describe SNMPv3 feature support.

- SNMPv3 enables message integrity, authentication and encryption
- SNMPv3 supports Trap and Inform messages

40. How is SNMP enabled on a Cisco network device?

   A. device(config)# snmp server community

   B. device(config)# snmp-host

   C. any **snmp-server** command

   D. device(config)# snmp enable

   E. SNMP is enabled as a default

Correct Answer (C)
Subject Matter: Device Monitoring Protocols

SNMP is enabled automatically on a Cisco device when any **snmp-server** command is configured.

41. What IOS command will configure an SNMP community string named *cisco* with read/write access?

   A. device(config)# snmp-server community cisco rw

   B. device(config)# snmp server community rw cisco

   C. device(config)# snmp server community password cisco rw

   D. device(config)# snmp-server community password cisco rw

Correct Answer (A)
Subject Matter: Device Monitoring Protocols

The following IOS command configures an SNMP community string named *cisco* with read/write access.

device(config)# snmp-server community cisco rw

42. Refer to the network topology drawing. Select the IOS command that configures an SNMP server for Router-2 with SNMPv3 and MD5/SHA authentication enabled?

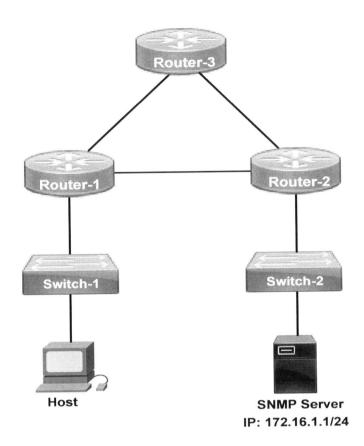

Host

SNMP Server
IP: 172.16.1.1/24

A. router-2(config)# snmp server 172.16.1.1 version 3 md5

B. router-2(config)# snmp-server host 172.16.1.1 version 3 auth

C. router-2(config)# snmp-server 172.16.1.1 version 3 auth

D. router-2(config-if)# snmp-server host 172.16.1.1 version 3 priv

Correct Answer (B)
Subject Matter: Device Monitoring Protocols

The following IOS command configures an SNMP server with IP address of 172.16.1.1 and enables SNMPv3. In addition it enables MD5/SHA authentication for optimized security.

router-2(config)# snmp-server host 172.16.1.1 version 3 auth

43. Select the IOS command that will configure an SNMP server named **nms.cisco.com** with version 2c and enable trap messages?

    A. snmp-server nms.cisco.com traps 2c

    B. snmp-server host nms.cisco.com enable version 2c trap

    C. snmp server nms.cisco.com traps version 2c

    D. snmp-server host nms.cisco.com traps version 2c

Correct Answer (D)
Subject Matter: Device Monitoring Protocols

The following IOS command will configure an SNMP server named **nms.cisco.com** with version 2c and enable trap messages.

    device(config)# snmp-server host nms.cisco.com traps version 2c

The Cisco network device will send all enabled notifications to the SNMP server. Enabling a lot of SNMP MIBs can cause high CPU utilization on Cisco devices. The number of queries (polling) increase with the MIBs enabled. The problem worsens particularly with polling of routing tables and ARP tables.

44. What two statements correctly describe Cisco ICMP echo-based IP SLA?

    A. application response time

    B. IP SLA responder is not required on the destination device

    C. Traceroute is used by ICMP echo service

    D. monitors network latency

Correct Answers (B,D)
Subject Matter: ICMP Echo-Based IP SLA

The following two statements are correct concerning ICMP echo-based IP SLA.

- IP SLA responder is not required on the destination device
- Monitors network latency

45. Select the correct statement that applies to ICMP echo-based IP SLA?

    A. default packet size is 64 bytes

    B. support for IPv4 hosts only

    C. UDP required

    D. support for IPv6 interfaces only

Correct Answer (A)
Subject Matter: ICMP Echo-Based IP SLA

The default packet size is 64 bytes for ICMP echo-based IP SLA operation.

46. Refer to the network topology drawing. What IOS command configures ICMP echo-based operation on Router-1 with a destination IP address of 172.16.3.1 and source IP address of 172.16.1.1?

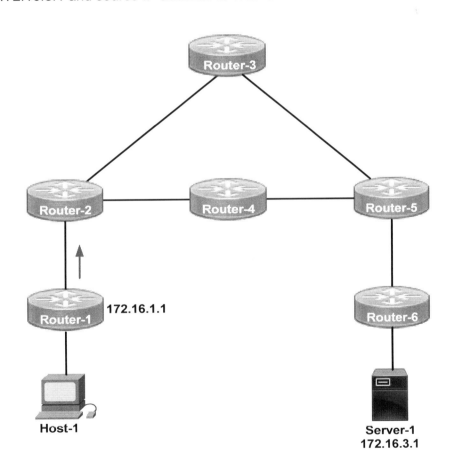

A. icmp-echo destination-ip 172.16.3.1 source ip 172.16.1.1

B. icmp-echo 172.16.3.1 source-ip 172.16.1.1

C. icmp echo destination-ip 172.16.1.1 source-ip 172.16.3.1

D. icmp-echo 172.16.1.1 source-ip 172.16.3.1

Correct Answer (B)
Subject Matter: ICMP Echo-Based IP SLA

The following IOS command enables ICMP echo on Router-1 with a destination IP address 172.16.3.1 and source IP address 172.16.1.1

router(config-ip-sla)# icmp-echo 172.16.3.1 source-ip 172.16.1.1

47. Match the file transfer method with the correct description?

FTP	adds encryption (SSH), supports larger files
SCP	server-based, not secure, UDP, single connection
TFTP	fast, network device slot, local copy
USB	server-based, username and password logon, TCP

Correct Answers.
Subject Matter: Device Maintenance

The following describe the characteristics of standard file transfer methods.

FTP	**server-based, username and password logon, TCP**
SCP	**adds encryption (SSH), supports larger files**
TFTP	**server-based, not secure, UDP, single connection**
USB	**fast, network device slot, local copy**

48. What command is used to verify the file integrity of an IOS image on Flash?

   A. device# verify /fcs [filesystem: filename]

   B. device# verify /md5 [filesystem: filename]

   C. device# verify /ios [filesystem: filename]

   D. device# verify /crc [filesystem: filename]

Correct Answer (B)
Subject Matter: Device Maintenance

The following command verifies the IOS image file integrity on Flash memory.

   device# verify /md5 [filesystem: filename]

49. Match the correct order when performing Cisco router password recovery?

Step 1:	Modify the configuration register to prevent the startup configuration file from loading: rommon > **confreg 0x2142**
Step 2:	Reboot router and press Ctrl-Break key to start ROMmon mode
Step 3:	Reboot the router and issue the following IOS command: router# **copy startup-config running-config**
Step 4:	Modify the configuration register with the following IOS command and reboot: router(config)# **config-register 0x2102**
Step 5:	Change the password and save changes with the following IOS command: router# **copy running-config startup-config**

Correct Answers.

Subject Matter: Device Maintenance

The following is the correct order for performing password recovery on a Cisco router or switch.

Step 1:	Reboot router and press Ctrl-Break key to start ROMmon mode
Step 2:	Modify the configuration register to prevent the startup configuration file from loading: rommon > **confreg 0x2142**
Step 3:	Reboot router and issue the following IOS command: router# **copy startup-config running-config**
Step 4:	Change the password and save changes with the following IOS command: router# **copy running-config startup-config**
Step 5:	Modify the configuration register with the following IOS command: router(config)# **config-register 0x2102** and reboot.

50. Match the Cisco device mode with the correct description?

user exec mode	router(config-router)#
enable mode	device(config)#
privileged exec mode	device#
rommon mode	device >
routing configuration mode	rommon >

Correct Answers.

Subject Matter: Initial Device Configuration

The following correctly match the Cisco device modes with prompts:

user exec mode	**device >**
enable mode	**device#**
privileged exec mode	**device(config)#**
rommon mode	**rommon >**
routing configuration mode	**router(config-router)#**

```
router > enable
router# configure terminal
router(config)# interface gigabitethernet0/0
router(config-if)#
```

51. What is the default source interface for the **ping** command when run from a
    Cisco network device?

    A. router loopback IP address

    B. highest IP address

    C. egress interface IP address

    D. ingress IP address

Correct Answer (C)
Subject Matter: IOS Troubleshooting Tools

The default source interface for the **ping** command is the egress interface IP
address.

52. What IOS command is used to start an Extended **ping**?

    A. device# ping /?

    B. device# ping -e

    C. device# ping /all

    D. device# ping

    E. device# ping -d

Correct Answer (D)
Subject Matter: IOS Troubleshooting Tools

The following command is used to start an Extended ping. The **ping** with no
destination IP address will cycle through dialog questions for individual ping
command settings.

```
device# ping
```

53. Match the Extended **ping** command feature with the correct description?

datagram size [100]:	specify exclusive hops to route ping path
data pattern [0xABCD]:	list addresses of hops that ping path use
target IP address:	number of pings sent
record:	destination host IP address
repeat count [5]:	egress interface for ICMP packets
loose:	enable packet fragmentation for MTU
strict:	troubleshooting serial lines
set DF bit in IP header? [no]:	packet size (bytes)
source address or interface:	specify addresses of hops to route ping

Correct Answers.
Subject Matter: IOS Troubleshooting Tools

The following describe each option available with an Extended ping:

datagram size [100]:	**packet size (bytes)**
data pattern [0xABCD]:	**troubleshooting serial lines**
target IP address:	**destination host IP address**
record:	**list addresses of hops that ping path use**
repeat count [5]:	**number of pings sent**
loose:	**specify addresses of hops to route ping**
strict:	**specify exclusive hops to route ping path**
set DF bit in IP header? [no]:	**enable packet fragmentation for MTU**
source address or interface:	**egress interface for ICMP packets**

476

54. What three events cause **traceroute** to terminate?

    A. destination host responds

    B. TTL value = 0

    C. maximum TTL is exceeded

    D. ctrl-shift + 6

    E. ctrl-break

Correct Answers (A,C,D)
Subject Matter: IOS Troubleshooting Tools

The following events will cause the IOS command **traceroute** to terminate:

- Destination host responds
- Maximum TTL is exceeded
- Escape sequence (Ctrl+Shift+6)

55. What two statements accurately describe the use of **traceroute** for troubleshooting purposes?

    A. Extended traceroute is not available from switches

    B. traceroute verifies the path packets take in order to get to a destination

    C. traceroute can troubleshoot routing issues including routing loops and packet filtering (ACL or firewall)

    D. Extended traceroute is used to determine the type of connectivity problem

    E. **tracert** command starts Extended traceroute mode

Correct Answers (B,C)
Subject Matter: IOS Troubleshooting Tools

The following statements describe the use of **traceroute** for troubleshooting purposes.

- Traceroute verifies the path packets take in order to get to a destination.

- Traceroute can troubleshoot routing issues including routing loops and packet filtering (ACL or firewall).

56. What two statements correctly describe Cisco device terminal logging?

A. Telnet/SSH sessions do not send logging messages to the terminal by default

B. Telnet/SSH sessions send logging messages to the terminal by default

C. console sessions do not send logging messages to the terminal by default

D. console sessions send logging messages to the terminal by default

Correct Answers (A,D)
Subject Matter: Configure Device Management

The following statements correctly describe Cisco terminal logging.

- Telnet/SSH sessions sending logging messages to the terminal is disabled by default.

- Console sessions sending logging messages to the terminal is enabled by default.

57. What two statements are true of the **ping** command?

A. ping can troubleshoot routing issues

B. Extended ping is used to determine the type of connectivity problem

C. ping is not ICMP-based

D. Extended ping tests network latency performance

Correct Answers (B,D)
Subject Matter: IOS Troubleshooting Tools

The following statements are true of the **ping** command.

- Extended ping is used to determine the type of connectivity problem.
- Extended ping tests network latency performance.

58. What IOS command enables terminal logging?

   A. device# terminal monitor enable

   B. device# terminal monitor

   C. device# terminal monitor on

   D. device(config)# terminal monitor

Correct Answer (B)
Subject Matter: Configure Device Management

Cisco devices do not send log messages to a terminal (VTY) session as a default. The VTY lines are used for Telnet and SSH sessions. The following IOS command enables terminal logging to send log messages to the terminal. That includes debug output and system error messages.

   device# terminal monitor

59. What IOS command lists the active VTY terminal lines for a router?

   A. router# show vty

   B. router# show term /all

   C. router# show vty 0 4

   D. router# show terminal

Correct Answer (D)
Subject Matter: IOS Troubleshooting Tools

The following IOS command lists the active VTY terminal lines for a router.

   router# show terminal

60. Match the Cisco Local SPAN component with the correct description?

source port	transmit, receive or both
destination port	interface or VLAN
forwarding traffic	interface
Local SPAN	source and destination port on same switch

Correct Answers.
Subject Matter: IOS Troubleshooting Tools

The following describe Cisco local SPAN characteristics and components.

source port	**interface or VLAN**
destination port	**Interface**
forwarding traffic	**transmit, receive or both**
Local SPAN	**source and destination port on same switch**

61. What three statements correctly describe Local SPAN operation?

   A. support for multiple source interfaces or a single VLAN

   B. support for 802.1X port security

   C. source interface must be an access port

   D. trunk source interface copies traffic from all VLANs

   E. configuring a destination port does not affect its running configuration

   F. packets from source interface/s are copied to destination interface

Correct Answers (A,D,F)
Subject Matter: IOS Troubleshooting Tools

The following statements correctly describe local SPAN operation:

- There is support for either multiple source interfaces or a single VLAN. There are at least two source interfaces defined. The hosts that are connected have established a network session.

- Trunk source interface copies traffic from all VLANs.

- Local SPAN is comprised of source and destination interfaces on the same switch. The SPAN copies traffic from source interface/s to a destination interface where a network analyzer is attached.

The following IOS commands will configure Local SPAN on a Cisco switch.

```
switch(config)# monitor session 1 source interface Gi1/1
switch(config)# monitor session 1 destination interface Gi1/2
```

62. Select the four correct statements for SDN programmability architecture?

A. SDN architecture decouples the control and data plane

B. control plane is a software module instead of a physical processor

C. SDN controller is a centralized control plane with a policy engine

D. network state is distributed

E. control plane is distributed

F. infrastructure is abstracted from applications

Correct Answers (A,B,C,F)
Subject Matter: Network Programmability

Software Defined Networking (SDN) is an architecture that separates the control plane from the data plane. The purpose for that is to abstract underlying network infrastructure. That allows programmability of supported network devices. It is similar to the hypervisor paradigm shift that abstracts (separates) server hardware from software components including operating systems, applications and virtual appliances. The same idea is applied to the network infrastructure with overlays and programmable services.

The following statements correctly describe SDN programmability:

- SDN architecture decouples the control and data plane.

- control plane is a software module instead of a physical processor.

- SDN controller is a centralized control plane with a policy engine.

- infrastructure is abstracted from applications.

63. What four statements are true of an SDN Controller?

A. network appears as a distributed switch

B. centralized management and network intelligence

C. network services are dynamically configurable

D. network appears as a single switch

E. centralized management and distributed intelligence

F. moves control plane from physical devices to software abstracted layer

Correct Answers (B,C,D,F)
Subject Matter: Network Programmability

The following statements accurately describe the SDN Controller:

- Centralized management and network intelligence.
- Network services are dynamically configurable.
- The network appears as a single switch.
- Moves control plane from physical devices to software abstracted layer.

64. What three statements are correct concerning SDN architecture?

A. SDN applications requests are sent via northbound APIs

B. data plane supports virtual (VM) network devices only

C. SDN controller relays information via southbound APIs to network devices

D. Cisco SDN controller provides routing and switching services

E. APIC-EM is the Cisco SDN controller

Correct Answers (A,C,E)
Subject Matter: Network Programmability

The southbound API provides connectivity between SDN Controller and data plane. The data plane includes the physical and virtual (VM) network devices. The SDN Controller relays information via southbound APIs to network devices. It is the translation point between the SDN policy engine and network infrastructure. Network equipment vendors such as Cisco now support OpenFlow southbound API. The policy engine is defined at SDN applications where requests are sent via northbound APIs. There are Cisco extensible network controller and agent for switches and routers and APIs.

The following statements correctly describe the purpose of SDN APIs:

- SDN applications requests are sent via northbound APIs.
- SDN Controller relays information via southbound APIs to network devices
- APIC-EM is the Cisco SDN Controller.

65. What three steps are required to backup an IOS image to TFTP server?

    A. upgrade TFTP server with IOS license to store image files

    B. create directory on TFTP server with security access

    C. verify file system on TFTP server

    D. assign a public IP address to the TFTP server

    E. verify disk space available on TFTP server

    F. configure access to TFTP server from ROMmon mode

Correct Answers (B,E,F)
Subject Matter: Device Maintenance

TFTP server support is available for managing IOS images and startup configuration files. It is an alternative to using memory on the network devices for storing files. Cisco supports loading IOS and the startup configuration file from TFTP server at bootup as well. Access to the TFTP server is only required at bootup to download files. The following are three recommended actions before doing an IOS image backup to TFTP server.

- Create directory on TFTP server with security access.
- Verify disk space available on TFTP server.
- Configure access to TFTP server from ROMmon mode.

66. Where does the Cisco device first attempt to load an IOS image based on a default configuration register setting?

   A. TFTP

   B. Flash

   C. ROM

   D. NVRAM

Correct Answer (B)
Subject Matter: Device Maintenance

   Step 1: The device starts and does Power on Self Test (POST) to verify hardware is operational. The bootstrap loader then determines where to load the IOS image based on the configuration register settings. The default setting loads the first IOS listed with any **boot system** command in the router startup configuration file. The **boot system** command points to a location of an IOS image stored in Flash memory. The file location configured with the first **boot system** command is used when multiple commands exist.

   Step 2: The first IOS image listed in Flash memory (where multiple IOS images exist) is loaded when there are no **boot system** commands.

   Step 3: IOS is loaded from TFTP server when no IOS images are on Flash.

   Step 4: ROMmon mode starts when there is no IOS image on TFTP server.

67. What action is taken by the router when no startup configuration file is found in the default location during bootup?

   A. IOS attempts to load the startup configuration file from NVRAM

   B. IOS attempts to load the startup configuration file from TFTP

   C. router starts initial configuration dialog mode (setup mode)

   D. IOS attempts to load the startup configuration file from ROM

Correct Answer (B)
Subject Matter: Device Maintenance

The following describes what the Cisco network device does when no startup configuration file is found during bootup:

Step 1: The Cisco network device first attempts to load the startup configuration from NVRAM (default location). There is a copy made of the startup configuration loaded to DRAM for active use. That is referred to as the running configuration.

Step 2: The network device attempts to load the startup configuration file from TFTP server if there is no startup configuration in NVRAM.

Step 3: The network device starts the initial configuration dialog mode if there is no configuration to a TFTP server or it is unavailable. That enables a start from scratch configuration. The preferred method is to restore the most recent startup configuration where available.

    --- System Configuration Dialog ---
    Would you like to enter the initial configuration dialog? [yes/no]: **yes**

68. What information is listed with the following IOS command? (select two)

    router# show inventory

    A. license

    B. serial number

    C. IOS version

    D. product ID (PID)

    E. DRAM (GB)

Correct Answers (B,D)
Subject Matter: Device Maintenance

The chassis serial number and product ID (PID) are available with **show inventory** IOS command. That information is useful when working with Cisco TAC. In addition all hardware modules installed have individual serial number and product ID numbers assigned.

69. Select the correct IOS commands to configure a management SVI on a layer 2 switch. Assign VLAN 100 to the SVI with an IP address of 192.168.1.254/24?

A. switch# conf t
   switch(config)# vlan 100
   switch(config-vlan)# management
   switch(config-vlan)# end
   !
   switch# conf t
   switch(config)# vlan 100
   switch(config-if)# ip address 192.168.1.254 255.255.255.0
   switch(config-if)# end

B. switch# conf t
   switch(config)# vlan 100
   switch(config-vlan)# enable management
   switch(config-vlan)# end
   !
   switch# conf t
   switch(config)# vlan 100
   switch(config-if)# ip address 192.168.1.254 255.255.255.0
   switch(config-if)# end

C. switch# conf t
   switch(config)# vlan 100
   switch(config-vlan)# management
   switch(config-vlan)# end
   !
   switch# conf t
   switch(config)# interface vlan 100
   switch(config-if)# ip address 192.168.1.254 255.255.255.0
   switch(config-if)# end

D. switch# conf t
   switch(config)# vlan 100
   switch(config-vlan)# vlan management
   switch(config-vlan)# end
   !
   switch# conf t
   switch(config)# vlan 100
   switch(config-if)# ip address 192.168.1.254
   switch(config-if)# end

Correct Answer (C)
Subject Matter: Initial Device Configuration

The default VLAN for an unconfigured Cisco switch is VLAN 1. All switch ports are assigned to VLAN 1. All network control traffic (CDP, VTP, PAgP etc.) is forwarded across VLAN 1 as well. The recommended best practice is to assign a separate unused VLAN for device management. The new management VLAN is assigned an IP address making it a layer 3 interface called an SVI. The purpose of the SVI on a layer 2 switch is to enable remote switch management.

The following IOS commands creates a new VLAN called management and assigns an IP address (SVI). The SVI must be in the same subnet as the upstream connected default gateway (router). The switch requires configuration of the **default-gateway** command. That provides a next hop address for reachability between the default gateway and switch. The default gateway is used as well for Inter-VLAN routing and ARP requests from the layer 2 switch.

```
switch# conf t
switch(config)# vlan 100
switch(config-vlan)# management
switch(config-vlan)# end
!
switch# conf t
switch(config)# interface vlan 100
switch(config-if)# ip address 192.168.1.254 255.255.255.0
switch(config-if)# end

switch# copy running-config startup-config
```

70. The network administrator recently added a new WAN connection to access a cloud service provider. The network administrator moved the router over to a new rack and now the application is not working. The internet and branch office connections are available however. What is the best explanation for the cause?

A. packet loss is occurring

B. IOS image file is corrupt

C. running configuration file is corrupt

D. running configuration file was not saved

E. startup configuration file was not saved

Correct Answer (D)
Subject Matter: Configure Device Management

The configuration changes for the new cloud connection were not saved before the router was rebooted during the rack move. The reboot causes the router to load the startup configuration. Changes were made to the running configuration for cloud connectivity. The network administrator however did not save (write) the running configuration changes to the startup configuration file.

    router# copy running-config startup-config

71. What two statements are correct concerning SDN architecture?

    A. Cisco APIC-EM is an SDN controller

    B. switches and routers are data plane devices

    C. SDN controller is an API

    D. routers are control plane devices

Correct Answers (A,B)
Subject Matter: SDN Controller

The SDN architecture is comprised of three primary layers. They include application layer, control layer and infrastructure layer.

Application Layer
SDN applications communicate with the SDN controller via northbound APIs.

Control Layer
SDN Controller provides control plane services and manage network service requests from applications to infrastructure devices. Cisco APIC-EM is an example of an SDN controller.

Infrastructure Layer
Comprised of data plane network devices such as switches. They communicate with the SDN controller via southbound APIs at the service abstraction layer.

49206484R00274

Made in the USA
San Bernardino, CA
16 May 2017